Markets and the Arts of Attachment

The collection explores how sentiment and relations are organised in consumer markets. Social studies of economies and markets have much more to offer than simply adding some 'context', 'culture' or 'soul' to the analysis of economic practices. As this collection showcases, studying markets socially reveals how attachments between people and products are engineered and can explain how, and why, they fail. The contributors explore the tools and techniques used to work with sentiment, aesthetics and relationships through strategies including social media marketing, consumer research, algorithmic profiling, personal selling, and call centre and relationship management. The arts of attachment, as the various contributions demonstrate, play a crucial but often misunderstood role in the technical and organisational functioning of markets.

Franck Cochoy is Professor of Sociology at the University of Toulouse Jean Jaurès and a member of CERTOP-CNRS, France. He works in the field of economic sociology, with a focus on the human and technical mediations that frame the relationship between supply and demand. He has conducted several projects and case studies on such topics as the role of marketing, packaging, self-service, trade press, and so on.

Joe Deville is a lecturer at Lancaster University, based jointly in the departments of Organisation, Work & Technology and Sociology. A major focus of his work has been the encounter between defaulting consumer credit debtor and debt collector, which was the subject of his first book *Lived Economies of Default*, published by Routledge in 2015. Other areas of interest include disaster preparedness, comparative and digital methods, behavioural economics, and theories of money.

Liz McFall is Senior Lecturer in Sociology and research lead for Digital Participation at the Open University in the UK. She is currently researching how the convergences surrounding digital disruption and the current global wave of health care reforms are forging new roles for states, insurance markets and marketing. She is author of *Devising Consumption: Cultural economies of insurance, credit and spending* (Routledge, 2014), *Advertising: A cultural economy* (2004) and Editor-in-Chief of the *Journal of Cultural Economy*.

CRESC
Culture, Economy and the Social
A new series from CRESC – the ESRC Centre for Research on Socio-cultural Change

Editors
Professor Tony Bennett, Social and Cultural Theory, University of Western Sydney; Professor Penny Harvey, Anthropology, Manchester University; Professor Kevin Hetherington, Geography, Open University

Editorial Advisory Board
Andrew Barry, University of Oxford; Michel Callon, Ecole des Mines de Paris; Dipesh Chakrabarty, The University of Chicago; Mike Crang, University of Durham; Tim Dant, Lancaster University; Jean-Louis Fabiani, Ecoles de Hautes Etudes en Sciences Sociales; Antoine Hennion, Paris Institute of Technology; Eric Hirsch, Brunel University; John Law, The Open University; Randy Martin, New York University; Timothy Mitchell, New York University; Rolland Munro, Keele University; Andrew Pickering, University of Exeter; Mary Poovey, New York University; Hugh Willmott, University of Cardiff; Sharon Zukin, Brooklyn College City University New York/ Graduate School, City University of New York

The *Culture, Economy and the Social* series is committed to innovative contemporary, comparative and historical work on the relations between social, cultural and economic change. It publishes empirically-based research that is theoretically informed, that critically examines the ways in which social, cultural and economic change is framed and made visible, and that is attentive to perspectives that tend to be ignored or side-lined by grand theorising or epochal accounts of social change. The series addresses the diverse manifestations of contemporary capitalism, and considers the various ways in which the 'social', 'the cultural' and 'the economic' are apprehended as tangible sites of value and practice. It is explicitly comparative, publishing books that work across disciplinary perspectives, cross-culturally, or across different historical periods.

The series is actively engaged in the analysis of the different theoretical traditions that have contributed to the development of the 'cultural turn' with a view to clarifying where these approaches converge and where they diverge on a particular issue. It is equally concerned to explore the new critical agendas emerging from current critiques of the cultural turn: those associated with the descriptive turn for example. Our commitment to interdisciplinarity thus aims at enriching theoretical and methodological discussion, building awareness of the common ground that has emerged in the past decade, and thinking through what is at stake in those approaches that resist integration to a common analytical model.

A complete list of titles can be viewed online here: www.routledge.com/CRESC/book-series/CRESC

The most recent titles in the series are:

Speculative Research
The Lure of Possible Futures
Edited by Alex Wilkie, Martin Savransky and Marsha Rosegarten

Markets and the Arts of Attachment
Edited by Franck Cochoy, Joe Deville and Liz McFall

Markets and the Arts of Attachment

Edited by
Franck Cochoy, Joe Deville and
Liz McFall

Routledge
Taylor & Francis Group
LONDON AND NEW YORK

E·S·R·C
ECONOMIC
& SOCIAL
RESEARCH
COUNCIL

Centre for Research on
Socio-Cultural Change

First published 2017
by Routledge
2 Park Square, Milton Park, Abingdon, Oxon OX14 4RN

and by Routledge
711 Third Avenue, New York, NY 10017

Routledge is an imprint of the Taylor & Francis Group, an informa business

British Library Cataloguing in Publication Data
A catalogue record for this book is available from the British Library

Library of Congress Cataloging in Publication Data
Names: Cochoy, Franck, editor. | Deville, Joe, editor. | McFall, Elizabeth
  Rose, editor.
Title: Markets and the arts of attachment / edited by Franck Cochoy, Joe
  Deville and Liz McFall.
Description: Abingdon, Oxon ; New York, NY : Routledge, [2017]
Identifiers: LCCN 2016050579| ISBN 9781138904293 (hardback) | ISBN
  9781315696454 (ebook)
Subjects: LCSH: Marketing–Psychological aspects. | Consumer behavior. |
  Consumption (Economics)–Social aspects.
Classification: LCC HF5415 .M32378 2017 | DDC 658.8/342–dc23
LC record available at https://lccn.loc.gov/2016050579

ISBN: 978-1-138-90429-3 (hbk)
ISBN: 978-1-315-69645-4 (ebk)

Typeset in Times New Roman
by Taylor & Francis Books

Printed and bound by CPI Group (UK) Ltd, Croydon, CR0 4YY

Contents

List of illustrations

Figures

Table

Box

Contributors

Tomas Ariztia is Associate Professor at the Sociology Department of Diego Portales University, Chile. His research is concerned with consumption studies – particularly marketing studies and sustainable consumption. He is interested in researching the infrastructures of consumption, especially marketing practices and devices, and is currently involved in a three-year research project focused on comparing big data, design thinking and market research as different knowledge grammars through which social entities are enacted in markets.

Michel Callon is Professor of Sociology at Mines ParisTech, Director of the Centre for the Sociology of Innovation from 1982 to 1994, and Chairman of the 4S (Society for Social Studies of Science) from 1998 to 1999. He is also, with Bruno Latour and John Law, one of the founders of Actor-Network Theory or the sociology of translation. His work covers a wide spectrum of issues connected to the interrelations between science, technology and society, including anthropologies of science, technology and markets, the socioeconomics of innovation, the sociology of medicine and health, and scientometrics and quantitative methods.

Franck Cochoy is Professor of Sociology at the University of Toulouse and a member of the CERTOP-CNRS, France. He works in the field of economic sociology and focuses on the different ways the encounters between supply and demand are framed, in both historical and contemporary markets. His latest books are *On the Origins of Self-Service* (Routledge, 2015), *Une histoire du ski* (Ref2C, 2016) and *On Curiosity: The Art of Market Seduction* (Mattering Press, 2016).

Joe Deville is a Lecturer at Lancaster University, based jointly in the Department of Organisation, Work and Technology and the Department of Sociology. A major focus of his work has been the encounter between defaulting consumer credit debtor and debt collector, the subject of his first book, *Lived Economies of Default* (Routledge, 2015).

Carolin Gerlitz is Professor for Digital Media and Methods at the University of Siegen and member of the Digital Methods Initiative, Amsterdam. Her research interests comprise platform and software studies, digital methods, economic sociology, digital culture, numbers, metrics, mobile and social media. She completed her PhD at Goldsmiths, University of London and worked at the University of Amsterdam as Assistant Professor.

Emmanuel Kessous is Professor of Sociology at the University of Nice-Sophia Antipolis, Researcher at Groupe de Recherche en Droit, Economie et Gestion and Associate Researcher at Groupe d'Etude des Méthodes de l'Analyse Sociologique de la Sorbonne. Previously, he worked for thirteen years at France Telecom's research and development centre (Orange Labs). He has edited and written numerous books and scientific journal papers in the field of digital economic sociology. At the University of Nice-Sophia Antipolis, he is co-convenor of a dual bachelor's degree in sociology and economics and of a Masters degree in 'the sociology and ergonomics of digital technologies'.

Hans Kjellberg is Professor of Marketing at the Stockholm School of Economics. His research focuses on economic organising, particularly the organising of markets. Recent publications include articles in *Consumption, Markets and Culture, Industrial Marketing Management, Journal of Marketing Management* and *Marketing Theory* and the co-edited volume *Concerned Markets* (Edward Elgar, 2014). Current projects include an interdisciplinary research programme on the digitalisation of consumption and a cross-country comparison of the valuation and pricing of pharmaceutical cancer treatments.

Alexandre Mallard is Director of the Centre de Sociologie de l'Innovation at the Ecole des Mines ParisTech. Originally trained as a sociologist of science and technology, he now works in the field of economic sociology. He has conducted research on sales activity, on very small businesses and on the rise of network interactions in the corporate environment. His current research projects investigate the social inscription of innovation, at the crossroads between economic sociology and political science.

Liz McFall is Head of Sociology at the Open University in the UK. She is currently researching how the convergences surrounding digital disruption and the current global wave of healthcare funding reforms are forging new roles for states, markets and marketing. Her book *Devising Consumption: Cultural Economies of Insurance, Credit and Spending* (Routledge, 2014) argues that states and markets were inevitable if uneasy allies in the promotion of public welfare and consumption. Liz is the author of *Advertising: A Cultural Economy* (SAGE, 2004), co-editor of *The Limits of Performativity: Politics of the Modern Economy* (Routledge, 2014), *Conduct: Sociology and Social Worlds* (Oxford University Press, 2008) and editor-in-chief of the *Journal of Cultural Economy*.

Kevin Mellet is a researcher at the Social Sciences Department of Orange Labs (Sense) and associate researcher at the Centre de Sociologie de l'Innovation (Mines ParisTech). His research is based primarily within economic sociology and science and technology studies and focuses on digital markets. He is particularly interested in the following research areas: online advertising and marketing, media economics with a focus on online social media, the different forms of participation and expression of consumers on the Internet, and more recently issues related to personal data. Since 2016, Kevin is an associate professor at the University Paris-Est Marnes-La-Vallée where he took co-responsibility for the Masters in "Communication and Social Networks".

José Ossandón is Assistant Professor at the Department of Organization, Copenhagen Business School. His current work focuses on two main areas: the encounter between households' mundane economic practices and calculative devices produced by financial firms and the recent rise of new models of economic knowledge used to evaluate, repair and govern market-based policy instruments.

Introduction

Markets and the arts of attachment

Liz McFall, Franck Cochoy and Joe Deville

One of the best-known stories sociologists and political economists tell about marketing is that it manufactures desire for things that people would not otherwise want. This is quite correct at one level but it is blandly tautological at another. Karl Marx (1980) knew better in the *Grundrisse* when he made his famous argument that a railway with no passengers is only a railway in prospect. Products, Marx explained, get their finishing touches only in consumption. Marketing is an integral part of the distribution of action that defines production and consumption by orchestrating markets. It is not, at least not only, the pretty lies of paid advertising, organised flash mobs and viral campaigns. As practised in the wild and taught in business schools everywhere, marketing also concerns the build, design, pricing and placing of the thing itself. This means that markets and marketing are in it together, as the work presented in Araujo, Finch and Kjellberg (2010) so painstakingly pointed out. By careful extension this also means that people are somehow *in* their products from the start.

There is an uncanny temporal logic in this argument. If a product is a product *only* in consumption what we are saying is that the consumption of marketed goods happens only when the arts and enterprises of marketing have successfully incorporated people, their prospective markets, within production. Marketing then is not an after the fact add-on, giving products the illusion of desirability – it can be found in the whole apparatus of production and consumption. This argument owes a great deal to earlier work that followed science, technology and markets across networks and actors.[1] What we aim to do in this collection is take this a little further by exploring markets as the outcome of various arts and devices of attachment that work with the avid propensities of all entities to associate.[2]

Markets work with avidity. This is to say something more than that they work through promoting greed – though they often do that too. What we mean by working with avidity is working with the propensity to 'have', that is, to associate, to relate, that can be found in all but the most inert entities. Markets proliferate attachments and attachments proliferate in markets. Antoine Hennion famously claimed 'attachment' for sociology as a term that signalled the dual action of relationship building.[3] Attachment, as he explained, is oriented towards the creation of both objective ties – attachment as a material link – and subjective ties – attachment as an affect, feeling or sentiment:

> Instead of measuring relations between elements considered as fixed, determined – cultural practices on the one hand, their practitioners, characterized by different variables, on the other – we have to reflexively question, from the amateur experience, how these relationships are formed, and how they are changing both the things valued and the people valuing them. This is why we prefer to talk about attachments. This beautiful word breaks the opposition between a series of causes that would come from outside – and the here and now of the situation and interaction. As for the amateurs, attachment insists less on labels and more on the state of persons; on the side of the works and tasted objects, it leaves open their right of reply, their ability to co-produce 'what is happening'.
>
> (Hennion, 2004: *Hennion's translation*)

In fact, attachment and avidity are inseparable. As Cochoy (2012, 2005) has pointed out in earlier contributions to this debate, from the perspective of certain, influential strands in sociological thought, the idea of market ties or attachments seems counterintuitive, almost oxymoronic. Surely, markets work to dissolve social ties so that atomised individuals can exchange freely without obligations to one another? For better and for worse, it is purported to be thanks to the market that we are able to free ourselves from exclusive, dependent relations and benefit from an infinity of choice. It is thanks to the market that we are deemed no longer united but alone, isolated from each other, subject to the competition of all against all. This idea (or ideal) of the market is also contained within the formalism of economic modelling, the same formalism, anthropologists among others object, that is always collapsing at the level of practice.[4] It is an idea that has, nevertheless, been formative in critiques of market relations from Durkheim to Polanyi.

Our aim in this introduction, and in the chapters that follow, is to enlarge the frame of the audit. We move beyond what markets do to pre-existing social ties, to explore also how the varied arts and devices of attachment – including those algorithmically grounded innovations that are fast developing within digital economies – compose and orchestrate markets. This includes, but is not limited to, considering how recognisably social ties of love, family, community or solidarity fare in markets. Also in the frame are questions about how attachments of all kinds – sentimental, affective, aesthetic, corporeal, physiological, psychosomatic, etc. – between people and things are worked into the arts and devices employed in markets.

In this sense, our project shares and pushes further the aims of Anne Schmidt and Christoph Conrad's recent book on *Affects, Bodies and Market Societies* (2016). In their book, the authors review the role of affects in the development of 'soft capitalism'. The authors of the book show how the puzzling opposition between affects as the expression of an invariant biological substratum and affects as ever shifting historical constructs is solved through various efforts aimed at activating our affects, depending on the power relationship between supply and demand, cultural orientations and economic goals (Schmidt and Conrad, 2016). In the following pages, we elaborate on the same idea, by stressing that the art of 'emotion management' is not only oriented at shifting individuals' inner states, but also at building ties with them and between them, hence deepening the social interconnections between people and economic realms and values. It is very important to stress that this process, far from being just top-down, from market professionals to ordinary consumers, often engages, and even sometimes starts from, the participation of lay people… including ourselves!

Inspired by Kjellberg's model in this collection, we begin in this spirit with a short diversion into an auto-ethnography of the Apple Watch. As a product in the emerging category of 'wearable' devices – devices that work through physical attachment to users – made by a company legendary for strong consumer attachment, the Watch offers a fitting departure point.

Who is attaching who? On wearing the Apple Watch

The launch of the Apple Watch, billed as the company's most personal device ever, was announced in March 2015. For us, this launch and the market fate of the watch was interesting for reasons which bear directly on our objectives in this collection. Apple is regularly ranked in the top five of the world's most valuable brands alongside the technology mega-corporations Google, Facebook, Microsoft and Amazon that increasingly structure what and how people buy.[5] Among these, Apple Inc. is a touchstone corporation, a shibboleth even, in the way it identifies and divides its followers and its critics. We editors are no exception to this. Perhaps the only Apple position we share is the view that the corporation offers an exceptional case study in the arts of market attachment. For all its devout following, Apple has, particularly since the ascendance that began with the launch of the iMac in 1998, faced a steady stream of critique for employing the dark arts of imitation, reverse engineering, patent infringement, litigiousness, off-shore production, questionable labour practices, excessive shareholder value extraction, consumer platform lock-ins, anti-competitive practices and especially slick marketing.[6] It is the character, the features and qualities of this slick marketing that make Apple, and its Watch in particular, such an instructive case for a collection exploring the arts and devices of how people attach to marketed goods (and how marketed goods attach to people).

One of us got attached in September 2015. She was always going to be the most prone. A long-time Apple fan, wilfully offsetting beheld beauty and intuitive usability against those dark rumours and open-source abuses, she would be the one to succumb. She was already accustomed to distributing her exercising self across another wearable device, a Fitbit with a 10,000 step target-setting and sleep-tracking function. But Apple's Watch was also a thing of beauty, at least she reckoned the version cast in rose gold aluminium was. Unlike the Fitbit, which she tucked into underwear whenever she dressed up, the Watch could be worn with anything. 'Can't you just take that ugly thing off for the wedding?' she used to get asked. Well, no, she hadn't been willing to let all those steps go to waste, unregarded, uncounted. It was bad enough that, placed in underwear, the device counted far fewer steps than when worn on the wrist. In point of fact, wearable devices don't count steps at all. Tracking devices use three-dimensional accelerometer systems to sense motion and motion intensity, which are then converted by algorithms into usable information rendered as 'steps'. Many of her steps are earned by typing angrily, even on one occasion by an intense patch of turbulence. Developers are well aware of this – activity trackers for the wrist are significantly less accurate than those worn on the trunk, or on the head. But they are much more *wearable*. People have a well-established tolerance for wearing little machines on their wrists, not so much, as Google Glass discovered, for wearing them along the central line where they more accurately capture bodily movement.

This is a first hint at how people are already *in* products. Becoming a product that endures, that gets 'into'[7] people, means fitting people, and their varied relations, into the product. As Cochoy (2016a) has described, in a different context, the innovator-producer is also, necessarily, a buyer. In the history/mythology of Apple, Steve Jobs occupies a position as the ultimate sovereign consumer, relentlessly pressing buttons to engineer and re-engineer user experience into the product. This distribution of producer/buyer/engineer/user/consumer relations is integral to the object's journey to becoming a marketed product. In the Apple Watch, the user is present even in the decision to call the device a watch. Unlike 'wearable devices', watches are a recognisable, liveable product category. Being called a watch might help counter resistance to body-borne machines among the many who are not 'early adopters' of technology, while at the same time hedging against the uncertain future of the 'wearable device' product category.

Yet Apple's Watch is no more a watch than any of the other trackers on the market with a time function are. It is more accurately described as a 'smart watch', another new product category that signals that its 'watch-like' functions play second fiddle to many other capabilities. For critics it's an overpriced, battery-greedy activity tracker that has yet to define the really crucial problem that it solves. Others point to its lower discard rate than that of competing devices which are fast becoming famous for ending up in drawers.[8] Notoriously secretive, Apple are not saying how many watches they have shipped. If early estimates are correct though the watch is selling faster than the first generation of the iPhone and taking over from Fitbit as the 'stickiest' of wearable tracking devices.[9] This raises intriguing questions about the nature of attachment. What is it about Apple's Watch, with its high price and functional limitations, that might be making it stick, or attach, faster to its users?

The price itself could be a factor (see Cochoy in this volume). Products may be stickier when they cost more, providing more motivation to resolve any post-purchase discomfort in their favour. But that is surely not all there is? There must be more in the attachment to Apple products to prompt those controversies about 'owned' consumers and cultish followings (Belk and Tumbat, 2005). Apple has certainly exercised unusual control through its development of multi-channel platforms that integrate content like software, music, video and apps with their hardware. Multi-channel platform integration locks consumers in 'by imposing high switching costs, as Apple content can only be played on Apple hardware' (Montgomerie and Roscoe, 2013: 293). It's a business model that provides operating synergies and a high level of influence over suppliers and customers. It also provides a device that helps to secure attachment, by making it possible to 'listen in' to customer conversations (c.f. McFall, 2014a). Apple's online iTunes and app stores give the company real-time access to lots of the things their customers are listening to, watching, reading, playing and working with. Its ranking and review systems aggregate this alongside the more detailed qualitative thoughts that customers share. As is the case with other tech giants, notably Amazon, this aggregate data is sorted using algorithms to produce sales 'rankings' or 'trends' that exert huge influence upon future purchases.[10]

Rankings are an important feature of attachment strategies in digital economies. At a glance, they appear to be measuring a straightforward data point, the number of purchases of a given product among all products, but, as Gillespie (2016: xx) explains, the process is 'bounded in oblique ways by timeframe, category, and other parameters determined by the platform, and fed back not just as information, but as an invitation to value that product because of its popularity'. Apple's Watch sits in an 'ecosystem' of devices that listen, sort, rank and value consumer habits, preferences and sentiments. Algorithmic ranking and trending devices provide a means of 'digitally objectifying' qualities (Mellet et al., 2013). These strategies of digital market attachment appear to push the boundaries of economics, scored, in Gabriel Tarde's terms, as a 'science of passionate interests'. They offer the capacity 'to calculate, with extremely sensitive mechanisms, the slightest mood variations' (Latour and Lepinay, 2009: 49) so that the kind of economic quantification of sentiment that Tarde aspired to seems, through this proliferation of new valuation techniques (c.f. Kjellberg and Mallard, 2013; Helgesson and Kjellberg, 2013), almost within grasp.

In this context of commercial digitisation, 'listening in' on prospective customers can claim to be looped back into production in a tighter temporal frame than imagined in most market models. The increased velocity of customer feedback and product adjustment cycles, particularly through user-generated online content, underscores the increasing prominence of co-production, co-creation and 'prosumption' in accounts of contemporary consumer capitalism (Zwick and Cayla, 2011; Ritzer and Jurgenson, 2010; also Mallard, Mellet and Gerlitz, this volume). Co-production plays a vital role in market attachment. The algorithmically powered valuation devices of digital retailing offer novel, and consequential, means of putting what people bought, and what they thought about it into the products they will buy next. And yet there has always been more than this going on when people attach to products.

In the end, it is not aggregated rankings and reviews, nor even the fact that the Watch design anticipates her interest in a more 'becoming' tracker (or to use an old-fashioned but apt phrase, a tracker that 'becomes her') that gets her. There is something in the way it takes on some of her burdens of responsibility. It reminds her when she has sat for too long with a gentle, haptic tap on the arm. In the progress towards closure of three coloured rings, a visually economical description of how close, or how far, she is from the day's targets for responsible, healthy movement is always waiting. More, it keeps her in touch with her other responsibilities: there is a gentle buzz when a meeting is about to start, a ringing vibration when someone is trying to get in touch. This places her geographically distant social relations in a new digital proximity – she can't miss them. If she was so minded she could even socialise her tracking by using a partner app to post her achievements on social media or even insert herself in live competition with other app users. It is for all these reasons that she has the Watch – and the Watch has her.

Devices, devisings and agencings

The case of Apple Watch attachment illustrates how the multiple, bifurcating lines connecting people and their products, products and their people can work. It is no surprise that the metricising qualities of devices like it (trackers, apps, smart phones, tablets, etc.) that work by translating huge rafts of human activity into data, has prompted rapidly circulating literatures exploring the political consequences, particularly through the idea of 'neoliberal' wellness industries.[11] There is something very compelling in these arguments and in what Bouk (2015) calls the corporate and financial interest in 'numbering' our days, but there is also something historically, empirically and sociologically unsatisfying in what this says about the 'us' who are so numbered.

Reaching back to what historians of science and technology had to say about how trust in numbers was accomplished, there is an important emphasis, particularly in Theodore Porter's (1996) account, on the role of rhetoric in establishing the sorts of cultures of objectivity in which quantified measures could thrive. Strategies of quantification, Porter notes, are not merely the tools of politics and public administration, they also 'work in an economy of personal and public knowledge, of trust and suspicion' (1996: 200). The important question is how to think about the ways personal and public knowledge are entangled in these strategies. In many critiques of the neoliberal commandeering of happiness, of wellbeing, of movement, of our very days on earth, by products and practices, of which Apple's Watch is just the tip of a fat iceberg, consumer selves are remarkably compliant, 'buffeted by forces over which they have no influence' (Davies, 2015: xx). There is a stark passivity to this version of the self who is 'done unto'. Personal and public knowledge feed into political and corporate action that moulds consumer identities such that the only available choices are between the hollow differentiations offered in the market. This gives a model of the individual whose fate might be wholly different without the ministrations of neoliberal capitalism. It is a model that also, logically invokes a separation of individual from society, of subject from object, such that the balance and origin of action is with the overweening structures of state and market interests to mould the kind of individuals they need.

It is reasonable enough to read history that way. Still, the empirical histories featured in this collection question what kind of an entity the individual who so mutely bears social relations is, and about what kind of an organising will is borne by social and political structures. In an early work, Ian Hacking put related questions about how particular sorts of individuals arose in particular sorts of societies in a Foucauldian frame:

> I do not believe there is a general story to be told about making up people. Each category has its own history. If we wish to present a partial framework to describe such events, we might think of two vectors. One is the vector of labelling from above, from a community of experts who create a 'reality' that some people make their own. Different from this is the vector of the autonomous behaviour of the person so labelled, which presses from below, creating a reality every expert must face.
>
> (Hacking, 1986: 168)

The idea of two interacting vectors, labelling from above and autonomous behaviour from below, that provide the conditions for particular sorts of person to emerge has been used before now to make sense of how consumers behave in retail spaces (du Gay and Negus, 1994). This partial framework offers a useful but not quite sufficient route into thinking about the multiple lines of action that come together in making up a consumer, a product, a market. It has since been developed much further in literature exploring the role of sociotechnical market agencements or devices in distributing action or agency across objects, practices, knowledges and people.[12] In this mode of analysis there is no hard, fixed separation between human and object, between technology and practice, between personal knowledge and political organisation. Instead, being an individual is accomplished through avidity. This means that it is the struggle to associate, relate, attach to other individuals and other things, that lies beneath all existence. Devices, devisings or 'agencings' provide the conceptual tools for thinking about the assemblages through which ways of having, and therefore of being, are figured out.

That this schema can slip into a tautology that has everything in the world participating in making everything in the world the way that it is, has been hazarded before.[13] It is certainly the case that the extended lines of reasoning that are given material form in devices can be difficult for the analyst to know where to cut, to limit.[14] Where is the end of a device's sphere of influence, of action, of consequences? Law and Ruppert's (2013: 229) discussion has devices as 'more or less patterned teleological arrangements' with function and purpose – they do things – though not necessarily, or only, the things they are supposed to. In Callon's terms, devices or 'socio-technical agencements' produce or perform their intended consequences in felicitous conditions of 'fragile and rare' alignment but 'the general rule is a misfire' (2010: 164).[15] This misfiring is what creates the political issues that surround markets and underpin the long controversies about what sorts of relations, ties or attachments markets should, and should not, get involved with.

The connections between device and consequence cannot be comprehensively described. What escapes tantalises analyses of how market attachment operates. Market devices may have functions and purposes that are designed to arrange market action in particular ways. They may fulfil functions across the long chain of activities that help build market attachment, for instance by incubating technologies, researching target groups, structuring sales pitches, securing early series funding, providing evidence of efficacy, recruiting influential advocates, publicising reviews, etc. (c.f. Latour, 1991). Such activities matter and specific devices, from focus groups to ranking algorithms, structure them in ways that can smooth 'pathways to market'. But devices also act in unaccountable, unfathomable ways. In the old Anglican prayer of confession an earlier sense of the word puts devices and desires together as an intricate collusion in those tricky and deceptive matters of the heart that distract individuals from their proper purposes, into doing '*those thinges which we ought not to have done* [sic]'.

This archaic sense has devices working internally, within a person – and also behind her back. This sense of the term is arguably closer to the word 'agencement' than contemporary usage, because it carries a sense of machinery, albeit internal machinery, *plus* motivated action. It also implies something about the hard limits to our understanding of how action – whether human, social, natural or scientific – is engineered and the consequences that ensue. Remembering this sense of devices does not mean abandoning careful, technical description of how they work. It does indicate pragmatic moderation, an acknowledgement that social, technical and political knowledge must necessarily be partial and subject to revision. In the context of market attachment this is a programmatic call to empirical description and analyses of the type collected here. Understanding how devices work to attach people to particular products, through processes of listening, co-production and addiction, as Callon explains in closing this collection, is essential to tackling the puzzle of the market. Market encounters are not meetings between agents and goods in waiting, they are 'shared but improbable adventures that take place in a multitude of sites and which shape the co-profiling of both goods and agents' (Callon, this collection, p. 180). These adventures have a quality to them that defies full accounting or reckoning. It is for this reason that we refer to 'the arts' of market attachment in our title.

Devices and arts

That some market attachments are defiantly, economically irrational is clearest in cases where the product is categorised as dependency inducing or addictive. In addition to contraband substances, mobile devices, smart watches, activity trackers, screens, games, prescribed opiate painkillers, subprime credit products, alcohol, sugared fizzy drinks and more have been referenced in this category. These are all products that attach people in ways that can lead them to neglect responsibilities, to leave core tasks undone. A common definition used in recovery programmes defines addiction as a habit that costs more, for example in damage to health, relationships, productivity, creativity, etc. than the money spent on it. Addictions that are structured through the devices of market attachment are arguably on the increase through the consolidated action of big sugar, big technology, big food, big finance, big pharma and big data as well as the more familiar culprit, big tobacco. A case can easily be made that such addictions, in mediating social experience in harmful and destructive ways, have net negative effects on health and wellbeing. The case that these addictions are *devised*, in the contemporary sense of the term, we suggest, is a little harder to make. Natasha Dow Schüll's account (2012; c.f. Poon, 2013) of how gambling addiction is technically, algorithmically designed into contemporary slot machines is powerful but there remains something that artfully resists explanation. This can be roughly summarised by reversing Callon's question in the Afterword from 'why do consumers attach themselves more to some goods than others?' to 'why do *some consumers* attach themselves more to goods than others?' Addicts have their 'drugs of choice', tech users tend to be platform loyal and even cola drinkers resist substituting their favourite brands. The reasons one brand, one product is more 'becoming' to one consumer than another lies somewhere between what we call the 'arts' and the devices of attachment.

This distinction between the arts and devices of attachment is artificial. If devices also involve the weird workings of machinery, the motives and consequences that escape description, then the term 'arts' is superfluous. That it survived the long period it has taken for this collection to come together indicates that we continued to find something useful, even necessary, in it. There are a number of reasons. The first reflects on the critique that encompassing definitions of devices, those that reach beyond the machine to incorporate dispositions, human beings, action, language, etc.,[16] risk a tautological collapse. This is Mirowski and Nik-Khah's (2007) particular point, but the more general argument that those concepts that purport to explain too much end by explaining very little has also been well rehearsed.[17] In using 'arts' we section off our interest in those tricky, tenuous, playful and often polarising elements of attachment that are somewhere in performative utterances like

'I'll have it', 'I'll take it!'. A second reason is that these dimensions have had far less attention in science and technology-focused market and finance studies in recent years. In this, we acknowledge the justification for Entwistle and Slater's (2014) complaint that actor-network theory, and by extension its close companion science and technology studies, has had much more to say about economy than it has about 'culture'. Our response is not a 'turn back' – again – to culture.[18] It is more an assertion that studying markets socially and technically means attending to *all* their elements, even those that most artfully defy empirical description.[19]

This matters because the action of avidity, as it takes place in market framings, relies on both device-like and more artful mechanisms working together. Whether devices are engineered *prima facie* to listen, to co-produce or to addict – as Callon's helpful programmatic distinction has it – how exactly they succeed – and fail – in making attachments between people and things is partly mysterious. Arts – aesthetic, pastoral, sentimental, unconscious, playful, dark – are often somewhere in the mix. Such arts, which stretch all the way from commissioning a 'fine' artist to work on a campaign, to regulating brand compliance to psychometric consumer profiling, could also be classified as a dimension or sub-function of devices. We have held on to the term anyway because while 'device' connotes something that works, that does things, 'arts' better signals the uncertainty, guesswork, sentiment, luck, mystery and failure that is also inherent in attachment. Markets work with avidity, as a general propensity, but deliberately attaching particular things to particular people, and particular people to particular things is, as our contributors in their different ways all show, fraught. The market work of making attachments is constant and relentless partly because detachment is its inevitable other (Callon et al., 2001). To have (something) is also always to have not (something else).

If the work of market attachment often goes unnoticed, it is, paradoxically, the process of detachment that sometimes reveals the strength of the tie. Attempting to change a car, bank, insurance company, credit, or internet service provider often unmasks an array of binding formalities (see Cochoy, this volume). We might consider that each time we buy a product it is possible to enter and leave the relationship as anonymous nobodies, in keeping with the ideal of market transactions. But even where anonymous entry is possible – and in an era of cashless payment, store loyalty cards and online shopping that all demand customer identification, anonymous transactions are becoming the exception – on exit we find a ball of ties that we did not suspect and that can be surprisingly difficult to undo. In participating in market transactions we enter a Gordian knot, passing from one node to another. Market attachments are simultaneously the outcome and cause of these transactions.

Behind the identification of these attachments lies an entire project, which consists of studying how markets 'make', 'unmake' and thus 'remake' society. In the pages that follow some of the varied and unusual types of attachment that arise in the encounters between partners in economic exchange emerge. Markets are extraordinarily rich in issues dear to sociologists. In order to capture these issues, it has been never more urgent to dispose of the idea that the sociological explanation of economy consists of mechanically tracing action in an institutionalised repertoire of more or less immutable entities and prior social properties (such as social class, gender, age, education, income, culture, institutions, etc.) that act as independent variables upon the course of economic action. To complete the analysis, and to capture the new forms of market action and the new social, technical and economic objects that are produced, our contributors study the distribution of action that culminates in exchange closely. This means following how arts and devices work to make, unmake and remake the attachments that comprise the always ready social market. It means remembering that people, whether advertising researchers, social media marketers, activists, call centre workers, savers, borrowers, online daters or expert hobbyists, are not the mute bearers of market relations. They are radically complicit. Which is to say that markets are contingent, all the way down, upon the associated action of individuals in attaching, rejecting, complaining, negotiating, reviewing, modifying, hacking, appropriating and refusing market offerings. Recognising this contingency, paradoxically, matters a great deal in regulating what markets should, and should not, have sovereignty over.

The chapters

Our work to unravel this paradoxical contingency begins with Franck Cochoy's analysis of the pasts and potential futures of the economic sociology of market attachment. As he notes, in its varied accounts of the relationship between societies and markets, sociology has tended to exhibit some confusion about precisely how the two are interrelated. The social, Cochoy argues, should be seen not as a substance that weighs over economic action but as a particular movement of association, the results of which can never be clear from the outset. Associations might produce what will be recognised as societies, they might produce what will be recognised as markets, but they might equally produce forms where the dividing line between society and economy is wholly unclear. This also raises the possibility that markets themselves might be intimately involved in the production of societies. The two conceptual poles of Cochoy's account are 'selection' and 'collection'. The former is the more familiar to students of the economy, encompassing some of the varied ways in which market agents, both individual and organisational, reach out to one another to form novel forms of association. The description of these forms of association matters, with Cochoy assessing the particular potential afforded by the vocabulary of both the 'tie' and the 'attachment'. Mechanisms of collection, meanwhile, have occupied scholars of markets to a far less extent. Cochoy points to just some of the highly diverse ways in which markets both depend on and constitute activities and movements of collectivisation. Opening up questions that the following chapters explore further in their own ways, Cochoy highlights the inherent multiplicity of products – that they might better be considered as 'bundles' than singular and autonomous. He also exposes the diverse ways in which people coalesce and are coalesced by and around various market processes, ranging from the highly strategic activities of the 'engines' of collection, to the opening up of markets to forms of political participation, at a range of scaler registers.

Tomas Ariztia explores the varied uses of Consumer Research (CR) in the making of advertising campaigns. His account reveals the use and value of CR in the practical work of making a useful 'truth' about consumers that might help foster attachment. CR, Ariztia shows, is not valued for its ability to mobilise or support 'evidence' about consumers but rather for its role in making a stable and specific truth about consumers. Different elements of CR are valued for their role in producing useful, negotiated and specific truths about consumers around which a campaign might be built. This very specific mode of engaging the consumer, Ariztia argues, can be thought of in John Dewey's terms as an inquiry – a mode of knowledge production that is problem-based, rather than based on uncovering an external reference or truth. The consumer 'truths' of CR are not stable or external but entirely contingent upon the specific problem or question posited by the campaign design process. This, Ariztia explains, is distinct from the role played by CR in other marketing devices, such as product development where CR functions mainly as a test to inform mutual adjustment between goods and consumers. More than a test, CR in advertising is a resource for imagining new (untested) attachments.

Kevin Mellet too focuses on marketing agencies, while at the same time shifting his analysis to how agencies exploit the potential of online forms of collectivity with particular attention to the role of social media. Mellet's case concerns a set of agencies that were grappling with what was, at the time of the study, a still new and highly uncertain domain. The challenge for such companies was how to transform the online social lives of groups of individuals into a source of extractable economic value. These are processes, Mellet shows, that rely on market professionals developing sophisticated understandings of the basis of social action, bringing them at times seemingly quite close to sociologists in their desire to understand, and ultimately exploit, what might cause and what might shape social action. Attachment in his case is effected through attempts, some inevitably more successful than others, by these experts to harness the potentially powerful forces of contagion, of influence and of community. How to achieve a 'buzz' amongst a particular group about a particular product, or how to make a video 'go viral' (contagion indeed!) is shown to be an artistic science (a scientific art?). This work is not without its tensions. The very fact that practical work of delivering contagion in markets is often characterised by creating cultural products – a video hoping for virality, for instance – that, to a greater extent than is the case in conventional advertising work, depend for their success on the unpredictable, on delivering that undefinable something that causes an individual not just to embrace a particular solicitation into their own lives but to share it with others, can push more conservative clients towards more dependable but perhaps less spectacular strategies. This is an important reminder, that market attachment involves processes that operate as much upstream as downstream (e.g. Cochoy, 2016a, 2016b), as much towards those that deliver products as towards those that use them, as well as multiple intervening agencies, each with their own goals and types of expertise.

Carolin Gerlitz's chapter draws attention to the multiple dimensions of attachment that such digitally aware expert-led activities can engender. Her focus is on the way that brands, in her case Dove and American Apparel, make strategic use of a diversity of actors that already, or could, have degrees of attachment to the brand in question. These attachments are not simply of desire or need, but extend to making use of apparent correspondences between the values exhibited by a particular brand, societal concerns and politically infused projects. A range of actors, from campaigning organisations to the actual and potential end users of the products the brands are trying to sell, and many of which are operating heavily online, are involved in these attachments. Through the imbrication of the politically infused passions of the stakeholders in the very mechanisms that reproduce these brands, it becomes possible to continually reshape the identity, meaning and indeed ontologies of the brands in question – thus making them ever more 'attachable'. What Gerlitz shows is that market attachment is never just attachment in and through markets. Market attachment is a process that works with, indeed thrives off, attachments already operative in a diversity of domains and settings, both informal and institutionalised. To put it in Gerlitz's terms, attachments are 'partible'. That is, they are at once always partial, in that an attachment inevitably attaches to multiple domains, and detachable, with no single domain able to assume that a particular attachment will, in the future, continue to attach the people and things that have been tied to it up until that point.

The resilience and diversity of attachments comes to the fore in Alexandre Mallard's account in a different way. Mallard uses his expertise on the role of the telephone in market and social life to provocatively reimagine commercial call centres as 'cord centres'. Telephones may have long abandoned their physical cords, but as Mallard reveals, they still play a distinctive role in making cord-like social ties. The telephone cord can *jouer sur la corde sensible*, or touch a soft spot. By enabling us to remotely hold but also hang up the line, telephones frame one of the smoothest and yet most fragile of social interactions. By focusing exchange exclusively on the voice, on the words, on 'what matters', they privilege communication, emotions and meaning. This is especially true in the case of call centres. On the surface, call centres seem more oriented towards instant, anonymous, functional and superficial conversations than towards the development of long-term, personal, social and meaningful relationships. But Mallard's sharp exploration of the technical framing of call centre conversations shows us precisely how these conversations can be managed to build consumer loyalty. The trick is in asymmetry but here of equipment rather than of information. The customer has just her phone and her questions. The call centre professional has her phone too, but she is also equipped with scripts and software that frame the exchange even before it starts. The customer is allocated to a segment in advance then streamed to a particular contact person and treated to a particular communication strategy. Mallard's account shows how attachments rest on the emerging balance between economic motives, underlying algorithms and market segments, interactional skills and social exchange. Phone-equipped commercial conversations, far from adjusting passive prepared questions to correspondingly passive pre-set answers, rely on a continuous and co-productive process of attachment. This requires the adaptability of the talkers but also the flexibility of the full system that works to frame their exchange.

The significance of the broader frame, the system, in which commercial conversation takes place is also prominent in McFall and Deville's chapter. They employ the conceit of markets 'having you' to place questions about the potency and intrusiveness of big digital marketing in an historical frame. Using the example of two companies trading in what have, at different times, been flashpoint industries, industrial assurance and online payday lending, they explore the idea that markets can only exist through 'having' customers who, in turn, must also 'have'. The art of markets, McFall and Deville argue, lies in how this having – of data, relations, associations, ties, 'us' – is practically accomplished. Digitisation generally, and digital marketing in particular, generate critical heat. For Wonga, a payday lender operating exclusively online and claiming a secret algorithmically personalised risk profiling as the basis of its business model, this heat was easily justified and particularly intense. That this heat, when it reached the level of governmental audit, missed its target, McFall and Deville suggest is partly a function of a misunderstanding of the extent and varied history of relationship-management strategies in both prime and non-prime financial services industries. The conversation between buyers and sellers is structured historically in a dynamic attempt to devise stable market attachments in spite of the asymmetries of information, technique and equipment between the parties. The variety of these techniques, their histories of success and failure, query some of the stronger epistemological claims made about the commercial uses of big proliferant data.

Ossandón's chapter stays with the low end of financial services and opens with a striking claim: credit cards assemble collectives. In this Ossandón echoes Gerlitz in exposing the diversity, and unpredictability, of the political attachments played out in market settings. The idea of a credit card getting involved in the formation of a collective seems almost counterintuitive. Credit depends on the certainty of a dyadic attachment – between a named creditor and a named borrower or, less commonly, borrowers. Ossandón shows that, in practice, such dyadic attachments can multiply and become distributed. His focus is on a particular pattern of credit card use in Chile. What he finds in the homes of families living in low-income areas of Santiago are credit cards on the move – both within and between households. Borrowers, he observes, are routinely acting as lenders, both of their own cards and of the access to credit that they afford. The shape of the consumer credit market in such places is thus conditioned by, and at the same time co-produces, collective circuits of social relations. But Ossandón's story is not just about the domestication of a technology by people as it enters their homes. As he observes, collectivisation in the consumer credit market, in Chile as much as pretty much anywhere else, profits from the data-driven assembly of populations, via the risk-driven management of current and future borrowers. The fact that only the lender can see and draw relations between the individuals brought together in their databases and modelled predictions creates the illusion that what is being produced by the database is somehow separate from the conduct and constitution of social life. As Ossandón notes, credit card sharing practices are equally invisible – not to their practitioners or curious ethnographers – but to the credit issuers dependent on assembling data traces. Like many of the contributions collected here, Ossandón's case lays bare not only the strangeness of what, for some, is a familiar, everyday practice but also how markets have, inevitably, to be made through social practices.

Emmanuel Kessous takes this point further still in examining the market for love and intimacy that operates on dating websites. Kessous' discussion enters two major debates in economic sociology. The first debate concerns how markets are best defined: as 'platforms' meant to bridge the two blocks of supply and demand or as involving the production of bilateral transactions aimed at attaching particular goods to particular agents (Callon, 2013). The second debate is about the 'contested' character of markets and the moral concerns that are provoked when market-like solutions are applied to certain 'goods'. 'Goods' here are not necessarily tangible products but may be any of a range of societally and individually significant functions, for example surrogacy, organs, biotechnical services, or in this case love (Steiner and Trespeusch, 2015). Kessous' study contributes to both debates. First, by unveiling the inner working of dating websites Kessous shows that, in some configurations at least, markets as platforms and markets as matching devices go hand in hand. The dating site is clearly designed as a market platform focused on pairing supply and demand for love (even if both sides are fully interchangeable), but it is also conceived as a manufacturer of love. Production and exchange are fully intertwined: the candidates for love are not pre-set products with given characteristics offered on a market, but full human actors who continuously and interactively adjust their properties in order to reach (hopefully) a successful encounter... or transaction. This latter hesitation brings us to the second debate and contribution. Kessous' case directly exposes the ambivalent meaning of 'attachments' as bonds that share the sacred value of human relationships and the technical dimension of material ties. Online dating, by favouring reflexive and strategic-like behaviours, also, simultaneously, favours a kind of exchange that misses its goal of real love-like 'attachments'. Almost as if the market for love was both fulfilling and contesting itself.

In the penultimate chapter Hans Kjellberg confronts the art of market attachment at its core by exploring the purest, most fascinating case: the hybrid bond that exists between a consumer and a product. Kjellberg's contribution is methodological, empirical and conceptual. It is methodological, in the way that auto-ethnography is used to generate a more illuminating close-up of this bond than may be possible through classic sociological inquiry. Instead of a well-chosen, representative sample or population, Kjellberg focuses on a pure idiosyncratic case, the purchase of a vintage Ford Thunderbird. He pushes the idiosyncrasy further by showing that the significance of this particular case can best be revealed through the particular experience of the researcher himself. This methodology gives Kjellberg's empirical contribution its force. His account shows that focusing on one single link – the relationship between the researcher and his car – unveils many, many others. Contrary to what economists and sociologists often think, the relationship between consumer and good is not an isolated dyad. It is just a first node leading to a huge network of unexpected encounters and socio-technical attachments. Just like Alice's talking rabbit, Hans' roaring car drives us into a wonderland. Following the car unveils an incredibly rich world, made of goods, contracts, pieces, but also interactions, friendship and love. At last, we discover that the economic attachment with a single good may end up reshaping a full society. The contribution is thus conceptual, since it shows that economic attachments, far from restricting people to a one-dimensional and predictable sphere of materialism and economic subordination rather associate and recombine technical and human dimensions to produce novel and often unexpected 'agencements', in the proper Callonian sense, indicating bundles of technical and human agencies (Callon, 2013).

The collection concludes with a commentary by Michel Callon that underlines the real necessity of considering the series of trials that result in market attachment. Understanding the puzzle of the market, he explains, means investigating the mixture of fragile and resilient attachments that underpin the success and failure of commercial transactions. This means giving up finally on the idea that producers and consumers, buyers and sellers just wait in their separate domains for a suitable place, an agora, they can go to. Instead markets happen in a wonderland, or a territory on which conscionable, and unconscionable, maps work together, not often in harmony, to transform or more accurately 'co-profile' goods and agents. The arts and devices we describe act as maps to market territory. As in Luis Borges' (1973 [1946]) well-used story, where the obsession with final exactitude in the scientific study of markets or society leaves only a mess of 'tattered remains', a useful and limited map makes for a navigable territory. Callon's taxonomy of three market devices focused primarily on listening, co-production and addiction works as a useful map to some of the predominant activity ongoing in the territory of contemporary market attachment. That these devices are artful in their inexactitudes, secrets and failures goes with the territory of attachment that Callon so precisely captures: 'the process of attachment is equally a process of expression, in which they learn what they are and what they are becoming, and whereby, symmetrically, things and goods express what they are or what they can do and "make do"' (Callon, this volume, p. 181).

Notes

1 The chapters by Cochoy, Mellet, Kjellberg and Kessous are updated and sub-stantially revised versions of chapters that appeared in *Du lien marchand* (Cochoy 2012).

2 In this regard the work by Hennion (2004, 2010), Hennion et al. (1989), Latour (1991), Cochoy (1998, 2005, 2008), Callon et al. (2001), Callon (2005a) and Mus-selin and Paradeise (2005) has been especially important and influential. Much of this is reprised in Callon et al. (2013) and see also McFall (2014a) and the contributions to Cochoy et al. (2016).

3 Building on earlier collaborative work, notably with Emilie Gomart, Geoffrey Bowker and Cécile Méadel (Gomart and Hennion (1999); Hennion et al. (1989)). Hennion's understanding of attachment marks a break with the extensive and, in Anglophone social science, more widely known discussion of attachment asso-ciated with psychologist John Bowlby's research on the bonds between parents and children and their effects. It is also largely distinct from the body of work within feminist theory concerned with questions of painful/problematic psychic and bodily attachment. A discussion of the points of correspondence between these different strands of work is beyond our scope here but see Deville (2015).

4 See Çalışkan and Callon (2009, 2010); Callon (2005a, 2005b); Miller (2002, 2005); Mirowski and Nik-Khah (2007); Musselin and Paradeise (2005).

5 In 2016 Google's parent company Alphabet passed Apple as the world's most valuable company, www.bloomberg.com/news/articles/2016-02-02/google-paren t-to-overtake-apple-as-world-s-most-valuable-company, but Forbes was still ranking as the most valuable brand www.forbes.com/powerful-brands/list/.

6 See Montgomerie and Roscoe (2013); Lazonick et al. (2013).

7 As an aside 'intu' was the brand chosen in 2013 by Capital Shopping Centres, one of the UK's largest centre management companies, as a way of signalling their 'new nationwide consumer-facing shopping centre brand and the transformation of its digital proposition'. www.intugroup.co.uk/investors/shareholders-bondholders/ transaction-archive/operational-initiatives-and-change-of-name/; http://uk.reuters. com/article/uk-csc-intu-idUKBRE90E00720130115.

8 There is even a high-profile campaign to rehome unused trackers run by Tufts professor Lisa Gualtieri, www.facebook.com/recyclehealth/.

9 'Stickiness' is used in the tech industry to refer to qualities, particularly in websites but also of devices like wearables, that encourage people to stay with, or attached to, the product for longer. www.wsj.com/articles/apple-watch-with-sizable-sales-ca nt-shake-its-critics-1461524901; http://bigstory.ap.org/article/2700956044de4517a 471a47c3243078b/strong-sales-high-abandonment-fitness-trackers; https://rockhea lth.com/reports/digital-health-consumer-adoption-2015/.

10 The iTunes ecosystem is a walled garden, where on the one hand, Apple has full control over what's accepted, while on the other, the iTunes chart algorithm deci-des which apps gain visibility. These charts continuously publish and update a list of 'top' applications split by categories. The higher an app is ranked in the charts, the more users see and download it. We don't know exactly how the ranking

algorithm works, but the general consensus is that both recent downloads and app usage affect it. https://medium.com/i-data/apple-s-app-charts-2015-data-and-trends-a bb95300df57#.d7k9tlv5q.

11 Beer (2015), Cederstrom and Spicer (2015), Davies (2015), Lupton (2014), Schüll (2016).

12 Cochoy et al. (2016), McFall (2014a), Çalışkan and Callon (2009, 2010), Callon (1998), Callon et al. (2001, 2007), Cochoy (1998, 2005, 2008).

13 Mirowski and Nik-Khah (2007), Law and Ruppert (2013).

14 See also Deleuze (1991) on reason and dispositive.

15 This misfiring is what creates issues and matters of concern 'in the form of controversies over the nature of relations between that which is delegated to the economy and that which remains outside of it. Saying and doing the economy because all economies are said and done (Çalışkan and Callon 2009) means entering into the agonistic field where the delimitation-bifurcation between the economy and politics is constantly being debated and played out' Callon (2010: 165).

16 See especially Callon (2007, 2010) and the introduction to Callon et al. (2007) for more on this.

17 See McFall (2014b) for a longer discussion of this critique.

18 Aside from adding to the dizzying succession of cultural, material, post-material turns we are hesitant about reinforcing a strong boundary between economies and cultures that in practice are constituent, contingent parts of each other until disentangled by their analysts. See also www.charisma-network.net/ and McFall (2015) for an overview of how the *Journal of Cultural Economy* and its contributors have tackled these questions.

19 This includes our own dispositional tendencies: the management of curiosity, for instance, has been described as the very 'art' of market seduction (Cochoy, 2016b).

Bibliography

Ahmed, S. (2004) *The Cultural Politics of Emotion*, New York: Routledge.

Araujo, L., Finch, J. and Kjellberg, H. (eds) (2010) *Reconnecting Marketing to Markets*, Oxford: Oxford University Press.

Beer, D. (2015) Productive measures: Culture and measurement in the context of everyday neoliberalism. *Big Data and Society*, 2(1): 1–12. http://doi.org/10.1177/2053951715578951.

Belk, R.W. and Tumbat, G. (2005) The cult of Macintosh. *Consumption Markets and Culture*, 8(3): 205–217. http://doi.org/10.1080/10253860500160403.

Berlant, L.G. (2011) *Cruel Optimism*, Durham, NC: Duke University Press.

Borges, J.L. (1973 [1946]). Of exactitude in science. In *A Universal History of Infamy*, trans. N.T. di. Giovanni, London: Allen Lane.

Bouk, D. (2015) *How Our Days Became Numbered: Risk and the Rise of the Statistical Individual*, Chicago, IL: University of Chicago Press.

Butler, J. (1997) *The Psychic Life of Power: Theories in Subjection*, Stanford, CA: Stanford University Press.

Çalışkan, K. and Callon, M. (2009) Economization, part 1: Shifting attention from the economy towards processes of economization. *Economy and Society*, 38(3): 369–398.

Çalışkan, K. and Callon, M. (2010) Economization, part 2: A research programme for the study of markets. *Economy and Society*, 39(1): 1–32.

Callon, M. (1998) Introduction: The embeddedness of economic markets in economics. In M. Callon (ed.), *The Laws of the Markets*, Oxford: Blackwell, pp. 2–57.

Callon, M. (2005a). Let's put an end on uncertainties. *Sociologie du Travail*, 47: S94–S100.

Callon, M. (2005b). Why virtualism paves the way to political impotence: A reply to Daniel Miller's critique of The Laws of the Markets. *Economic Sociology European Electronic Newsletter*, 6(2): 3–20.

Callon, M. (2010) Performativity, misfires and politics. *Journal of Cultural Economy*, 3(2): 163–169. http://doi.org/10.1080/17530350.2010.494119.

Callon, M. (2013) Qu'est-ce qu'un agencement marchand? In M. Callon et al., *Sociologie des agencements marchands*, Paris: Presses des Mines, pp. 325–440.

Callon, M., Meadel, C. and Rabeharisoa, V. (2001) The economy of qualities. *Economy and Society*, 31(2): 194–217.

Callon, M., Millo, Y. and Muniesa, F. (eds) (2007) *Market Devices*, Oxford: Wiley-Blackwell.

Callon, M., Akrich, M., Dubuisson-Quellier, S., Grandclement, C., Hennion, A., Latour, B., Meadel, C., Muniesa, F. and Rabeharisoa, V. (2013) *Sociologie des agencements marchand*, Paris: Presses des Mines.

Cederstrom, C. and Spicer, A. (2015) *The Wellness Syndrome*, Malden, MA: Polity.

Cochoy, F. (1998) Another discipline for the market economy: Marketing as a performative knowledge and know-how for capitalism. In M. Callon (ed.), *The Laws of the Markets*, Oxford: Blackwell, pp. 194–221.

Cochoy, F. (2005) A brief history of 'customers', or the gradual standardization of markets and organizations. *Sociologie Du Travail*, 47: e36–e56. http://doi.org/10.1016/j.soctra.2005.08.001.

Cochoy, F. (2008) Calculation, qualculation, calqulation: Shopping cart arithmetic, equipped cognition and the clustered consumer. *Marketing Theory*, 8(1): 15–44.

Cochoy, F. (ed.) (2012) *Du lien marchand: comment le marché fait société*, Toulouse: Presses Universitaires du Mirail.

Cochoy, F. (2016a). L'innovateur comme acheteur: Howard Head et l'invention du marché des skis composites (1947–1949). *Sociologie du travail*, 58(2): 115–137.

Cochoy, F. (2016b). *On Curiosity: The Art of Market Seduction*, Manchester: Mattering Press.

Cochoy, F., Trompette, P. and Araujo, L. (2016) From market agencements to market agencing: An introduction. *Consumption Markets and Culture*, 19(1): 3–16. http://doi.org/10.1080/10253866.2015.1096066.

Davies, W. (2015) *The Happiness Industry: How the Government and Big Business Sold Us Well-Being*, London: Verso.

Deleuze, G. (1991) What is a dispositif? In *Michel Foucault, Philosopher: Essays Translated from the French and German*, trans. T.J. Armstrong, Harlow: Pearson Educational.

Deville, J. (2015) *Lived Economies of Default: Consumer Credit, Debt Collection and the Capture of Affect*, London: Routledge.

Du Gay, P. and Negus, K. (1994) The changing sites of sound: Music retailing and the composition of consumers. *Media, Culture and Society*, 16(3): 395–413.

Entwistle, J. and Slater, D. (2014) Reassembling the cultural. *Journal of Cultural Economy*, 7(2): 161–177. http://doi.org/10.1080/17530350.2013.783501.

Gillespie, T. (2016) #trendingistrending: When algorithms become culture. In R. Seyfert and J. Roberge (eds), *Algorithmic Cultures: Essays on Meaning, Performance and New Technologies*, London: Routledge, pp. 52–75.

Gomart, E. and Hennion, A. (1999) A sociology of attachment: Music amateurs, drug users. In J. Law and J. Hassard (eds), *Actor Network Theory and After*, Oxford: Sociological Review and Blackwell, pp. 220–247.

Hacking, I. (1986) Making up people. In C. Heller, D. Wellerby and M. Sosna (eds), *Reconstructing Individualism: Autonomy, Individuality, and the Self*, Stanford, CA: Stanford University Press, pp. 222–236.

Helgesson, C.-F. and Kjellberg, H. (2013) Values and valuation in market practice. *Journal of Cultural Economy*, 6(4): 361–369.

Hennion, A. (2004) Une sociologie des attachements, D'une sociologie de la culture à une pragmatique de l'amateur. *Sociétés*, 85(3): 9–24.

Hennion, A. (2010) Loving music: From a sociology of mediation to a pragmatics of taste. *Comunicar*, 34(XVII): 25–33.

Hennion, A., Meadel, C. and Bowker, G. (1989) The artisans of desire: The mediation of advertising between product and consumer. *Sociological Theory*, 7(2): 191–209.

Kjellberg, H. and Mallard, A. (2013) Valuation studies? Our collective two cents. *Valuation Studies*, 1(1): 11–30. http://doi.org/10.3384/vs.2001-5992.131111.

Latour, B. (1991) Technology is society made durable. In J. Law (ed.), *The Sociology of Monsters*, London: Routledge, pp. 103–131.

Latour, B. and Lepinay, V.A. (2009) *The Science of Passionate Interests: An Introduction to Gabriel Tarde's Economic Anthropology*, Chicago, IL: Prickly Paradigm Press.

Law, J. and Ruppert, E. (2013) The social life of methods: Devices. *Journal of Cultural Economy*, 6(3): 229–240.

Lazonick, W., Mazzucato, M. and Tulum, Ö. (2013) Apple's changing business model: What should the world's richest company do with all those profits? *Accounting Forum*, 37(4): 249–267. http://doi.org/10.1016/j.accfor.2013.07.002.

Lupton, D. (2014) Health promotion in the digital era: A critical commentary. *Health Promotion International*, 30(1): 174–183. http://doi.org/10.1093/heapro/dau091.

Marx, K. (1980 [1857–1858]). *Marx's Grundrisse*, selected and edited by D. McLellan, London: Paladin.

McFall, L. (2014a). *Devising Consumption: Cultural Economies of Insurance, Credit and Spending*, London: Routledge.

McFall, L. (2014b). What have market devices got to do with policy instruments? In C. Halpern, P. Lascoumes and P. Le Galés (eds), *L'instrumentation de l'action publique. Controverses, résistances, effets*, Paris: Presses de Sciences Po.

McFall, L. (2015) What's changing cultural economy? *Journal of Cultural Economy*, 8(1): 1–15. http://doi.org/10.1080/17530350.2014.988670.

Mellet, K., Beauvisage, T., Beuscart, J.-S. and Trespeuch, M. (2013) A "democratization" of markets? Online consumer reviews in the restaurant industry. *Valuation Studies*, 2(1): 125–146. http://doi.org/10.3384/vs.2001-5992.14215.

Miller, D. (2002) Turning Callon the right way up. *Economy and Society*, 31(2): 218–233. http://doi.org/10.1080/03085140220123135.

Miller, D. (2005) Reply to Michel Callon. *Economic Sociology European Electronic Newsletter* 6(3): 3–13.

Mirowski, P. and Nik-Khah, E. (2007) Markets made flesh: Performativity, and a problem in science studies, augmented with consideration of the FCC auctions. In D. Mackenzie, F. Muniesa and L. Sui (eds), *Do Economists Make Markets*, Princeton, NJ: Princeton University Press, pp. 190–224.

Montgomerie, J. and Roscoe, S. (2013) Owning the consumer: Getting to the core of the Apple business model. *Accounting Forum*, 37(4): 290–299. http://doi.org/10.1016/j.accfor.2013.06.003.

Musselin, C. and Paradeise, C. (2005) Quality: A debate. *Sociologie du Travail*, 47: S89–S123.

Poon, M. (2013) For financial certainty, try machine gambling. *Journal of Cultural Economy*, 7(4): 516–523. http://doi.org/10.1080/17530350.2013.840668.

Porter, T. (1996) *Trust in Numbers: The Pursuit of Objectivity in Science and Public Life*, Princeton, NJ: Princeton University Press.

Ritzer, G. and Jurgenson, N. (2010) Production, consumption, prosumption: The nature of capitalism in the age of the digital "prosumer". *Journal of Consumer Culture*, 10(1): 13–36. http://doi.org/10.1177/1469540509354673.

Schmidt, A. and Conrad, C. (eds) (2016) *Affects, Bodies and Market Societies*, Tübingen: Mohr Siebeck.

Schüll, N.D. (2012) *Addiction by Design: Machine Gambling in Las Vegas*, Princeton, NJ: Princeton University Press.

Schüll, N.D. (2016) Data for life: Wearable technology and the design of self-care. *BioSocieties*. doi:10.1057/biosoc.2015.47

Steiner, P. and Trespeusch, M. (eds) (2015) *Marchés contestés. Quand le marché rencontre la morale*, Toulouse: Presses de l'université du Mirail.

Zelizer, V.A. (2005) *The Purchase of Intimacy*, Princeton, NJ: Princeton University Press.

Zwick, D. and Cayla, J. (2011) *Inside Marketing: Practices, Ideologies, Devices*, Oxford: Oxford University Press.

1 From social ties to socioeconomic attachments

A matter of selection and collection

Franck Cochoy

Prologue. October 2010. I buy an iPhone from the mobile phone company Orange, without a subscription. I connect the device and realize that I am stuck: even though it was bought free of subscription, my phone is attached to the operator who sold it to me. I discover on the operator's website that releasing it is possible for a cost. But the process fails, for practical reasons: the machine that answers my call requires an Orange phone number that I obviously do not have! After further surfing on the web and looking for other numbers to dial, I reach another call centre, which also asks for this famous Orange phone number, but that for once does not cut me off after waiting but switches the call to an operator. I interact with a kind person, who makes me wait for a long time because my case is complicated. She returns with instructions from her supervisor and suggests I should call a number at Apple. Apple tells me to go back to Orange, advising me to go to a shop and insist. After pulling ties from the ball of links that binds me to the market, I decide to buy a prepaid card for 15 euros that allows me to use my device as a WiFi hotspot, while relying on my existing smartphone for phone calls, and waiting for six months until I am finally untied from the relational trap into which my apparently 'free choice' purchase locked me into for so long.

How should the economic sociologist deal with the social relationships involved at the heart of market exchanges? Let's say that two options (at least) are available. The first option is well known: it is the one that has been offered for thirty years by the now not so 'new economic sociology' and the paradigm of 'embeddedness' (Granovetter, 1985). This research stream assumes that (social) ties precede (economic) exchanges. Accounting for economic action is thus about uncovering the social configurations that pre-determine exchange and give shape and meaning to it. Describing, characterising and quantifying the nature of these ties – undertaking the structural analysis of social networks – is the means to establish the causal relationship which goes from interpersonal relationships to the nature of trade. A particularly famous example is Granovetter's analysis of 'the strength of weak ties' (1973), which shows how different types of social relationships play a key role in the search for jobs in the labour market. This strong and improved analytical framework, armed with rigorous and efficient methodological tools, has proved its validity and effectiveness: see the long series of works driven by Harrison White and pursued by Granovetter and their various successors.

Yet, when reading Granovetter carefully, one discovers that the author himself subtly weakened the type of ties he contributed to build. The embeddedness he proposes does not unambiguously refer to the metaphor of an economic object embedded in a social body. It depends rather on a more balanced and symmetric view of the relationship, where the embeddedness is itself seen as the result of the exchange: 'The middle of the road I have travelled is more arduous than either requiring as it does, detailed analysis of social structure and of the complex way social and economic motives are intertwined' (Granovetter quoted by Steiner, 2002).

This idea of 'intertwined' social and economic motives supplements the more traditional idea of the embeddedness of economic matters into an encompassing 'social structure'. Behind this view lies the possibility of discussing 'classic' definitions of embeddedness and purely 'socialized' ties. For Bruno Latour (2005), the social is better defined not as a substance overhanging action (as if there was a kind of 'social stuff' into which everything else was plunged), but as the movement which characterises the process of 'association' between heterogeneous entities, which are in themselves neither 'social' nor 'natural'. In the very same way one could, in economic sociology, put aside the idea of a subordination of the economy to society, and see how the exchange itself produces varied forms of ties, in the sense of 'connections' between various entities. This is the second option that I would like to explore. Such an option can help in understanding why and how market professionals, like my phone provider, continuously build some ties in order to cut others (for instance, by attempting to break a long-standing relationship with one of their competitors). I will examine how a tie can be the result rather than the starting point of trade, by uncovering the dynamics of *market collection* that is inseparable from the process of *selection* too often exclusively associated to market mechanisms. I will also explain why this leads us to move from social ties to socioeconomic attachments.

Selection

Since Polanyi (2001), it is as if economists and sociologists agreed to consider the market mostly as an operator of tie selection/dissolution. Sociologists express their concerns about such processes, while economists, even if they do not praise them, then at least study their workings. From this point of view, and without offending sociologists, it is economists who have taken the lead, by describing with great force and clarity (at least) three mechanisms of selection. The first is that of *market selection*, also named the 'law of the market': when qualities and prices are known, *good products drive out bad ones*. This is the great legacy of classical liberalism, of Adam Smith's model of the invisible hand, of Spencer's economic Darwinism and of pure and perfect competition formalised by neoclassical economics. The second mechanism is that of '*historical selection*', a process better known as 'path dependency'. In this case, *the most popular products drive the others out of the marketplace.* Indeed, the value of some goods grows in proportion to their use by other people, regardless of their intrinsic value: this is the case, for instance, with 'network technologies', such as computer operating systems. For such goods, there is a tendency to prefer the most widely distributed system because it maximises opportunities for exchange between users, even if the chosen solution is from a strictly technical point of view not the most effective. The third mechanism is that of '*adverse selection*' which, as its name suggests, is the opposite of the first: in a situation of asymmetric information (for example, when the seller knows more about the product than the buyer), *bad products drive out good ones.* Indeed, in the absence of information about quality, the buyer has no reason to pay more than the average market price, so that the good products, being more expensive, are 'trapped' by the lack of information: unable to find a buyer, they end up leaving the market (Akerlof, 1970).

Market selection

Studying these different forms of selection has kept economic sociology very busy. On such matters, this sub-discipline somewhat trails in the wake of the very economic theories it comes to refute, criticise, discuss, qualify, supplement and extend. This is despite the fact that economic sociology nevertheless borrows from economic theories the basic findings and proposals it puts under scrutiny (such borrowing of course being in no way a problem!). In sociology, market selection is always and everywhere the subject of a pretty unanimous rejection. The proposition is either that market selection does not exist or would not work, or because it does exist and works too well, by provoking disastrous effects and/or social, moral and political problems. Citing works on these points would mobilise the entire corpus of international economic sociology! Yet, at the level of the layman, market selection is not always considered a horrifying monster. Indeed, some people invoke competition in the name of a certain idea of justice, even if these same people are not great fans of liberalism. This might be because their own political preferences are opposed to it or because they are not necessarily aware that their discourse is in fact an appeal to market mechanisms! One may for instance refer to the protestations of many PhD students against the functioning of French university hiring committees, deemed 'collusive' and/or 'opaque'. Denouncing the 'proximity' and 'networks' they suspect dominate the job market for academic positions (Musselin, 2010), these candidates ask for more 'transparency', 'clear criteria', more rigorous procedures, based primarily on a review of personal merits. This type of 'objective call for the market rationale' opens an interesting research programme aimed at studying, in the wake of the sociology of justification (Boltanski and Thévenot, 2006), not only the 'dissonance' between different types of orders of worth (Stark, 2009) – in this case, the market world of competing candidates versus the domestic world of academic networks – but also and foremost the points at which, in practice, market rationality may be anchored. This varies from the arguments of those who believe it at least partially joins their own vested interests (large companies eager to secure fluid markets, small agents keen to protect the pro-small-size dogma that sits behind much free competition, consumers praising competition and transparency, etc.) to specify the rules and technologies designed to support and develop market rationality's physical expression. See, for instance, internet price engines (Bourreau and Licoppe, 2007).

Historical selection

Historical selection (or path dependency) combines the economics of innovation on the one hand and the history and anthropology of techniques on the other. Of course, the sociohistorical 'path' followed by technical objects can challenge the stylised representations of economists, as shown in the controversy between Paul David (1985) and Stan J. Liebowitz and Stephen E. Margolis (1990) about 'the fable of the keys'. The first author claims that the QWERTY keyboard is in fact an arbitrary and suboptimal solution whose 'irreversible' hegemony is due to its early and widespread adoption. The latter provide specific historical details liable to set this view in question. But social history can also complement and enhance the model in hand. For example, a careful study of the technical evolution of supermarket trolleys highlights the existence of 'nested' innovations besides the 'locked-in' innovations of path dependency. As Catherine Grandclément (2006) has shown, the trolley's design has proved flexible over time. However, this flexibility could only be achieved by fitting new solutions to the preceding design, without coordination or preparedness, and by simply adjusting to competing solutions. The trolley designed by the pioneer Goldman juxtaposed two vertically stackable baskets that could be arranged freely on a folding frame. This solution was followed by the trolley of the innovative competitor Watson. Watson's trolley was also composed of two baskets, but this time they were welded onto the frame, in which trolleys could interlock laterally or 'telescope' with one another through a hinged back door. Then came the well-known single basket telescoping trolley, imagined in turn by Goldman by copying and simplifying his competitor's solution. The study of such objects is interesting because it points towards the importance of 'combinatorial' processes driven by the market, alongside the more traditional selection process and halfway between imitation and differentiation. This is a key aspect of the 'market *agencement*'. The term describes a type of market which is neither the pure abstract 'interface' mechanism imagined by economics, nor the large 'embedded' institution proposed by sociologists, but singular and transient combinations of varied social, economic and technical resources, of both large (Callon, 2013, 2016) and local extension (Calvignac and Cochoy, 2016).

Adverse selection

Adverse selection opens a breach in the idea of 'perfect market' that numerous sociologists – including the author of these lines! – have willingly swallowed, delighted to be able to add their own criticism to that of economists. In particular, the idea that quality is variable, and that this variation has a significant impact on the functioning of markets, has motivated the conduct of a large number of sociological studies on issues of quality, especially in France. Recently, this has led to the launch at an international level of the journal *Valuation Studies* (Helgesson and Muniesa, 2013). In France, it is probably Lucien Karpik who played the leading role in the sociology of quality. The author distinguished a 'judgement-market' from a 'price-market'. Being deprived of price and standardised information (like the French market for lawyers, where advertising was until recently forbidden), judgement-markets are based on reputation and trust. Karpik also insisted on the role of specific technical devices, like buying guides, which help products' 'singularities' to be adjusted to consumers' 'modes of engagement' (Karpik, 2010). The task of sociology is thus to uncover the different cognitive and technical elements that help subordinate the market relationship to a classic type of embeddedness. This type of analysis has been extended in two ways. First, Michel Callon and his colleagues (2002) further examined the process of product 'qualification', which is about transforming a hot, malleable 'product' into a cold, stable 'good'. More specifically, qualifying a product consists in assembling (producing) a set of human and physical entities into a 'stabilised' form (a good) that producers and marketers seek then to 'attach' to customers (this often requires a symmetric operation aimed at 'detaching' these goods from their competitors).

Perhaps because the sociology of quality has proved cumulative, but also probably because it has for this very reason reached a point of saturation, further research then turned to the dimension of price dimension (for a literature review, see Beckert, 2011), the analysis of calculative devices (Callon and Muniesa, 2005), and the political sociology of statistics (Didier, 2012). Paradoxically, the contribution of these works is perhaps less the extension of the 'sociology of quality' by adding to it a sociology of prices and measurement, than the restoration of a continuum that should never have been broken between the two. On the one hand, on the supply side, these studies show that price is finally a quality among all the others and therefore depends on a more general work of qualification. On the other hand, on the demand side, the same studies help show that processes of consumer choice rest on a special type of cognitive operation that I described in terms of 'qualculation'. By qualculation, I mean a valuation process which is mostly grounded in purely qualitative dimensions because of a lack of price information. As such, it works only transiently (as soon as it becomes possible, calculation takes over again) and with a spirit which is very close to regular calculation (comparing, classifying, selecting, etc.), albeit equipped by the surrounding environment and qualitative reference points (Cochoy, 2008a).

From social ties to socioeconomic attachments

These processes, because they insist on transformative activities rather than on the effect of pre-set social forces on instant transactions, bring two major changes into the picture. First, they introduce another perspective on embeddedness: what matters now is not so much embeddedness – i.e. a given state of entanglement – than the process of embedding, i.e. the actions aimed at building connections. What counts are not so much social 'networks' but rather 'networking' activities, in the sense of building, assembling and more recently 'agencing' social but also material and economic elements (Cochoy et al., 2016). These agencing practices place the shaping of bilateral relationships at the core of the market game, well beyond the construction of anonymous contacts by standard market platforms (Callon, 2016). As a result, this changes the meaning of what we consider as a social relationship, to the point where it is better to shift terminology and to talk instead in terms of 'socio-economic attachments', rather than, as previously, of pure 'social ties'. There are at least four reasons for such a shift.

First, whereas in the social sciences 'ties' have become the exclusive expression of social connections, 'attachments' open the repertoire of who and what is linked to hybrid forms of associations between persons, between things, and between persons and things. This occurs without *a priori* a clear distinction between what is social and what is economic, with the economic and the social being the outcome rather than the starting point of the attachment process. This is why I suggest talking in terms of 'socioeconomic' attachments.

Second, as Antoine Hennion, who theorised the notion, shows, attachments are connected to bodily practices. As such, they are a matter of taste, i.e. a practice where what is involved is not just some pre-set social forces or char-acteristics, but the physical encounter between the body of the amateur and the materiality of what is tasted, and the new links that emerge from such a meeting: 'This beautiful word [attachment] destroys the opposition that accentuates the dualism of the word "taste", between a series of causes that come from outside and the "hic et nunc" of the situation and the interaction' (Hennion, 2010: 26).

Third, Hennion's lesson can be extended: 'attachment' is most often used to designate a kind of relationship governed by affects, beyond the mere emo-tions of taste (McFall, 2009; McFall, 2014; McFall and Deville, this volume). This brings us to the theory of 'captation' I formulated a few years ago. Captation comes from the French '*capter*', which means attracting and attaching someone or something to oneself without forcing him or her (Cochoy, 2007). As I have shown, the market captation of customers rests on the use of devices (*dispositifs*) that bet on the targets' dispositions. In other words, it rests on attachment devices. For instance, a loyalty card is a device (it's a plastic tool) that enacts the existing disposition for making an instant calculation (if I obtain the card, i.e. if I attach it to myself, I will obtain a set rebate on my purchases) in order to build the new long-term disposition of loyalty (repeated gains are expected to create a strong attachment between the consumer and the supplier; see Coll (2012), Araujo and Kjellberg (2014)). In other words, captation is about 'heating' some dispositions to 'melt' existing attachments and thus to detach and then attach them otherwise, as Joe Deville (2012, 2014) brilliantly shows through his studies of debt collection: in order to reattach debtors to the payment of their debt, collectors play with sophisticated combinations of letters, shaming practices, phone calls, emotional threats and so on.

Last but not least, the word 'attachment', like the related notion of '*agencement*' (Calvignac and Cochoy, 2016), has the great advantage of being both a noun (it points to a given configuration) and a gerund: it designates not only the attachments, but more importantly the process of attaching, of, thus, collecting.

Collection

Indeed, with attaching activities, we reach the less travelled and most promising theme of 'market collection'. This is a theme with which economic sociology should feel much more comfortable, since it better fits the interests and skills of sociologists who, after all, like to define themselves as experts of 'collective matters'. This aspect of the economic dynamics would probably not have been left dormant for so long had we not forgotten Tarde's *Economic Psychology*, which brilliantly pointed to the issue more than a century ago:

> It was rightly an objection to Darwin that the struggle for life presupposes the association for life, that is to say, the *organization* that the multiplying repetitions of organisms and the struggles that ensue do not explain but involve. [Of course,] *opposition* is a general fact, but yet less general than adaptation and repetition. As such, it must take place between them, below them, as a mere intermediary or auxiliary which is frequently necessary... Everywhere in the living and social world, even in the physical world, we see harmonious things which, by multiplying themselves, come to fight against each other, adaptations that oppose: germs against cells, organisms against organisms, corporation against corporation, the State against the State, molecules against molecules, and also everywhere, as the result of this crisis, we see oppositions that are adapting: commensalism and acclimatization phenomena, fertilization, alliance treaties, chemical combination.

> (Tarde, 1902: 32–3, my translation)

We cannot establish more clearly the tension that brings together selection (here 'struggle for life', 'opposition') and collection (here 'association for life', 'organisation'). The one does not go without the other. As Tarde puts it, life does not preclude isolated entities but harmonious collections of simple elements.

These collections are not immune to competition and do not invalidate it: 'collections' 'select' each other. But they are also one of its alternatives or unforeseen outcomes: 'opposition' can certainly lead to selection, that is to say, to the elimination of one of the opposed elements, but also to 'organisation', 'commensalism', 'acclimation', 'fertilisation', 'alliance' and 'combination'. From this point of view, the choice between 'market' and 'organisation' dear to new institutional economics appears only as a late and impoverished extension of Tarde's intuition. In the latter, organisation, far from being reduced to the narrow figure of the firm, embraces a much more diverse range of 'harmonies' that cannot be reduced to human ones. Tarde speaks of 'germs' and 'corporation', of 'state' and 'molecules', of many entities to which he would certainly add today 'GMOs', 'teams', 'vaccines', 'segments', 'unions', 'Airbus', 'catalogues', 'derivatives', 'standards', 'consumer organisations' and so on. I would like to focus on two figures of this movement of collection which are irreducibly related to selection, and without which the latter cannot be understood.

Bundles of characteristics and objects

The first figure is the collection of product characteristics. As far as such collections are concerned, it is worth remembering the lessons of the economist Kelvin Lancaster. Lancaster greatly enriched the theory of consumer choice. He did so by noting that consumer preferences do not point towards the products themselves, but rather to some of their inner characteristics. These can only be obtained by acquiring the whole aggregate that contains them. Indeed, Lancaster presents the product as a 'bundle', that is to say, as a collection of characteristics (Lancaster, 1966): a product appears as a small, very stable, cohesive and ordered society of things, whose rules of association – complementarity, functionality, interchangeability, interoperability, substitutability, rigidity, 'optionality', etc. – determine the mechanisms of its adoption. The ability to 'tinker' or not a product, to add or to substitute a particular component to it, impacts heavily on the direction of economic behaviour and the shape of market structures. The sociologies of industrial standardisation (Brunsson and Jacobsson, 2000) or financial products (Lépinay, 2011; MacKenzie, 2006) are led by their objects to explore combinations of human properties, product specifications and commercial demands. For this reason, they show vividly that, on such matters, economic sociology can no longer sustain any great divide between people and things. It becomes impossible to limit the 'social' to a set of facts or narrowly defined relationships. At the same time, economic sociology cannot set aside objects or stop at their outer edges. Indeed, the social lies not at the periphery of objects, but at their heart, and points towards a composite and dynamic process that collects and combines human and non-human 'constituencies' (Neyland and Simakova, 2010). As collections of characteristics, products are themselves supplemented by collections of products. Sandrine Barrey's study on merchandising and the 'work of collection' in the retail sector (Barrey, 2007), or my own work on the history of self-service (Cochoy, 2008b), help in understanding that the retailing business is not only, as it is often thought, about submitting suppliers and products to a hard game of selection, to a series of arm wrestles exclusively focused on putting price pressure on each individual item. The retailing business, more surprisingly, is also about 'managing collections'; it is about building product assortments, establishing coherent and eye-catching displays, in order to master the grammar of an aisle, according to a 'cohesive' logic which prepares and favours the consumer's next singular 'selections'.

Collections of people

The second figure of market collection focuses more on people, even while objects continue to play a crucial role. Economic transactions, far from opposing and continually separating actors, rather mobilise and encourage the formation of a series of groups of producers, consumers, market intermediaries, etc.

On the side of producers and market intermediaries, which are very familiar with the benefits for competition of agreements and alliances, we may quote the historical examples of cartels (Chandler, 1977), customer–supplier relationships (Yates, 2006), the practice of 'cooperative marketing' – one of the first innovations of this discipline (Hobson, 1921) – and also professional associations (Strasser, 1989). In brief: the economy is full of collective and more or less organised bodies (among which networks are only one manifestation among others). Such organisational collections remind us that competitors are also defined mostly as colleagues and thus fall within the larger umbrella of 'co-opetition' (Bruno, 2012). The collectives of producers are supplemented by the collections of consumers they attempt to create as soon as they work to take over a market. In fact, establishing a commercial relationship amounts less to addressing familiar 'clients', as in local markets, or the undifferentiated mass of consumers in the global market, and more to attempting to capture customer groups of varied extension – ranging from the individual to large assemblies – which have been cleverly identified and constructed by marketers (Tedlow, 1990).

Contemporary marketing thus appears as an activity of true social engineering. Marketing is a matter of sociological expertise, a pure act of creating collective entities that compete, recombine and challenge the social groups deemed stable by official statistics, and undermine the so-called isolation of market actors. However, it is very important to note that this kind of expertise aimed at tracing, understanding and 'devising' the various 'attachments' which connect innumerable social and technical factors to actual individual consumer practices, is subject to ceaseless puzzles, misfires, failures and other mysteries (McFall, 2014). Paradoxically such problems are not always seen as unexpected 'unknowns' or 'overflows' (Czarniawska and Löfgren, 2012) but are sometimes surprisingly generated 'on purpose' by market researchers, according to a professional logic in which 'More data creates more *non*-knowledge which needs to be attacked by creating more data' (Schwarzkopf, 2015).

The side of producers therefore holds (more or less, as we just saw) that of consumers. The new collective entities made by merchants range from the segments of marketing, which are theoretical groups more or less performed by market dynamics (Sunderland and Denny, 2011), to the establishment of genuine customer communities ('virtual' in form, but very real in their exchanges). Indeed, some companies implement internet blogs and discussion forums designed to allow consumers to express themselves but also to exchange their views about brands and products.[1] These companies are of course acting in the hope of channelling and directing these exchanges if not in a positive sense, at least to limit the spontaneous proliferation of 'wild' and therefore less controllable similar forms of expression (Raimond, 2012). Other firms go further by enlisting communities of users in the production of the same services by means of 'crowdsourcing' devices (Dujarier, 2014) or by deliberately mobilising interest groups connected with particular societal concerns to shape a brand identity (Gerlitz, this volume). This type of relationship blurs the traditional boundaries between producers and consumers. Brand communities revive, to some extent, the self-production economy that reigned before the advent of the mass market and the concomitant dissociation of production from consumption (Strasser, 1989).

This said, the new forms of self-production are not private and unique, but public and collective. They are not about the production of basic goods (food and clothing) but of highly sophisticated services (software, expertise, creation, etc.); they also result in a logic of 'bottom-up innovation' (Von Hippel, 2002). On the one hand, the ability of user communities to enter a game of organised production joins the strategic interests of the business side, as in the case of 'crowdsourcing' systems (Dujarier, 2014). On the other hand, it also competes with them, as shown in the case of open-source software development. The closed 'proprietary logic' of profit companies, which hides behind the exclusivity of patents and licences, contrasts with the open and collective logic of 'epistemic communities' (Cross, 2013), based on the free sharing of the results of their collective productive effort. In these transformations, the role of technical interfaces is essential insofar as their characteristics allow not only collaborative and sharing activities, but also more or less fine adjustments of participants' interests and community imperatives. That is to say, they make it possible to subordinate the production of social networks to technological arrangements, as in relational marketing and brand community management (Mellet, this volume).

Collecting engines

This brings us to the fascinating topic of collecting engines or market machines. Granovetter (1973) was right to show that market encounters, far from resting on market processes alone, largely involve prior pure social ties. But he was wrong to abandon the remaining part of market ties – those born from anonymous encounters – to the sole expertise of economics. These ties, far from depending on 'nature-like' and abstract market mechanisms, also rest on fully social processes, techniques and institutions, and thus require the full attention of sociologists. See the job market dear to Granovetter: the author was quick to evoke spontaneous candidacies and jobs as residual alternatives to social networks, as if they were unquestionable generic market-like processes, deprived of any social dimension. The irony is that it is to (heterodox) economists that we owe the sociology of job ads: Marchal et al. (2007) showed, for instance, that these ads are true social institutions which take very different formats across time and places, and thus create different types of job attachment. More generally, the market is full of 'collecting engines' which have the ability, depending on their particular logic and way of working, to collect supply and demand actors in a given way and shape their attachments accordingly. Some are very classic and range from mundane shop windows (Cochoy, 2016), trade publications (Cochoy, 2015) and trade shows (Favre, 2014), to sophisticated relational marketing techniques (Ariztia and Mellet, this volume), auction places (Garcia-Parpet, 2007), trading rooms (Lépinay, 2011), market algorithms (Callon and Muniesa, 2005) and financial formulas (MacKenzie, 2006). Others are more original, like, for instance, the devices imagined for 'heart attachment' operations, both in the literary and figurative versions of what a 'heart' means. As far as literal hearts are concerned, I refer to the complex algorithms imagined to be able to allocate heart transplants and to realise their best attachment (technically, logistically and ethically), in situations where price-matching mechanisms are out of the question (Steiner, 2010). And for figurative hearts, I may reference those dating websites whose varied designs and features play a growing role in love encounters and further possible attachments (Kessous, this volume). All these devices, whatever their differences and particularities, show that new social relations may emerge from anonymous encounters, i.e. away from existing social ties, and that marketplaces (or alternative 'matching' systems) and market devices play the leading role in collecting the necessary resources, then organising their subsequent attachment.

Collection politics

The emergence of market collections, rather than being solely dependent on technical arrangements, and far from being confined to the world of new technologies of information and communication, involves more general political issues. The constitution of collective market groups raises the question of the size of the 'agencies' that operate in markets, and of the inevitability of the division and asymmetry that emerges between, on the business side, macro actors and, on the user side, micro actors. One can of course consider liberalism as the expression of a broad and old movement, supported by both economic and political forces. Economics and politics did the upstream work necessary to establish market and democratic institutions, and a lot of symmetric downstream work needed to construct *homo economicus* from mundane self-interests (Hirschman, 1977) and *homo politicus* from material ballot boxes and polling booths (Cochoy, 2008a). But this downstream work partially failed. *Homo economicus* is a bifurcated figure, since it adopts either the face of the entrepreneur or the consumer. Now, the logics of accumulation and the requirements of management have gradually come to dominate one of these faces, that of the individual entrepreneur, who gave birth to big business and behind it the collective of salaried managers (Chandler, 1977). Ultimately, if the entrepreneur still exists, it is rather as the hypostatic figure of the collective forces that support it (Giraudeau, 2008). In front of large companies, the only singular figure that remains is that of the individual citizen, the user, the consumer, the customer.

This asymmetry is laden with risks of dominating and excluding people who thus become 'orphan groups' (Callon, 2007). The emergence of such groups raise political and scientific concerns (Harrison et al., 2015), but also the concerns of the actors themselves, who often do not wait for academics and other socially conscious actors to counter attack. Since the rise of big capitalism, small demand side actors have attempted to turn themselves into large consumer collectives: cooperative movements at the end of the nineteenth century (Strasser, 1989; Furlough, 1991), consumer associations and consumerism in the twentieth (Cohen, 2003; Dubuisson-Quellier, 2013a). These rebalancing efforts continue today in new ways, not only through technologies that reduce the cost of collective action, as we have seen above, but also through the support of law, as shown by the emergence of 'class actions'. This type of legal arrangement not only helps to aggregate individual complaints into collective ones but, in so doing, brings about societal changes worthy of attention (see the paradoxical alliance between the affirmation of a collective consumerist consciousness on the one hand and the progress of individual market utilitarianism on the other hand; see also the 'judiciarisation' of society, the shift of protests from the sphere of work to that of consumption) (Dubuisson-Quellier, 2013b).

However, it would be wrong to reduce the aggregation of consumers to its most visible and institutionalised forms. The anthropologist Daniel Miller has shown that even the most isolated, the most personal and the most trivial act of consumption often takes a highly social and collective meaning, such as when a mother goes shopping to please her children (Miller, 1998). This intuition is worth pursuing, by studying the collective dimension of acts of consumption not only as mental orientations of isolated consumers, but also as physical properties of these same acts, when consumers interact and choose their goods collectively in the marketplace. In fact, commercial scenes often evidence not a single 'consumer' selecting products alone, as is more or less explicitly supposed by most consumption theories and studies (whatever the discipline: economics, psychology, sociology, consumer research, etc.). It is rather small collections of consumers – family, friends or simply occasional groups – who gather in retail spaces to share the experience of choice. Here, studying the interactions between buyers deserves attention, as soon as one assumes that the outcome of the discussions between people about the choice of a given object is unlikely to be reducible to the average of their respective intentions and individual properties (Cochoy, 2008a).

Conclusion

All in all, we see that the selective and the collective, far from being the 'edges' of the exchange, the one addressing the economy, the other society, are rather two engines driving the same socioeconomic activity. Here lies an entire project, which ultimately aims at studying how the market 'does', 'deconstructs' and thus 'redoes' society. The market has never been so rich in issues dear to sociologists. However, in order to address these issues, it has never been more urgent to abandon the idea that the sociological explanation of the economy consists in mechanically tracing the actions of a set of pre-given and quasi immutable entities and properties (such as social class, gender, age, education, income, culture, institutions, relational forms) that are supposed to act as independent variables on the course of economic action. In order to complete the analysis and seize new market forms of action, and new social, technical and economic objects that this action produces, we should also study the associations produced by the market. This would imply a move from explanation to description, a shift from economic sociology to economic sociography, in order to capture socioeconomic attachment processes in the making and, ultimately, to explore the consequences of such transformations.

Note

1 See for example the case of the Panasonic bread machine: http://panasonic. typepa d.com/machineapain/.

Bibliography

Akerlof, G.A. (1970) The market for 'lemons': Quality uncertainty and the market mechanism. *Quarterly Journal of Economics*, 84(3), August: 488–500.

Araujo, L. and Kjellberg, H. (2014) Enacting novel agencements: The case of the FFP schemes in the US airline industry (1981–1991). University of Lancaster and Stockholm School of Economics, working paper.

Barrey, S. (2007) Struggling to be displayed at the point of purchase: The emergence of merchandising in French supermarkets. In M. Callon, Y. Millo and F. Muniesa (eds), *Market Devices*, Oxford: Blackwell, pp. 92–108.

Beckert, J. (2011) Where do prices come from? Sociological approaches to price formation. *Socio-Economic Review*, 9(4): 757–786.

Boltanski, L. and Thévenot, L. (2006) *On Justification: The Economies of Worth*, Princeton, NJ: Princeton University Press.

Bourreau, M. and Licoppe, C. (2007) On-line bidding and on-line buying on the same website: Implications and consequences of the internet homepage proximity of two modes of commercialization. In N. Curien and E. Brousseau (eds), *Internet and Digital Economics*, Cambridge: Cambridge University Press, pp. 510–536.

Bruno, I. (2012) Quand s'associer, c'est concourir. Les paradoxes de la 'coopétition'. In F. Cochoy (ed.), *Du lien marchand. Essai(s) de sociologie économique relationniste*, Toulouse: Presses Universitaires du Mirail, pp. 54–78.

Brunsson, N. and Jacobsson, B. (eds) (2000) *A World of Standards*, Oxford: Oxford University Press.

Callon, M. (2007) An essay on the growing contribution of economic markets to the proliferation of the social. *Theory, Culture and Society*, 24(7–8): 139–163.

Callon, M. (2013) Qu'est-ce qu'un agencement marchand? In M. Callon, M. Akrich, S. Dubuisson-Quellier et al., *Sociologie des agencements marchands*, Paris: Presses des Mines, pp. 325–440.

Callon, M. (2016) Revisiting marketization: From interface-markets to market-agencements. *Consumption, Markets and Culture*, 19(1): 17–37.

Callon, M. and Muniesa, F. (2005) Economic markets as calculative collective devices. *Organization Studies*, 26(8): 1229–1250.

Callon, M., Méadel, C. and Rabeharisoa, V. (2002) The economy of qualities. *Economy and Society*, 31(2): 194–217.

Calvignac, C. and Cochoy, F. (2016) On vehicular agencies: Lessons from the quantitative observation of consumer logistics. *Consumption, Markets and Culture*, 19(1): 133–147.

Chandler, A.D., Jr. (1977) *The Visible Hand: The Managerial Revolution in American Business*, Cambridge, MA: Belknap Press of Harvard University Press.

Cochoy, F. (2007) A brief theory of the 'captation' of the public: Understanding the market with Little Red Riding Hood. *Theory, Culture and Society*, 24(7–8): 213–233.

Cochoy, F. (2008a). Calculation, qualculation, calqulation: Shopping cart's arithmetic, equipped cognition and clustered consumers. *Marketing Theory*, 8(1): 15–44.

Cochoy, F. (2008b). Hansel and Gretel at the grocery store: Progressive grocer and the little American consumers (1929–1959), *Journal of Cultural Economy*, 1(2): 145–163.

Cochoy, F. (2015) *On the Origins of Self-Service*, London: Routledge.

Cochoy, F. (2016) *On Curiosity: The Art of Market Seduction*, Manchester: Mattering Press.

Cochoy, F., Trompette, P. and Araujo, L. (2016) From market agencements to market agencing: An introduction. *Consumption, Markets and Culture*, 19(1): 3–16.

Cohen, L. (2003) *A Consumers' Republic: The Politics of Mass Consumption in Postwar America*, New York: Alfred A. Knopf.

Coll, S. (2012) Le marketing relationnel et le lien marchand: le cas des cartes de fidélité suisses. In F. Cochoy (ed.), *Du lien marchand, Essai(s) de sociologie économique relationniste*, Toulouse: Presses Universitaires du Mirail, pp. 197–218.

Cross, M.K.D. (2013) Rethinking epistemic communities twenty years later. *Review of International Studies*, 39(1): 137–160.

Czarniawska, B. and Löfgren, O. (eds) (2012) *Managing Overflow in Affluent Societies*, London: Palgrave.

David, P.A. (1985) Clio and the economics of QWERTY. *American Economic Review*, 75(2): 332–337.

Deville, J. (2012) Regenerating market attachments. *Journal of Cultural Economy*, 5(4): 423–439.

Deville, J. (2014) Consumer credit default and collections: The shifting ontologies of market attachment. *Consumption, Markets and Culture*, 17(5): 468–490.

Didier, E. (2012) Cunning observation: US agricultural statistics in the time of laissez-faire. *History of Political Economy* (HOPE Annual Supplement on Observation), 44(1): 27–45.

Dubuisson-Quellier, S. (2013a). A market mediation strategy: How social movements seek to change firms' practices by promoting new principles of product valuation. *Organization Studies*, 34(5–6): 683–703.

Dubuisson-Quellier, S. (2013b). *Ethical Consumption*, Halifax: Fernwood Publishing.

Dujarier, M.-A. (2014) The three sociological types of consumer work. *Journal of Consumer Culture*, April, 1–17.

Favre, G. (2014) Des rencontres dans la mondialisation. Réseaux et apprentissages dans un salon de distribution de programmes de télévision en Afrique sub-saharienne. PhD thesis, Paris, Université Paris-Dauphine.

Furlough, E. (1991) *Consumer Cooperation in France: The Politics of Consumption, 1834–1930*, Ithaca, NY: Cornell University Press.

Garcia-Parpet, M.-F. (2007) The social construction of a perfect market: The strawberry auction at Fontaines-en-Sologne. In D. MacKenzie, F. Muniesa and L. Siu (eds), *Do Economists Make Markets? On the Performativity of Economics*, Princeton, NJ: Princeton University Press, pp. 20–53.

Giraudeau, M. (2008) The drafts of strategy: Opening up strategic plans and their uses. *Long Range Planning*, 41(3): 291–308.

Grandclément, C. (2006) Wheeling food products around the store... and away: The invention of the shopping cart, 1936–1953. Paper presented at the Food Chains Conference: Provisioning, Technology, and Science, Hagley Museum and Library, Wilmington, Delaware, 2–4 November. www.csi.mines-paristech.fr/working-papers/WP/WP_CSI_006.pdf (accessed 8 August 2016).

Granovetter, M. (1973) The strength of weak ties. *American Journal of Sociology*, 78(6): 1360–1380.

Granovetter, M. (1985) Economic action and social structure: The problem of embeddedness. *American Journal of Sociology*, 91(3): 481–510.

Harrison, D., Geiger, S., Kjellberg, H. and Mallard, A. (eds) (2015) *Concerned Markets*, Cheltenham: Edward Elgar.

Helgesson, C.-F. and Muniesa, F. (2013) For what it's worth: An introduction to valuation studies. *Valuation Studies*, 1(1): 1–10.

Hennion, H. (2010) Loving music: From a sociology of mediation to a pragmatics of taste. *Comunicar*, 17(34): 25–33.

Hirschman, A.O. (1977) *The Passions and the Interests: Political Arguments for Capitalism before Its Triumph*, Princeton, NJ: Princeton University Press.

Hobson, A. (1921) Fundamentals of coöperative marketing. *Journal of Farm Economics*, 3(1), January: 24–29.

Karpik, L. (2010) *Valuing the Unique: The Economics of Singularities*, Princeton, NJ: Princeton University Press.

Lancaster, K.J. (1966) A new approach to consumer theory. *Journal of Political Economy*, 74(2): 132–157.

Latour, B. (2005) *Reassembling the Social: An Introduction to Actor-Network Theory*, Oxford: Oxford University Press.

Lépinay, V.-A. (2011) *Codes of Finance: Engineering Derivatives in A Global Bank*, Princeton, NJ: Princeton University Press.

Liebowitz, S.J. and Margolis, S.E. (1990) The fable of the keys. *Journal of Law and Economics*, 33(1): 1–25.

MacKenzie, D. (2006) *An Engine, Not a Camera: How Financial Models Shape Markets*, Cambridge, MA: MIT Press.

Marchal, E., Mellet, K. and Rieucau, G. (2007) Job board toolkits: Internet matchmaking and changes in job advertisements. *Human Relations*, 60(7): 1091–1113.

McFall, L. (2009) Devices and desires: How useful is the 'new' new economic sociology for understanding market attachment? *Sociology Compass*, 3(2): 267–282.

McFall, L. (2014) *Devising Consumption: Cultural Economies of Insurance, Credit and Spending*, Abingdon: Routledge.

Miller, D. (1998) *A Theory of Shopping*, Ithaca, NY: Cornell University Press.

Musselin, C. (2010) *The Market for Academics*, New York: Routledge.

Neyland, D. and Simakova, E. (2010) Trading bads and goods: Market practices in fair trade. In L. Araujo, J. Finch and H. Kjellberg (eds), *Reconnecting Marketing to Markets*, Oxford: Oxford University Press, pp. 204–223.

Polanyi, K. (2001) *The Great Transformation: The Political and Economic Origins of Our Time*, Boston, MA: Beacon Press.

Raimond, É. (2012) Le travail du lien entre l'entreprise et ses clients sur internet: la socialisation des clients à la marque sur les blogs. In F. Cochoy (ed.), *Du lien marchand. Essai(s) de sociologie économique relationniste*, Toulouse: Presses Universitaires du Mirail, pp. 175–196.

Schwarzkopf, S. (2015) Data overflow and sacred ignorance: An agnotological account of organizing in the market and consumer research industry. Copenhagen Business School, working paper.

Stark, D. (2009) *The Sense of Dissonance: Accounts of Worth in Economic Life*, Princeton, NJ: Princeton University Press.

Steiner, P. (2002) Encastrements et sociologie économique. In I. Huault (ed.), *La construction sociale de l'entreprise, Autour des travaux de Mark Granovetter*, Colombelle: Management et société, pp. 29–50.

Steiner, P. (2010) Gift-giving or market? Economists and the performation of organ commerce. *Journal of Cultural Economy*, 3(2): 243–259.

Strasser, S. (1989) *Satisfaction Guaranteed: The Making of the American Mass Market*, New York: Pantheon Books.

Sunderland, P.L. and Denny, R.M. (2011) *Consumer Segmentation in Practice: An Ethnographic Account of Slippage*. In J. Cayla and D. Zwick (eds), *Inside Marketing*, Oxford: Oxford University Press, pp. 137–161.

Tarde, G. (1902) *Psychologie économique*, vol. 1, Paris: Alcan.

Tedlow, R.S. (1990) *New and Improved: The Story of Mass Marketing in America*, New York: Basic Books.

Von Hippel, E. (2002) Horizontal innovation networks – by and for users. MIT Sloan School of Management, Working Paper No. 4366-4302, June.

Yates, J. (2006) How business enterprises use technology: Extending the demand-side turn. *Enterprise and Society*, 7(3): 422–455.

2 Manufacturing the consumer's truth

The uses of consumer research in advertising inquiry

Tomas Ariztia

One of the few matters advertising professionals agree on is the key place of the consumer during a campaign design.[1] Understanding consumer desires and imagining how to reach them is regarded as their key task. As one advertising planner explained to me:

> In the end, the driver is what conducts, what inspires, what motivates your campaigns and the campaign developments. And, in the end, in this case the driver is the consumer. For all products and campaigns the driver is the consumer, the consumer is what makes you feel motivated, inspired, producing the necessary insights to develop and carry on with a product.

According to these advertising professionals, good advertising 'reaches the consumer's mind', touches a 'nerve' or 'puts itself in the consumer's shoes'. This is nothing new. Historically, advertising and marketing have placed the consumer at the centre of their work, both at the practical and the discursive level (Schwarzkopf, 2009).[2] The consumer is at the beginning and at the end of any advertising campaign.

However, in spite of this centrality, the consumer is still an elusive figure during the manufacturing of advertising campaigns. Unlike other marketing activities that routinely interact with consumers in market encounters, such as Customer Relationship Management (CRM) systems (Zwick and Denegri Knott, 2009), shopping carts (Cochoy, 2008) or insurance sellers (McFall, 2011), advertising campaigns often lack a direct encounter through which campaigns can be calibrated and redefined before being released. In other words, the process of manufacturing an advertising campaign lacks the most defining test of its success: the purchase. Second-hand consumer knowledge thus plays a critical role in the advertising production pipeline as it provides a working hypothesis on consumer qualities. This type of knowledge is used throughout the creative process long before the final campaign is implemented and 'tested' in the market. In fact, from the first stages of an advertising campaign, different types of knowledge about the consumer are used to qualify the 'target' and to mobilise creative and commercial ideas to create a campaign that works. A key type of knowledge used for this purpose is consumer research (CR). By the term CR I am referring to the array of documents and figures used in advertising agencies to provide representations of consumer qualities. This encompasses a wide collection of epistemic objects presenting diverse types of knowledge. CR often takes the form of short reports and PowerPoint slides and includes surveys that measure attitudes towards brands or goods; qualitative market research – often using focus groups – that offers 'depth' descriptions of a particular type of consumer; consumer data coming from social media (such as Twitter or Facebook) or consumer trends documents describing broad patterns in marketing and consumption.

This chapter focuses on exploring the practical uses and valuation of CR in advertising agencies. Based on forty interviews and ethnographic fieldwork in a mid-sized advertising agency in Santiago, Chile, I describe here the practical process of using CR during the design of advertising campaigns. By describing this process, I show how CR is mobilised in relation to a creative/imaginative process through which a specific reality about consumers is enacted.[3] I argue that the manufacturing of advertising campaigns involves producing and mobilising an internal and specific 'truth' about the consumer which is the outcome of a fluid and practical problem-solving process. Relying on John Dewey's (1938) concept of inquiry, I describe the use of CR in advertising agencies as related to a logic of internal inquiry through which a particular truth about the consumer is generated.

The chapter is structured as follows. The following section briefly describes some theoretical aspects regarding advertising as well as the use of CR in marketing practice. I take a pragmatic approach that focuses on examining the manufacturing of advertising campaigns as a practical accomplishment. More particularly, I suggest examining the uses of CR in advertising as related to the production of an emotional 'truth' about the consumer that works for specific advertising campaigns. Based on the previous reflection, the third section describes empirically how CR is used and evaluated during the design of advertising campaigns in Chile. I describe two aspects of this process. First, I describe how advertising professionals choose and evaluate consumer research for its use in campaign design. In particular, I describe how CR is valued in terms of its ability to display and circulate 'novelty' between the advertising agency and its clients. Second, I describe how different types of consumer research material are combined in order to produce a coherent and useful 'truth'. I argue that this process of 'curating' consumer research involves stabilising particular qualities of consumers while discarding others, thus producing a shared background between advertising professionals and clients. I describe how this process involves not only mobilising pure 'facts' about consumers but also producing and circulating emotional interpretations about consumers and their potential attachments.

Marketing devices and producing the truth about the consumer

Recent years have seen an increasing amount of scholarly work focused on exploring ordinary marketing and advertising practices, knowledge and devices (Hennion et al., 1989, McFall, 2004; Araujo, 2007; Cochoy, 2007b; Cronin, 2000, 2008, 2010; Nixon, 2003; Slater 2002; Zwick and Cayla, 2011; Moor, 2012; Ariztia, 2014, 2015a, 2015b). A common starting point for this so-called 'pragmatic turn' in the sociology of marketing has been to approach marketing as a collection of practices, knowledge and devices that helps define economic goods, agents and market encounters (Araujo, 2007; Çalışkan and Callon, 2010; Cochoy, 2007b). By seeking to produce attachment, marketing devices are understood here as key players in the creation of consumer markets.

Perhaps the most famous marketing device is advertising. Advertising has long been a subject of interest for the sociology of consumption. It has been described as the key device connecting production and consumption (Nixon, 1997) or the main vehicle for the expansion of consumerist ideology (Sklair, 2002). In this chapter, however, I focus instead on a previous step: the process through which advertising, as a marketing device, is manufactured (Hennion et al., 1989). In doing so, I approach advertising campaigns as practical accomplishments (Araujo et al., 2010). I am thus more interested in how advertising is made than in what it can do. In doing this, I am following in the footsteps of a long research tradition that has focused on studying ordinary advertising practices (Hennion et al., 1989; Nixon, 2003; Mazzarella, 2003, McFall, 2004; Moeran, 2009; Malefyt and Moeran, 2003; Miller, 1997; Slater, 2002).

Specifically, I look at the knowledge practices and devices that play a role in the manufacturing of advertising campaigns before they are deployed, used and tested in market encounters. I focus on describing one specific aspect of this manufacturing: the way in which consumer knowledge is used and evaluated throughout the campaign design. By focusing on this, I seek to enrich our understanding of how 'the consumer' is enacted in marketing devices. As McFall (2014: 28) recently put it:

> It is clear that devices are meant to include human dispositions by equipping, formatting or 'agencing' them. Yet very little attention has been spared on examining precisely how the habits, beliefs, attitudes, ideas, practices, skills and competences, the whole shooting match of private fact, are practically incorporated within devices.

This chapter seeks to discuss how what McFall, after William James, labels 'private fact' is mobilised through CR during the production of advertising. By mapping this process, I aim to unpack how marketing devices such as advertising work by producing and mobilising a particular type of reality about consumers, that is, by mobilising some specific beliefs, affects, habits and competences throughout the process of manufacturing a campaign.

Consumer knowledge in advertising

The manufacturing of marketing devices, such as advertising, relies on producing and using an extensive amount of knowledge about consumers often from market research companies.[4] When it comes to the practical work of marketing experts, this knowledge can be of different types and can be used in different stages of the design and orchestration of market encounters. This knowledge plays a central role in the practical task of organising market encounters, the qualification of goods and the marketing devices designed to bring goods and consumers together inside the agency.

CR is one of the most critical types of this knowledge (Nixon, 2009; Schwarzkopf, 2009) and includes applied research on consumer attitudes, values and qualities, as well as 'social' backgrounds (knowledge about general social and cultural trends that might affect or inform consumer dispositions). CR involves elements such as quantitative and qualitative consumer research studies – often produced by market research companies – social media data, as well as general reports or presentations commonly described as 'consumer trends' which depict specific transformations and qualities of consumers of specific categories.

As argued by Grandclément and Gaglio, CR mobilises the consumer through different representational techniques in order to bring it 'back' into the marketing organisation (2011). Since the classic work of Miller and Rose describing the use of psychology and motivation research to mobilise consumers (Miller and Rose, 1997), social science scholars have increasingly explored the place of CR in marketing practices (Schwarzkopf, 2009; Grandclément and Gaglio, 2011; Nixon, 2009; Cochoy, 1998). A key contribution of this literature, which might be called 'the social studies of market research', lies in showing how CR enacts the consumer inside marketing organisations. In fact, authors have explored how different devices help to create specific versions of the consumer that suit different – and in some cases contradictory – aspects of marketing work, for example by using focus groups to mobilise the consumer persona as opinions that suit marketing objectives (Grandclément and Gaglio, 2011), or by provoking a specific type of reality that acts as a proxy for consumer behaviour (Muniesa and Trébuchet-Breitwiller, 2010). It is worth noting here that the consumer, as produced and mobilised by CR, is not a unified entity (Cova and Cova, 2012). Instead, the consumer is enacted by means of a complex and distributed process of qualification(s) where many different versions of consumers and goods are addressed. This was nicely exemplified by Dubuisson-Quellier in her account of the uses of CR in the multiple qualification processes that occur during the development and marketing of new goods (2010).

The place and value of CR is particularly interesting for thinking about advertising, often portrayed as the most self-referential type of marketing devices (McFall, 2014), where the final outcomes (campaigns) also depend on the agency's anxieties concerning its clients and the competition. With this in mind, then, some authors posit that CR occupies a secondary and/or instrumental role in the process of defining a final campaign. In fact, it is a common claim that CR plays an instrumental role in advertising work. Some authors have asserted that CR is mobilised as legitimate knowledge that helps agencies understand consumers, thus helping calm producers' anxieties (Lury and Warde, 1997). Furthermore, it has been argued that CR is strategically used by advertising professionals as part of a 'commercial' imperative that guides the relationship with clients (Cronin, 2004) or manages power struggles in the field of advertising (Kaptan, 2013). From this viewpoint, the 'truth' about consumers mobilised by CR in advertising campaigns is a strategic operation through which advertising professionals seek to enhance their commercial position when dealing with clients or competition. In other words, the 'truth' about consumers mobilised in advertising is approached in relation to its uses rather than how it is produced.

In this chapter, however, I want to explore a different path of analysis. Instead of relating the uses of CR exclusively to commercial and strategic logic in the advertising field, I focus on the practical uses of CR during the campaign design. This means focusing more on how CR is situated in the mundane process of producing a campaign and looking at the practices and devices through which CR is mobilised. In other words, I place CR within the practical work of producing a campaign, as a specific knowledge process (Knorr-Cetina, 1999). Thus, more than describing how CR is used in instrumental terms, I focus here on the practical production of a specific truth about the consumer that CR helps to produce in advertising practice (Muniesa, 2014). This perspective should help to unravel some of the specificities of advertising as a marketing device. In fact, as I describe in the next section, what prevails throughout the process of using CR is not an effort to produce or test a campaign based on a scientific and/or external description of the consumer but, instead, an effort to produce and mobilise a truth that works within the process.

The next two sections will develop this argument empirically. To do so, I rely on forty interviews with advertising professionals as well as participant observation in agencies. The description is based on practitioners' accounts and practices concerning the use of CR in their daily activities in the agency. Consequently, I leave aside the production and use of other types of knowledge in advertising, such as tacit (Schwarzkopf, 2008; Kaptan, 2013) or creative knowledge (Nixon, 2003; Moeran, 2009). The description focuses on two particular aspects of how CR is used. The first part addresses the process of finding and choosing CR during the design of advertising campaigns. The second part describes how CR is used throughout the manufacturing process as a tool for supporting and imagining a truth that works.

Finding and choosing consumer research

Advertising companies obtain CR studies and data from different sources. The main sources are the clients who produce CR studies on a regular basis. During the first stages of any campaign, existing studies on the 'target' and the category are circulated between the clients and the agency and within the agency. This is often done by sending PowerPoint slides or Word documents by email. Depending on the size of the clients, this exchange of studies might involve an enormous amount of information which is sent compressed into a zip file, or just the exchange of a few key 'numbers' about the 'target' written in the body of an email.

CR studies received from clients are often complemented by other sources of information.[5] For example, some agencies have alliances with market research companies through which they externalise research when required. In any case, I was told by my interviewees that advertising agencies seldom buy CR for themselves; rather, they 'broker' studies for their clients if needed. As one planner explained to me:

> Coca Cola has people in a research area, Entel [a local mobile phone company] has people in a research area, GM has people in a research area, BCI, all of them do, so generally we get all market research from our clients, and what we agencies do is to suggest some research with external consultant agencies, which could address the health of a brand or a specific consumer.[6]

Another key source involves the use of international networks of applied consumer research and consumer trends. Big advertising agencies are often members of private global networks of consumer knowledge that circulate applied studies relating to consumer trends and different marketing categories. The use of this type of resource was described by some of my interviewees as an indicator of the agency's level of sophistication, as it is common for big agencies to be a part of well-known international networks. These networks run password-protected webpages containing an extensive amount of reports about different targets and trends in marketing as well as general documents that synthesise cultural and social transformations in different areas of the world or social groups. An important feature of this type of knowledge is that it is often organised to produce or suggest a clear marketing action. For example, one company 'Trend Watching'[7] specialises in producing and circulating vast amounts of relatively short and straightforward documents on marketing and consumer trends.

These sources of CR are often complemented by the more informal use of Google and social networking sites. 'Googling' and internet searches in general are regarded by most interviewees as the most common (and useful) tool for finding CR and general information that might help the campaign.

Choosing novelty

Overall, these sources provide a collection of different elements that help both to describe the consumer and to suggest potential ways of addressing him/her. Some of them provide knowledge regarding the purchasing habits of particular 'targets', others describe the inner motives and new motivations of consumers, while in other cases the studies and reports provide 'only' some hard sociodemographic data. In most cases, through these various means, it is possible to amass a huge amount of CR with potential significance for the campaign design. Because of this, searching for and selecting CR for use in a campaign also involves having to assess the value and utility of this knowledge in relation to the advertising campaign being designed. What is at play is a process of valuation where some CR pieces are valued as worthy and others are discarded (Muniesa, 2011; Stark, 2009).

A key element in defining the worth of a particular consumer research piece regards the novelty and specificity of both its contents and the research techniques that were used to produce it. On the one hand, new studies are highly valued because they are thought to provide fresh descriptions of the consumer. As part of this process, CR pieces are often placed and compared in terms of wider circuits of CR knowledge production and consumption. One advertiser, for example, explained that research is good if it is new partly because it has not circulated among other actors in the industry. Some agencies rely heavily on this ability to surprise clients with new studies, as a way of avoiding general or generic descriptions of consumers. Here both novelty and specificity are critical. As one planner explained to me:

> Macan is an agency that stands out for doing CR studies that are then opened up to the market. It first gives exclusivity to its clients and then makes them widely available. It presents them at ANDA, at ICARE [these are renowned marketing conferences in Chile]. For example, we are now presenting a new study called 'Macho/Men'. In general, these studies that are too generic, such as 'this person spends this amount of time, uses media at this time of day' are not helpful for me, they're too generic.

But the value of novelty for evaluating and choosing consumer research is not only related to the content of the studies. The freshness of the methodological devices used to produce the studies is also key. Indeed, it can be noted that the social research techniques used to produce CR reports are subject to an ever changing status. While some specific methodological devices have fallen out of favour, others are considered a 'must'. For example, as a sociologist doing fieldwork in an agency, I engaged in several conversations about the worth of different techniques. During these talks, some advertisers said that focus groups are old-fashioned and that ethnographic techniques are a 'better way to depict' consumers. In this same vein, I was told that now even ethnographic techniques are becoming somewhat out of fashion. The following answer from an advertising professional gives a clear example of the value of 'novelty' in the selection of CR studies:

> What is better, to use all studies or to use different types for different clients? Why do we show a [statistical] graph or a very cool ethnography? Well, the fashion a year, maybe year and a half ago started to be word clouds. I'm still using word clouds; the last one involved transforming all Cruz Verde advertisements, Salco Brand, FASA advertisements [well-known

pharmacy brands in Chile], into word clouds, and the clients were very happy.

Against this backdrop, it is worth noting that for many of my interviewees the new 'hype' in CR concerns social media. Social media and social media data gathering were being defined by some advertisers as the final technology that, as I was told on several occasions, are providing the definitive space for a 'real encounter' with consumers.[8]

Supporting and imagining the consumer's truth

Up until now, I have described how advertising agencies search, choose and value CR for use in a campaign. In this section, I discuss a second aspect, namely, the uses of CR during the process of defining and mobilising key campaign concepts. Given the different sources that are used to obtain studies, a key practice in the use of CR studies consists of organising these different collected materials into a narrative. This task often takes the form of a patchwork in which different sources are combined into a single coherent argument regarding the consumer and the brand/good to be promoted in a specific campaign. 'Making the most' of existing sources is a critical part of the work to be carried out at this stage. The final outcome is a composition that relies on multiple – and often divergent – CR sources composed of studies, specific figures, polls, news articles and whatever other sources are useful in terms of the process of defining a consumer:

> We need to make the most of all of it, if the brands give you something, if they give you a CR study, what I prefer is not to rely just on that but to also search for other things or trends that are shaping things and that help me 'complement' [that information], otherwise you end up with bias.

Different aspects of the consumer are organised to provide a single coherent narrative that links the description of the consumer with the core concept of the proposed campaign. What prevails, then, is a practical approach to the use of different types of sources.

A key device in this process is the brief. The brief often consists of a Power-Point presentation that sums up the main aspects of a campaign (such as objectives, targets and driving concepts). With respect to CR use, the brief is key in at least two ways. On the one hand, it functions as a framing device. That is, it defines the scope of relevance of the material, the type of studies and data that are useful. It also helps to maintain a given framework throughout the whole manufacturing process. With the brief, useful studies and facts and figures create a stable version of the consumer that 'travels' through the process. In fact, to indicate the evolution of the brief during campaign manufacturing, agencies often use different names for different stages, namely client briefs, planning briefs and the final creative briefs. The brief, thus, acts as a type of narrative device, a mobile immutable (Latour, 1986), that ensures coherence and frames the process. This is equivalent to other market devices such as the business models described by Doganova and Eyquem-Renault (2009). On the other hand, the brief, as a device, also serves as a backdrop for assembling the CR studies into a final version. PowerPoint presentations with relevant consumer research data are exchanged by email and presented and reworked in internal meetings until they are ready to move to the next step. Much of the work in advertising can be defined as mediated by this device; 'this is a presentation industry', one informant once told me. 'We generally arrive at a meeting or presentation, and we work in these meetings with a PowerPoint presentation. The client can take this PowerPoint, for example, and review it or share it; the PowerPoint becomes a shareable element.'

Throughout the process of collecting CR studies, a central task is to adapt, recombine and mould selected consumer research studies into a coherent narrative that allows the campaign design to progress. An almost artistic ability is needed to blend different pieces of data to articulate a feasible and useful version of the consumer and a potential attachment to the consumer is required. This role – the 'curation' of existing consumer research to produce a useful description of a consumer – is often assigned to one type of advertising professional: the planner. During my fieldwork, I was involved as a planner in the design of a campaign for a non-governmental organisation. When doing so, an informant explained how to arrange the different pieces of CR as well as the ideas for the campaign design. He described how he had to integrate, quite precisely, all the different data and make it coherent in order to produce the final concept and insight. He also told me that this process often involves using different sources and, importantly, different voices.

Besides the practical dynamic of composition that prevails in the organisation of different sorts of CR during a campaign design, advertising professionals' accounts allowed me to define two further critical uses. First, CR is put to work to support and promote a particular idea, that is, to maintain some stability throughout the process. Second, CR is often deployed to create new potential versions of the consumer. In what follows, I describe how these two uses operated in my fieldwork.

Producing background

CR is used as a resource in the negotiation of key campaign concepts. Here it takes on a critical role in providing support for a particular strategy or concept throughout the campaign design process. A crucial element is the version of the consumer that is being mobilised. CR can offer 'background' for a particular hypothesis about consumer qualities. As one informant said, in many cases CR data are used to provide necessary support to enable the client and the agency to move fast on 'obvious' elements, thus helping them to create a common baseline and to agree on a shared description of consumer qualities and potential ways of attaching them:

When the work is done with good support you say 'See, consumers are approaching this, from this and that perspective, the tendencies are making people more interested in this way rather than in this other way. This links up better with your brand promise and your strengths. So this is how we get here.' [and he might say] 'Ahh, I understand, well, I don't like this little phrase there, we can change it', but everything is well supported, so the guy understands.

Specific pieces of data are used in this context to foster a line of argumentation that supports a particular version of the consumer. This is a key element, not only in relations with clients, as described by Cronin (2004), but also in internal agency meetings during the work process. Against this backdrop, quantitative data and devices are resources in the process of creating a common, shared background for the different participants in the process. As one interviewee stated:

[We use] indices for understanding our brand situation, people's loyalty, what type of people they are... Data that helps to contextualize the brand situation a little bit, the consumer, everything. These are contexts, basically, but they are not that relevant at the end of the day... You have to be reasonable in terms of the brands you are working for. In the end, statistics and data help a little bit to contextualize where you are and who you are talking to.

As this quote shows, there is thus a need to manage the 'objectivity' of consumer research during the campaign design process and negotiation. In some cases, hard, statistical data was used to create a common understanding with clients (particularly if they are engineers or more inclined to quantitative measures). In other cases CR, often relying on qualitative data, was used to mobilise more emotional components:

It all depends on the person you have in front of you. Some people are tougher, more quantitative as clients, so you have to come up with arguments based on 'surveyology' [a neologism used in the interview] with hard data, or we can call it a hard reference, and then based on that, produce softer interpretations... In other cases, you only have to provide a more theoretical conceptualization, say, more emotional, based on phrases. So the sources [you use] depend on your taste.

It is important to emphasise that the type of emotions being mobilised and orchestrated are not only those of the consumers. They are also the emotions of the clients and the professionals involved in the campaign design. Against this backdrop, one specific use of CR is associated with the need to move beyond or break up stereotypes about consumers, thus allowing better support for new creative ideas during meetings. An example provided by an advertising professional described this very clearly. Some years ago, they had a client who wanted them to develop an advertising campaign for the 'Pension Fund Company'. To that end, they began collecting different types of studies regarding how people view the retirement fund trust in Chile. Their clients, the Pension Fund Company, also provided them with several CR studies they had developed over the years. In those studies, a key theme was that consumers were not happy with the retirement funds industry. While the idea that consumers held negative attitudes towards pension funds was widely accepted by their clients, agency staff felt they needed to portray this feeling in a different way to support their creative idea. To that end, they used photographs of the different users of private pension funds in order to push clients beyond their quantitative descriptions and hypotheses about their customers. They did so by setting up a performance during a meeting in which they presented clients with a 'rougher' and a more 'flesh and blood' version of consumers. As I was told, by doing so they managed to agree on a particular type of advertising strategy:

> Look, we did a CR project with Adimark, here are the graphics, but, this is nothing new, you understand? So [the pictures] helped us to show a face, an attitude, the anger, and therefore to convince them that they have to make a significant communication effort from a radically different starting point. From there, we designed a campaign with Julio Jung [a famous Chilean actor].

As described in the previous example, presenting the right piece of CR can help prevent stagnant moments during negotiations about the value of a proposed campaign or idea when clients and agency staff disagree. CR therefore is used in the process of managing and controlling not only a selected version of consumers, but the whole process of defining the campaign. As described in this case, by bringing a different type of CR into the meetings they were able to smooth out the negotiation of the campaign strategy.

Using CR, then, is part of a very practical process of negotiating and agreeing on a common truth about the consumer. CR enacts a type of consumer reality that gives context and stability to the version of the consumer that is proposed to be mobilised in a campaign. In other words, CR is used to produce a common space in which hypotheses about consumer qualities can advance during the manufacturing of the campaign. In doing so, CR helps maintain some specific types of reality and also opens up new possibilities during meetings and presentations.

Enacting the consumer: broadening connections, nurturing intuition

Previously I described the uses of CR in supporting and stabilising some specific consumer qualities, but CR is also used in a second way: to increase inspiration and open up further possibilities in the definition of consumers. A key part of using CR in this way is the ability to 'read' it properly, that is, to use it to find new creative ideas. Being able to read and interpret CR properly can foster new affective connections with consumers (Deville, 2012). In one case, for example, it was explained to me that the key use of CR is finding a more emotional and subjective tone in the information coming from focus groups, even if this means paying attention to more than the specific topics of the focus. This is very clear in how one interviewee explained her approach to using CR focus groups:

> I learned that in Spain, not in Chile. I was part of a Cuali [qualitative research project] and I met with my boss. I was always thinking about the findings in terms of what I was assessing, hard information; I was the rational type. But she asked me 'what was the group like, how did you feel with them, how did they relate to each other... describe them to me, what they were like, how they did their hair'. So, after that it was clear to me, I put together a picture of the group, how they related to each other. This was the foundation for their conversation. From this type of analysis, you can say, OK. If they like or don't like some specific shoe is another issue. You have to see what these women are like inside the life they have.

An element that is common to a number of different descriptions of CR use is the search for an 'in-depth connection' with the consumer, to reach the consumer's inner soul. The search for depth, however, is not related to the type of knowledge being mobilised, nor its objectivity, but to the potential to produce a specific truth about consumers that is useful to the campaign. In this way, CR is the starting point of a process of 'theorising' and imagining who the consumer is and how to reach him/her:

> Based on the basic data they give you, you have to research the person [a consumer], go out and search, search for different information, attempt to do some research that, in the end, helps you understand him/her a little more. From there you start extracting some theories about them. It can be 'this guy has this attitude about this issue. He doesn't fit in this category. Why don't we change the message, we use his message, or why don't we say this to him. This guy is searching for this in his life.' This is how it goes. Searching, trying to search. But you never stick just with what they give you, because if you do that, you'll know if the guy is 25 or 45, but beyond that you won't know anything.

In this context, a critical use of CR is as a space for nurturing 'intuition'. In fact, as argued by one informant, the key 'utility' of CR is its ability to help produce a new distinctive truth about the consumer.

CR's core value and use in advertising, ultimately, is its practical place throughout the process of qualifying the consumer and defining a potential attachment. This role is twofold. On the one hand, CR is associated with the process of producing and mobilising a truth about the consumer by producing a common context and background throughout the process, a context that moves through different meetings and negotiations, thus making the campaign possible. On the other hand, CR is linked with opening up new possibilities and spaces for describing and imagining consumer qualities. In other words, it helps enact a consumer that might fit in the practical and distributed process of producing a campaign. In both cases, there is not one final criterion that defines the value of CR. It depends on how it fits into the very practical process through which consumers' truths and potential attachments are manufactured.

Discussion

> Inquiry is the controlled or directed transformation of an indeterminate situation into one that is so determinate in its constituent distinctions and relations as to convert the elements of the original situation into a unified whole.
>
> (Dewey, 1938: 104–5)

In this chapter I have described the uses of CR during the process of manufacturing advertising campaigns. By doing so, I have tried to unpack how marketing devices are manufactured. The description shows how the use and value of CR lies within the very practical process of manufacturing a useful 'truth' about consumers that might foster an attachment. In advertising, CR is not valued in terms of its ability to mobilise or support 'evidence' about consumers. Instead, the value of CR depends on the practical role it plays throughout the campaign design in helping to enact a stable and specific truth about consumers. Here, elements such as 'novelty' and the role played in the process of negotiating consumer qualities among different stakeholders are key. Another key value of CR concerns how it helps advertisers imagine potential attachments/links with consumers by mobilising affective connections and inspirations that give rise to creative ideas. It is valued for its help in engendering an 'in-depth connection' with consumers. This concept of 'in-depth' is not about 'objective' or external accounts or about testing campaigns with consumers. Rather it means helping to produce a useful, negotiated and specific truth about consumers on the basis of which a campaign can be developed.

Thus the use of CR in advertising involves a specific mode of engaging with consumer knowledge. Perhaps a good way to define this mode is to use the concept of inquiry developed by John Dewey (1938). In Dewey's terms, inquiry denotes a process of knowledge production that aims at solving a problem rather than pointing to an external reference or truth (Talisse, 2002). In the inquiry process, emphasis is placed on an active process through which the final truth is produced. Therefore, more than reflecting an external truth, the outcome of an inquiry process involves moving from a moment of indetermination to a moment of closure in which the final truth is the one that works for a determined problem (Dewey, 1938: VI).

Applying Dewey's concept of inquiry to the role of CR in advertising highlights how the use of CR is guided more by the logic of problem solving than the logic of discovering an 'external' truth about the consumer to guide campaigns. CR does produce a 'truth' about the consumer, but it is one that is entirely contingent upon the specific problem or question posited by the campaign design process. This argument does not imply that CR in advertising is instrumentally deployed in order to maintain a commercial position. What it means is that making advertising involves producing specific versions of consumers that cannot be disentangled from the internal inquiry of crafting an advertising campaign.

This differs from the place of CR – and consumer knowledge in general – in other marketing devices, such as, for example, those related to the qualification of goods or those that take part in the final encounter. In the case of product development, as described by Dubuisson-Quellier (2010), CR functions mainly as a test of goods in order to produce a mutual adjustment between goods and consumers. Similarly, in the case of selling devices, like showrooms for example, there is a regular encounter with, and feedback from, consumers and goods. This functions as an ongoing test of success or failure. In these cases, consumer knowledge is a device for discovering and/or testing potential attachments.

In advertising, the place of CR is somewhat different. Instead of providing advertising work with an external reality about consumers that acts as a test, the value of CR lies in producing truths that enable the everyday processes of producing a campaign. More than a test, CR in advertising is a resource for imagining new (untested) attachments. Thus I concur with Cronin in arguing that CR in advertising can be better understood as mediating a process of (internal) imagination rather than a process of (external) discovery (Cronin, 2000: 44). In advertising, in sum, CR is used less as a source of evidence than as a tool for fostering a process for which useful truth is the outcome.

Notes

1 This chapter draws on research funded by the Chilean National Fund for Scientific and Technological Development (Fondecyt Project 1140078).
2 This centrality has lately been inflated by recent marketing discourses such as 'co-creation' or 'prosumption' (Zwick et al., 2008), which coincide in seeing the consumer as the key actor in advertising and marketing practices (see also Gerlitz, this volume).
3 I concur here with other researchers who have explored how marketing practices involve producing and mobilising a particular type of reality (Muniesa and Trébuchet-Breitwiller, 2010; Grandclément and Gaglio, 2011; Cronin, 2008; Muniesa, 2014).
4 In this chapter I am interested mostly with secondary knowledge because it can be argued that in their ordinary operation, marketing devices also produce knowledge about consumers (for more on this argument see McFall, 2014: Chapter 1).

5 Interestingly, academic consumer research was not mentioned by my interviewees. The only type of academic source mentioned were general social reports such as the United Nations Development Programme reports. In fact, for most advertising agencies, as CR is not the core of their work, they seldom know about more academic spaces where CR is being produced.
6 All interview quotes are my own translations.
7 http://trendwatching.com/.
8 For more on this anxiety, see McFall, 2014.

Bibliography

Araujo, L. (2007) Markets, market-making and marketing. *Marketing Theory*, 7(3): 211–226.

Araujo, L., Finch, J. and Kjellberg, H. (eds) (2010) *Reconnecting Marketing to Markets*, Oxford: Oxford University Press.

Ariztia, T. (2014) Housing markets performing class: Middle-class cultures and market professionals in Chile. *Sociological Review*, 62(2): 400–420. doi: 10.1111/1467-954X.12144

Ariztia, T. (2015a). The 'reference' as an advertising device. In I. Farias and A. Wilkie (eds), *Studio Studies: Operations, Topologies and Displacements*, London: Routledge, pp. 40–55.

Ariztia, T. (2015b). Unpacking insight: How consumers are qualified by advertising agencies. *Journal of Consumer Culture*, 15(2): 143–162.

Çalışkan, K. and Callon, M. (2009) Economization, part 1: Shifting attention from the economy towards processes of economization. *Economy and Society*, 38(3): 369–398.

Cochoy, F. (1998) Another discipline for the market economy: Marketing as a performative knowledge and know-how for capitalism. In M. Callon (ed.), *The Laws of the Markets*, Oxford: Blackwell, pp. 194–221.

Cochoy, F. (2007a). A sociology of market-things: On tending the garden of choices in mass retailing. *Sociological Review*, 55(s2): 109–129.

Cochoy, F. (2007b). A brief theory of the 'captation' of publics: Understanding the market with Little Red Riding Hood. *Theory, Culture and Society*, 24(7–8): 203–223.

Cochoy, F. (2008) Hansel and Gretel at the grocery store. *Journal of Cultural Economy*, 1(2): 145–163.

Cova, B. and Cova, V. (2012) On the road to prosumption: Marketing discourse and the development of consumer competencies. *Consumption, Markets and Culture*, 15(2): 149–168.

Cronin, A.M. (2000) *Advertising and Consumer Citizenship: Gender, Images and Rights*, London: Routledge.

Cronin, A.M. (2004) Currencies of commercial exchange: Advertising agencies and the promotional imperative. *Journal of Consumer Culture*, 4(3): 339–360.

Cronin, A.M. (2008) Mobility and market research: Outdoor advertising and the commercial ontology of the city. *Mobilities*, 3(1): 95–115.

Deville, J. (2012) Regenerating market attachments: Consumer credit debt collection and the capture of affect. *Journal of Cultural Economy*, 5(4): 423–439.

Dewey, J. (1938) *Logic: The Theory of Inquiry*, New York: Henry Holt and Company.

Doganova, L. and Eyquem-Renault, M. (2009) What do business models do? *Research Policy*, 38(10): 1559–1570.

Dubuisson-Quellier, S. (2010) Product tastes, consumer tastes: The plurality of qualifications in product development and marketing activities. In L. Araujo, J. Finch and H. Kjellberg (eds), *Reconnecting Marketing to Markets*, Oxford: Oxford University Press, pp. 74–93.

Grandclément, C. and Gaglio, G. (2011) Convoking the consumer in person: The focus group effect. In D. Zwick and J. Cayla (eds), *Inside Marketing: Ideologies, Practices, Devices*, Oxford: Oxford University Press, pp. 87–114.

Hennion, A., Meadel, C. and Bowker, G. (1989) The artisans of desire: The mediation of advertising between product and consumer. *Sociological Theory*, 7(2): 191–209.

Kaptan, Y. (2013) 'We just know!' Tacit knowledge and knowledge production in the Turkish advertising industry. *Journal of Consumer Culture*, 13(3): 264–282.

Knorr-Cetina, K. (1999) *Epistemic Cultures: How the Sciences Make Knowledge*, Cambridge, MA: Harvard University Press.

Latour, B. (1986) Visualization and cognition: Drawing things together. *Knowledge and Society*, 6: 1–40.

Lury, C. and Warde, A. (1997) Investments in the imaginary consumer. In M. Nava, A. Blake, I. MacRury and B. Richards (eds), *Buy This Book: Studies in Advertising and Consumption*, Abingdon: Routledge, pp. 87–102.

Malefyt, T.D.W. and Moeran, B. (2003) *Advertising Cultures*, London: Bloomsbury Academic.

Mazzarella, W. (2003) *Shoveling Smoke: Advertising and Globalization in Contemporary India*, Durham, NC: Duke University Press.

McFall, L. (2004) *Advertising: A Cultural Economy*, London: Sage.

McFall, L. (2009) Devices and desires: How useful is the 'new' new economic sociology for understanding market attachment? *Sociology Compass*, 3(2): 267–282.

McFall, L. (2011) A 'good, average man': Calculation and the limits of statistics in enrolling insurance customers. *Sociological Review*, 59(4): 661–684.

McFall, L. (2014) *Devising Consumption: Cultural Economies of Insurance, Credit and Spending*. London: Routledge.

Miller, D. (1997) *Capitalism: An Ethnographic Approach*, Oxford: Berg.

Miller, P. and Rose, N. (1997) Mobilising the consumer: Assembling the subject of consumption. *Theory, Culture and Society*, 14(1): 1–36.

Moeran, B. (2009) The organization of creativity in Japanese advertising production. *Human Relations*, 62: 963–985.

Moor, L. (2012) Beyond cultural intermediaries? A socio-technical perspective on the market for social interventions. *European Journal of Cultural Studies*, 15(5): 563–580. https://doi.org/10.1177/1367549412445759.

Muniesa, F. (2011) A flank movement in the understanding of valuation. *Sociological Review*, 59(s2): 24–38.

Muniesa, F. (2014) *The Provoked Economy: Economic Reality and the Performative Turn*, London: Routledge.

Muniesa, F. and Trébuchet-Breitwiller, A.-S. (2010) Becoming a measuring instrument. *Journal of Cultural Economy*, 3(3): 321–337.

Nixon, S. (1997) Circulating culture. In P. Du Gay (ed.), *Production of Culture/Cultures of Production*, London: Sage/Open University, pp. 67–118.

Nixon, S. (2003) *Advertising Cultures: Gender, Commerce, Creativity*, London: Sage.

Nixon, S. (2009) Understanding ordinary women: Advertising, consumer research and mass consumption in Britain, 1948–1967. CRESI Working Paper Number: 2009–03, Essex University.

Schwarzkopf, S. (2008) Creativity, capital and tacit knowledge. *Journal of Cultural Economy*, 1(2): 181–197.

Schwarzkopf, S. (2009) Discovering the consumer market research: Product innovation, and the creation of brand loyalty in Britain and the United States in the interwar years. *Journal of Macromarketing*, 29(1): 8–20.

Sklair, L. (2002) *Globalization: Capitalism and Its Alternatives*, Oxford: Oxford University Press.

Slater, D. (2002). Capturing markets from the economists. In P. Du Gay and M. Pryke (eds), *Cultural Economy: Cultural Analysis and Commercial Life*, London: Sage, pp. 59–77.

Stark, D. (2009) *The Sense of Dissonance: Accounts of Worth in Economic Life*, Princeton, NJ: Princeton University Press.

Talisse, R. (2002) Two concepts of inquiry. *Philosophical Writings*, 20: 69–81.

Thrift, N. (2005) *Knowing Capitalism*, London: Sage.

Tironi, M. (2014) Atmospheres of indagation: Disasters and the politics of excessiveness. *Sociological Review*, 62: 114–134.

Zwick, D. and Cayla, J. (eds) (2011) *Inside Marketing: Practices, Ideologies, Devices*, Oxford: Oxford University Press.

Zwick, D. and Denegri Knott, J. (2009) Manufacturing customers: The database as new means of production. *Journal of Consumer Culture*, 9(2): 221–247.

Zwick, D., Bonsu, S.K. and Darmody, A. (2008) Putting consumers to work: Co-creation and new marketing govern-mentality. *Journal of Consumer Culture*, 8(2): 163–196.

3   Marketing and the domestication of social media

Kevin Mellet

Introduction

The development of computer-based communication produced a strong surge of interest in the potential of word-of-mouth marketing (Gladwell, 2000; Keller and Berry, 2003; Sernovitz, 2006). Today, online word-of-mouth marketing encompasses a plurality of practices, from media advertising to public relations and customer relationship management. Most of these marketing practices take place on 'web 2.0' or 'social media' websites such as blogs, content-sharing sites (video, photo) or social network services. These websites provide users with features that allow them to organise and display their social relations (boyd and Ellison, 2007). Moreover, these sites include features (such as embedding, liking and sharing content) that facilitate the social spreading of media material (applications, games, links, videos, etc.). Thus, social media makes the social activity of internet users more visible, measurable and possibly manipulable.[1]

A number of authors have described the development of a 'viral culture' associated with social media websites like YouTube, Facebook or Twitter (Wasik, 2009; Berger, 2013; Jenkins et al., 2013). Brands are very much part of this phenomenon: commercials appear regularly in the rankings of the most viewed and shared online videos. For example, the 'Evian Roller Babies' video ad has gathered more than 86 million views on YouTube since it went online in July 2009. From a slightly different perspective, Starbucks Coffee had over 35 million 'likes' on Facebook and more than 8 million 'followers' on Twitter as of June 2015. These exceptional figures are often cited in the trade press as examples of the potential of web 2.0 for marketing, and seem to justify the use of the epidemiological metaphor.

Websites promote the circulation of brands and products by offering users access to apparently 'free' content that is in fact mainly funded by revenue drawn from advertising and marketing (Beuscart and Mellet, 2008). Conversely, advertisers are attracted by the growing audience of these sites[2] and the opportunity to place their brands and products at the very centre of online conversations. However, this incentive does not eliminate the uncertainties inherent in an emerging and unstabilised field of activity. This raises the question of how marketing works to 'domesticate' social media.[3]

In 2008 and 2009, when the market for social media marketing services was still in its experimental phase, companies attempted to use social media in a variety of ways that were not always clearly thought out. These ranged from using it for brand-awareness purposes to direct response advertising, public relations and customer relationship management. These companies viewed social network sites as a medium of communication that could not be ignored (due to the large audiences, or because their competitors were there), but did not fully understand how the various functionalities of these sites could help brands achieve their marketing objectives.

This chapter focuses on a set of actors who played a crucial role in the domestication of social media by marketing. Most of them are start-ups that were created in the 2000s. I call them social media marketing (SMM) agencies, since the label has gained ground among professionals. The purpose of this contribution is to examine the 'marketisation' activities (Callon, 1998; Araujo et al., 2010) carried out by SMM agencies: what are their products, and who are their customers and competitors? How do they market their products? How do they equip and implement their work (advertising formats, monitoring and evaluation measurement instruments)? The chapter relies on qualitative empirical material consisting of twelve interviews conducted with SMM agency managers (France, June–October 2010) and fifteen interviews conducted with advertisers (France, June–July 2009).

SMM agencies share both the same playground, i.e. social media, and a concern for word of mouth. Their raw material is the 'social activity' of internet users – namely the discussions, expressions and recommendations that take place on social media. SMM agencies are not interested in the consumer as described in standard economic theory – namely as an isolated and self-sufficient individual; on the contrary, they consider her as a fundamentally social and talkative being. Agencies seek to market this social activity to advertisers either by indexing it or by provoking it. However, marketisation requires a certain degree of standardisation, including the definition of products and measurement tools with precise and stable contours, in order to comply with the usual qualifications of the advertising market and to achieve a significant volume of business. In other words, these agencies must transform a raw and multifaceted input – the social activities of internet users – into one output which takes the form of relatively standardised communication actions. This work requires them to clarify what the nature of this social substrate is and how it operates. My hypothesis is that the investments made by SMM agencies equip and manipulate representations of the consumer as 'homo sociologicus', with these representations themselves (sometimes explicitly) deriving from social theories. The representations concern the nature of social relationships; they take the form of ontologies, that is to say simplified, reductive and somehow exclusive conceptions of the link established between individuals in online social worlds. These figures of social relationships allow professionals to filter among the heterogeneous and uncoordinated expressions of internet users, to give them relief and meaning, and in the end to act on them.

Analysis shows that the emerging market for SMM services is organised around three specialties: contagion, influence and community. Each specialty stems from a specific feature of social relation, and is translated into a 'marketing promise' and embodied in products and measuring instruments. *Contagion specialists* rely on personal relations networks to provoke the fast and large-scale spreading of content such as viral videos or game applications. They belong to the segment of advertising whose purpose is to generate product and brand awareness. These specialists promise advertisers that they will maximise visibility while minimising paid advertising because the spreading of messages is outsourced to internet users. *Influence specialists* concentrate their efforts on the identification and targeting of individuals who exercise an influence on their circle of acquaintances. The support of this figure of social relationships leads them towards a marketing practice which is close to the domain of public relations. *Specialists of the community* are experts in the management of online communities. This specialty consists essentially nowadays in running brands' fan pages on Facebook. In what follows, this chapter examines the roles of each of these major specialisations in this still emerging industry in turn.

Experts in contagion

The first type of specialisation that we identify is viral marketing in the strict sense. Viral marketing relies on social networks to provoke the rapid spread, on a large scale and through word of mouth, of content such as promotional videos or gaming applications. Experts in contagion connect to the field of media advertising by promising advertisers that they will generate brand awareness while minimising the purchase of advertising space – a promise they fail to keep most of the time because of the unpredictable nature of 'buzz'.

The figure of social relationships: contagion and epidemiology

Contagion is the figure of social relationships that underlies this area of SMM. The individual is seen as being inserted into networks of relationships; she can infect or be infected by the individuals who are connected to her. She is the vehicle of a form of contamination that extends, step by step, to the whole of society. This is a metaphorical representation of the social world, borrowed from epidemiology, but here that which is transmitted is not an infectious disease or a virus, but information.[4] Indeed, the web can be seen as a network in which pieces of information (content) move horizontally, following a mechanism of replication. In this digital environment, a video will be classified as viral if it reaches a certain level of visibility through word of mouth. The goal of the marketer is of course to reproduce this mechanism.

This figure of the social relationship has led to the emergence of a large body of literature in social science, which has later been translated into the science of marketing. Work on the diffusion of innovations (Coleman et al.,

1966; Rogers, 1962; Bass, 1969) has shown that the structure of social networks affects the flow of information, and that a specific class of individuals, qualified as innovators or opinion leaders, plays an important role in the initiation of mechanical diffusion. These diffusion models have been the basis for works that are interested in the mechanisms of viral marketing on the web (Mellet, 2009). A controversial issue in this literature, which had a direct impact on the activities of SMM agencies, concerns the role played by opinion leaders in the initiation of viral dynamics. Some authors (Gladwell, 2000) argue that a small class of individuals, the 'super-influencers', play a key role in spreading (or not) ideas and trends online because they are highly connected and have a strong influence on those around them. Advertisers should therefore focus their efforts on identifying and targeting these happy few.[5] However, research on the online diffusion of innovations or ideas challenges the role of such opinion leaders. For example, computer simulations carried out by Watts and Dodds (2007) reveal that viral diffusion depends essentially on the existence of a critical mass of easily influenced individuals, rather than on a few select influentials.

The marketing field: media advertising

The results of these studies on viral spreading have had two operational consequences. First, they reconcile the viral marketing approach with advertising that uses mass media. From this perspective, it is not necessary to target and tailor a personalised communication to a small number of influentials. Instead, communication should be initiated using many different 'entry points', which are what media advertising is usually designed to provide. Second, the challenge of viral distribution lies mainly in encouraging individuals to share the message: the 'pass-along effect'. Of course, there are a great variety of mechanisms, contexts or strategies designed to encourage the message to spread virally: financial incentives, humour and creativity, an event, mystery, etc. In the context of the internet, social media sites play a critical role in this because they incorporate sharing functions (such as the 'share' and 'like' buttons on Facebook; 'retweet' and 'favourite' on Twitter).

Viral marketing agencies' own practices, as we observed from the interviews, support the case made by Watts and Dodds. Agencies anchor their activities in the field of advertising in order to maximise brand or product awareness. Their approach to viral marketing typically consists first of combining paid media advertising and word of mouth. Viral campaigns always receive a paid media boost at the start and word of mouth is then supposed to take over. The audience gained through word of mouth is, to use a native term, 'earned media' and represents money saved on 'paid media' or publicity that is purchased through advertising. Second, the expertise of agencies is concerned with the 'pass-along effect'; that is, the ability to produce content that is attractive enough for individuals to want to share it with those around them.

These two aspects appear very clearly in the economic equation outlined by this viral marketing or 'buzz' agency:

> When you make a buzz campaign, you're going to invest a lot more in content creation, it will cost you more initially. After that, you'll also buy media, because buzz does not happen alone… The most amazing campaign we have done is what we did for Orange, *Monfestival* [MyFestival] … We had a budget of €150,000. We took the risk of saying that rather than, for example, putting 100,000 in (paid) media and 50,000 in the creation [of an ad], we would take 150,000 to create really great content. Since Orange has a huge customer database, Orange could already send [it] to a few people, so the ad was sent to 200,000 people. Except that these 200,000 video views have turned into 10 million.
>
> (George, CEO, buzz agency A, twenty employees)

Another example of a viral campaign that had significant success is the 2010 video campaign 'A hunter shoots a bear' (by Buzzman agency, for Tipp-Ex): it consists of an interactive video on YouTube (in fact, a custom Flash application embedded in YouTube) which puts a bear and a hunter face to face, offering the viewers the choice of which ending they want to see by erasing the word 'shoots' in the title using a Tipp-Ex corrector and replacing it with a word chosen by them.[6] In order to give as many responses as possible to the viewers' queries, more than forty different endings were produced and filmed. The campaign is often cited as an incredibly successful viral phenomenon. Over time, its different versions have gathered a total of 30 to 40 million views, and the creative material received multiple awards in professional advertising festivals. A professional who participated in the design of this campaign stresses the importance of the quality of the creation for its future viral success:

> So in fact, it really is the social web, for once, that launched it, but we had content that was very strong, which worked very well… We still purchased advertising space on YouTube UK and Italy, it was also a kind of deal with YouTube, since they did something custom for us. And it worked.
>
> (Mick, community manager, Buzzman agency, thirty employees)

The previous two examples cleverly connect the traditional video format with an interactive device that produces a personalised effect. They belong to what one interviewed expert calls content-based buzz ('*le buzz de contenu*'): 'So content-based buzz, it's typically the surprising video. It's not technique, it's all about creativity' (Ron, social media marketing manager, advertiser).

Another means of domesticating virality comes under the category of what the same expert calls mechanical virality ('*le viral de mécanique*'), as opposed to content-based buzz. Mechanical virality is solely based on incentives. The best example of mechanical virality is the contest concerning a Facebook application a company has created. First, the contest is advertised through (paid) Facebook ads. Then, internet users are forced to 'like' the page to be eligible to participate. Finally, they are encouraged to share the app with friends, since it increases their chances of winning as well as those of their friends. However, the content is very poor: it is limited to a basic quiz with standard questions; only the potential prize varies, depending on the campaign.

Measuring the success of viral campaigns

Viral marketing metrics are fairly similar to their media counterparts, namely the number of videos viewed or the number of quizzes played. These metrics are used to make comparisons between purchased audience and audience acquired through word of mouth. In order to refine the measure of virality, agencies have also developed viral coefficient that give an indication of people's willingness to share the message: 'Each day we had a table telling us the number of video viewers, the number of earned viewers [those viewers that were not acquired through paid advertising but through word-of-mouth referrals]… and at the end the viral coefficients [the relationship between earned and paid views]' (George).

Contagion cannot be decreed

Both of the campaigns just mentioned – Orange and Tipp-Ex – are the biggest hits of their respective agencies. They are loss leaders to attract new advertisers. They cannot, however, be reproduced campaign after campaign, precisely because of their exceptional nature: 'There's a Tipp-Ex effect, for sure. Advertisers think we can do it again, and they are disappointed that it has not been done with them. Except that there are things that are a bit special anyway, even if we try to do as well every time' (Mick).

Most campaigns produce little or no word of mouth. The uncertainty of the viral success of the campaigns and the (measurable) extent of this success is very problematic for agencies. Indeed, advertisers allocate their advertising budgets depending on the size and quality of the audience they hope to reach. They want guarantees. Can agencies manage to secure a measured viral audience? This problem is essentially concerned with content-based buzz.[7] Agencies strive to reduce uncertainty in two ways. First, they develop a specific knowledge of why things catch on, in terms of format and content. For movies, they prefer a short format – less than thirty seconds – and for it to appear to be an amateur production ('low fi'). These specifications, however, are not sufficient to ensure the viral success of an advertising campaign. As emphasised by this agency employee, content 'must be brilliant, otherwise it will not work' (Mick). Genius cannot be reproduced and standardised, campaign after campaign.

The temptation of artificial virality

The most radical solution – but also the most delicate to pursue from an ethical standpoint – is to buy an audience that has been labelled 'viral'. Several advertising networks sell advertising space that serves as a seeder for viral marketing campaigns. But they can, more discreetly, give a boost to agencies in the second part of a campaign, the part that is supposed to be based on word of mouth. The fact that advertisers ultimately demand a certain volume of total audience means that the ambiguity is maintained between a purchased audience and an audience that is generated by word of mouth:

> Goviral and others, like e-Buzzing, or BlogBang, their principle is to say that today, just for a buzz to start, you have to buy a first part of the audience, for the media material to be seen by the first people who will pass it along… But it is not prohibited, if you are struggling, if you feel that it [the content] does not work or that the content is not strong enough, [then] you resort to these players. But it is not so much in the genes of the agency [i.e. the agency Mick worked for].
>
> (Mick)

For another expert, the temptation to use artificial virality – even though it may be justified by advertisers' risk aversion – is a denial of the principles of viral marketing:

> Not to name them, E-buzzing, BlogBang, those people made us believe we were going to use the viral power of bloggers… They clearly say in their sales pitch: yes, do not worry, it's bloggers. Ah, so this is a new world. But beyond that, what do they say? What promise do they sell? They sell 2 million certified views, irrespective of the video, for €10,000… That is, they rely on a misunderstanding, and they managed the perfect hold up, while, at the same time, selling the dream of social media to their customers, by telling them you'll see, social media, it means the loss of control. Oh, okay, it's the loss of control. Yes, but do not worry, I'll sell you the dream of the loss of control, and you will stay in control. Ah, well, that's cool, I have the cake and eat it too, that's even better.
>
> (Keith, CEO, social media research agency, twenty employees)

Consequently, we observe a very strong tension between the logic of pure virality, which can produce success but is primarily characterised by unpredictability, and the rationality of media advertising, in which predictability prevails. From the point of view of agencies, advertisers' expectations result in the temptation to reduce the viral audience to a specific medium, to make it measurable and marketable just as with any other media.

Experts in influence

Specialists in influence focus on the identification and targeting of individuals who are supposed to be able to influence those around them. This focus leads these specialists to a marketing practice that is very different from that of experts in contagion. This links them to the field of public relations (PR), whose contours – though not the trade itself – have been redefined by social media.

A figure of social relationships that equips public relations

> Wherever there are games of influence, what you called earlier word of mouth, it's about us, it is our business.
>
>   (Ringo, 'Digital influence' manager, PR branch of an advertising company)

For this 'digital influence' manager in a PR agency, word of mouth comes down to games of influence. This feature of social relationships is associated with a representation of the social world that is different from the horizontal and egalitarian concept that animates experts in contagion. The world of influence is vertical and hierarchical: individuals can be differentiated according to their ability to exert influence in networks of relationships. A small number of individuals, qualified as influentials or opinion leaders, are supposed to have a high ability to influence those around them.

This view of the social world, based on influence, is shared by public relations specialists. For the latter, the tracking and targeting of influencers are the strategic entry points to shaping public opinion. Founders of this business, like Edward Bernays in the United States in the early twentieth century, worked to establish the best practices of 'spin doctors'. Among these, the goal of influencing the influencers appears prominently:

> Those interested in fashioning public opinion must be sociologically and anthropologically informed; they must be meticulous students of the social structure and of the cultural routines through which opinions take hold on an interpersonal level. They must consider the imprint of sex, race, economics, and geography on public attitudes. It was also important to understand existing networks of influence – family, community, education and religion for example – as well as the undeclared patterns of leadership that operate within each of them. 'If you can influence the leaders', Bernays instructed, 'you automatically influence the group which they sway'.
>
>   (Ewen, 1996: 168)

We will not describe here the different facets of a field whose goals and methods are multiple and sometimes conflicting (Ewen, 1996). Note, however, that the internet and social media are of particular interest to PR professionals to the extent that they expand the boundaries of public space. Indeed, as pointed out by Cardon (2010), the internet weakens the position of the traditional 'gatekeepers' – journalists, publishers, personalities – who are responsible for monitoring and maintaining the boundary between public space and the space of sociability. Over time, gatekeepers have become the almost exclusive focus of attention for media relations, the central tool of public relations. Now, a number of amateurs and quasi-professionals have increased access to public space, for example by blogging. Moreover, ordinary and personal conversations can achieve visibility online. Consequently, as their voice becomes part of a broader public space, new people are likely to achieve the status of being 'influential':

> We came to the conclusion that it was necessary to offer something different to customers, because there was a great danger, in a way, because not only journalists could express themselves about a brand; the impact could come from elsewhere, with equal force, and sometimes even cause disasters for some brands.
>
> (Janis, CEO, RP 2.0 agency, four employees)

The influence specialist's toolbox

The influence specialist's toolbox differs significantly from that of the expert in contagion. The service being sold is not an advertising product, combining a commercial and a short-term campaign. It more closely resembles a support and consulting contract with a company or institution, which extends over the long term. This support is based on two main types of expertise.

The first is to identify and qualify those who may access the status of influencer. This is called 'profiling'. It is traditionally focused on journalists, of whom PR professionals have a regularly updated database. Profiling extends to influentials that can be identified on social media websites such as Twitter, Facebook or on blogs. To perform this profiling operation, quantitative 'counters' indicating the number of friends or 'followers' are useful, but cannot replace the interpretative work of the professional spin doctor:

> You see if the person has 5,000 followers on Twitter, and half of these 5,000 followers are journalists, to take an example, one can say that [on a scale] from 1 to 10, there is an influence of 9. Because it means something. Same thing on Facebook. In fact we look at people. It is not the volume, that's the idea. I'm never going to say: '5,000 on Twitter, 2,000 on Facebook, so that's great influence'. Now if those 2,000 Facebook friends are teens, aged 14–15, it could interest me for Nintendo, but it's not going to be interesting for Perrier-Dita Von Teese. So, every time, the profiling work really involves the individual. But in the same way as it happened before for a journalist. Actually for a journalist, we know what she personally cares for. We know if she has children, we know her interests in life, beyond what is technically visible to everyone, that is to say what she wrote, just to be sure to talk her while being on top of her mind.
>
> (Ringo)

In a social world reduced to 'influence games', the PR professional is looking to fill a position that allows her to influence the influentials whom she has identified. This is the second area of expertise. Thus, most professionals we met publish a blog and have an active Twitter account ('I have 4,000 followers'). These tools help them maintain a 'dialogue' in the sense of 'being part of the conversation' about various issues. In addition, experts in influence mobilise classic media relations devices: sponsorship contracts, gifts, invitations to events, etc. They organise events such as Apérotweets (cocktail parties with Twitter influencers) or Goldenblog Awards (blogger awards), for which the invite list has an exclusive dimension.[8]

The extension of the domain of influence?

How do customers, advertisers and brand managers measure and assess the work of influence specialists? In the field of media relations, the two most commonly used metrics are press coverage – media coverage resulting from the action of press agents – and the advertising value equivalency rate, which estimates what editorial coverage would cost if it were advertising space. These measures are also mobilised to assess the actions of experts in influence on the web:

> Trying to find common metrics that will demonstrate that there is an influence, it's very complicated. This is a subject that is 100 years old in global PR and it exists today within digital PR. No one has found a good answer. So much so that in traditional PR, the only measurement system I know of that is actually used is the advertising value equivalency. And it's the worst thing you can do. Making an advertising equivalency, this is the very antithesis of our business. But so far, this is what we find, this is the standard.
>
> (Ringo)

If PR professionals explore the dynamics of how influence affects new media, such as blogs or Twitter, they still use traditional assessment tools. Consequently, the efforts of these specialists are rewarded – and their clients are satisfied – only when their actions produce visible effects in mainstream media. For an operation to be successful, it must loop on traditional media: 'What's funny is that by dint of creating this buzz on the web, we hit the jackpot: Jerome Bonaldi [a well-known French journalist] on France 2 [a French broadcast TV network]' (Janis).

Finally, we observe a strong tension between talk that emphasises the need to address the emerging influentials in social media and practices that are deeply rooted in traditional public relations. Thus, experts in influence will look at Twitter not because it highlights the expansion of the public space, but rather because the social network is populated by journalists and politicians: 'Twitter is an absolutely key influence tool, because it is an elite which is an elite group of decision makers. These are exactly the targets that I'm interested in, which can be journalists – there are a lot of journalists on Twitter – or politicians or opinion leaders, whoever they are' (Ringo).

Community specialists

Contagion and influence are not the only social relationship figures on which SMM agencies build their business. Some agencies are experts in managing online communities. This specialty now essentially consists of managing brand pages on Facebook. Community managers are, however, torn between the ideal of strong engagement with community members and the poverty of online interactions… which leads them to elicit more instrumental forms of mobilisation.

The figure of social relationships: commitment to community

Facing the ephemeral bubbles of collective attention based on contagion, which follow each other, the expert in community instead favours stable links and relationships that last. But, unlike the hierarchical representation that is expected to result from influence games, this vision of the social world is egalitarian. If it is possible to differentiate between people according to their level of involvement or participation, the main issue at stake is the separation between community members and non-members. 'On one hand, when we try to talk to influencers, we try to obtain coverage [media coverage] from them. On the other hand, when we speak to fans, we try to get engagement from these fans. These are two different concepts' (John, online agency, subsidiary of an independent advertising company).

The concept of 'community' as it is mobilised and equipped by SMM agencies does not have the same meaning as is given to it by sociologists since the works of Tönnies and Durkheim. Brand communities (Cova and Cova, 2001; Muniz and O'Guinn, 2001) are described as stable and structured groups, based on a shared interest in a brand or a product. The forms of commitment associated with these communities are compatible with con-temporary individualism and consumerism, whose values they share. Web-pages and forums that are fed and managed by internet users support many brand communities (Amine and Sitz, 2007).

The conversation established between brands and consumers organised in communities can be linked to the field of customer relationship management. Indeed, records of interactions between internet users on social media web-sites can fuel the remote monitoring by an organisation of the quality of their products and services. Social media can also be used to support the development of loyalty programmes:

> However for a brand, it's still interesting enough to have all this feedback, because for once, even if it's sometimes scary, there are hard facts, there

are real consumer insights that come to the surface... At the risk of caricature, a guy who says 'it's a crappy product', how can we reply? And a guy who says 'the product is great', it would be nice to answer. Brands do not know what to answer, but today we are entering a logic of community that requires management.

> (Paul, CEO, online niche marketing agency, forty employees)

The community manager's toolkit

For the community manager as for the influence specialist, the interaction has to be maintained over time ('Today, we are more in a year-long contract logic'). This positioning is consistent with a critique that is made against the expert in virality, unable to maintain a lasting relationship with the internet user beyond the initial campaign:

> When looking for example at Tipp-Ex, which is today's buzz, there is no connection to Facebook. It's weird not having a Tipp-Ex fan page... I do not want to rewrite history, but now, in the end, what I find unfortunate is that this is a campaign that was very successful, which is great and all, [but] it will stop and will struggle to bounce back because it did not create its legend. They could have, perhaps, tried to group some fans [i.e. page likes] together, or at least people who found this video funny, before eventually reactivating them later.
>
> (John)

The management of brand pages on Facebook is the typical product marketed by those who are experts in community. These pages gather Facebook members who have declared themselves 'fans' of the brand by clicking the 'like' button. This membership gives them the opportunity to like, comment and share content (news, photos, videos, contests) published by the page manager – content that appears directly in their newsfeed, alongside the news of their friends. Thus, the functioning of the 'community' is based on engagement. Customers agree to become members of the community. They agree to receive the information, but they can also unsubscribe. They eventually agree to become the voice of the brand among their friends. They thus differ from influentials, who are usually solicited against their will, and often repeatedly, once they have been recorded in the files of the influence specialists:

> Today it will be mostly the management of Facebook pages. At the start, we were working with blogs. We did a lot of things, sending small gifts, organizing parties, things like that, for bloggers. It had a certain limit. There have been so many that it made for big budgets. I recognize that they are true influentials, but as they were over-solicited, it did not really work... I recognize that with the rise of social networks... platforms like Facebook, we're really in this logic of community management. And for

once, the social networking part has a real meaning, because we have reached what was originally our dream when we tried to reach influentials: to group together those in love with a brand. Now, we manage them directly. Well, they are not necessarily 'in love' with a brand, but in any case these people have a great deal of sympathy for the brand.

(Paul)

Of course, community management presupposes the existence of a community. The most common way this process is configured involves a company that engages the agency's services because it does not know how to handle an existing fan page:

So people come to us saying 'well, what can we do?' Often they have existing communities, but they never made them lively… This was the case when we got the management of Petit Bateau [an old French clothes brand that has become fashionable in the past 20 years], for example. We have run Petit Bateau's page for about six months. They had done nothing with it. We took it over and we really made it lively. And this is the most common case.

(Paul)

Facebook page management has two main dimensions. First, it is necessary to moderate fans' discussions. This form of control implies removing insulting or outlandish comments and responding to questions or criticisms. Second, it is necessary to maintain the relationship and to encourage likes and comments by regularly publishing content. This work is based on a clever arbitrage between soliciting attention and maintaining a certain distance between the publications, in order to prevent the defection of fans whose newsfeed could be overloaded. Maintaining a high level of attention and participation depends not only on the quality and consistency of published content, but also on the publishing strategy:

So that's basically how to reach out better in the newsfeeds. For example, we know that the inclusion of photographs is a plus, that kind of thing. It is true that we have to write open questions in order to maximize the number of likes or comments. The more comments or likes I receive, the more relevant my post will be. The more relevant it is, the more it will go up in Facebook's visibility algorithms. That's an emerging field.

(Paul)

Facebook's engagement metrics

The value of the community to the client depends of course on the number of its members, but also on their level of engagement. The community manager's objective is to 'maximize the interaction rate' (John) on his or her page. To assess the activity of members and adjust their work accordingly, managers have a dashboard featuring numerous quantitative insights on the community's activities: number of new fans; number of active members – those who have, at least once during the previous week, visited the page, commented or 'liked' a post; number of comments and likes, etc.:

> Basically, to continue on my Danone [*Dannon*] example, I have a fan base on my page, my Danone yogurt fan page. I connect with them several times a month with messages that I publish on the Facebook page. And I observe all this very, very closely. I check the number of likes, I check the number of comments, I check the percentage of interactions [with a post] with respect to their reach. These are the first KPIs [Key Perfomance Indicators]. Then I check the churn rate [the proportion of Facebook users who stop liking the page over a given period of time], I refine the editorial line in terms of themes, photos, videos, links, content, etc. I actually look to refine my editorial strategy and my Facebook presence in order to maximize interaction rates while minimizing my churn.
>
> (John)

'Engagement, that's fine; but then what do they do, all these fans?'

With Facebook, experts in community have a very powerful toolbox for measuring the activity of members and adjusting their management work. The representation of the activity of users produced by quantitative indicators is very valuable. It allows them to reduce uncertainty in planning their activity and to provide precise accounts to customers who wish to obtain a measurable return for each dollar spent. Finally, these indicators have a performative effect to the extent that they form a 'community' made up of more or less 'engaged' fans. Since it is measurable and comparable, it is not necessary to consider the nature of the 'engagement' of people, or to question what 'being a fan' or clicking 'Like' on Facebook means. However, as forms of attachment, these are extremely thin and inexpensive, and they drain the concept of community – even when used in the modern sense of brand community – of any real substance.

The community managers I interviewed say their job often consists of trying to maintain 'fans' who have been manufactured artificially and in large quantities through quizzes based on practices of mechanical virality (see above). Thus, they find themselves caught in the tension between the ideal of participation and dialogue associated with the 'community', and the need to generate revenue at the risk of betraying this ideal in favour of a utilitarian logic.

This tension is also reflected in the relationship between SMM agencies and their clients. As underlined by one advertiser, 'engagement, that's fine, but then, what do they do, all these fans?' 'Engagement' and conversation are not conventional marketing objectives. They must, at some point, convert or transform; in other words, they must lead to sales. This tension between the conversational ideal and economic necessity can lead to more open conflicts concerning page management. In the case of Petit Bateau's page management, this opposition led to a jurisdictional dispute, which ultimately resulted in the client recovering the Facebook page management function:

> Then, there is a skills problem, about who will be in charge. For example, I know that at Petit Bateau they have taken over the page, saying 'hey, it's no use'. Everything is finally nice and after all we had done to engage users, basically they said 'we do not care. What we will do from now on is send coupons every week, and also publish pictures of the catalog with the leading products of the moment that are top sellers.' It's an approach. Honestly, it works, but hey, if after all that the Facebook pages become newsletters for coupons and sales promotions, this is not what I call conversation.
>
> (Paul)

Conclusion

This chapter has presented an exploration of the business of social media marketing agencies. We have seen how these players have emerged, positioning themselves at the junction between a new, 'conversational' form of media – social media – and a market – the market for advertising and marketing services. In this conclusion we come back to the issue of 'domestication' of sociability by marketing, as raised in the introduction.

The domestication of word of mouth on social media sites by marketing is not self-evident. It involves multiple investments not only to design and equip marketable means of action, but also to incorporate these innovative products in a market with stabilised formats and measurement indicators. We identified three modes of intervention. Each is derived from a basic figure of social relationship, each results in a 'marketing promise', and each is materialised in a product and measuring instruments. The emerging market for social media marketing services is thus organised into three specialties: contagion, influence and community. However, efforts to build products that meet advertisers' expectations are not always sufficient. There is an irreducible tension between the metrics that are specific to these innovative products – the 'virality ratio', the measure of 'online influence', 'engagement' rates – and traditional marketing metrics. Agencies sell potential contagion, but advertisers demand a guaranteed audience level. Agencies sell online influence, but advertisers ultimately look at the benefits of traditional media (TV, print media). Agencies sell a dialogue with fans, but advertisers demand promotions that convert into sales. Agencies are therefore constantly tempted to give up their promise of 'alternative marketing' based on virality, online games of influence or dialogue. It is here that we finally realise that the adventure of social media marketing is – or at least it is when one adopts the perspective of professionals – the history of the domestication of marketing by marketing, rather than the history of the domestication of word of mouth by marketing.

Notes

1 Word-of-mouth marketing originated with the research carried out at the Department of Sociology of the University of Columbia by Paul Lazarsfeld's team in the 1940s and 1950s. Their surveys revealed the limited impact of short-term media-based initiatives on people's attitudes, and the influence of networks of personal relationships on purchase or voting decisions. While everybody is exposed to media, we have varying relationships with these information flows. 'Opinion leaders' are characterised by an active attitude combining a systematic quest for information with attention paid to understanding it. The conversation between opinion leaders and those they influence then begins, leading to decisions being made by some. Word-of-mouth marketing, which developed in the late 1950s in the wake of the work by Lazarsfeld's team, is in fact the application of this model to marketing: the implementation of targeted communication designed for individuals who are identified as influencers and are therefore likely to play a key role in the purchase decisions made by the other people around them (Brooks, 1957). As the reader shall see below, social media marketing redefines and greatly widens this restrictive approach.
2 In June 2014, Facebook was the second-most visited website in France with almost 28 million monthly internet users (Médiamétrie-Netratings). Video-sharing site YouTube occupied the third rank with more than 25 million users. Blog-publishing service Blogger was ranked 16th (10 million users).
3 The term 'domestication' must be understood both literally – marketers seek to exercise tight control over *a priori* uncontrolled ordinary conversations – but also figuratively, in the formulation proposed by Callon (1986). Callon places particular emphasis on definition and interessement mechanisms, and on devices that support them.
4 Experts in contagion implicitly refer to Gabriel Tarde's ontology. Indeed, as pointed out by Latour and Lépinay, Tarde's conception of social science focuses on the dynamics of contamination which spread from individual to individual. They are even more directly – but certainly unknowingly – Tardians when they implement the 'conversations among idlers' [*les conversations des badauds*] in their activity as their main 'factor of production' (Latour and Lépinay, 2009: 2).
5 As we will see in the next section, this representation is mobilised by the influence specialists.
6 www.youtube.com/profile?annotation_id=annotation_820885&feature=iv&src_vid=4ba1BqJ4S2M&user=tippexperience.
7 Indeed, the recommendation is more predictable when obtained through economic incentives, which is the case of gaming applications on Facebook – hence the term 'mechanical' virality.
8 'Without some form of censorship, propaganda in the strict sense of the word is impossible. In order to conduct a propaganda, there must be some barrier between the public and the event' (Lippman, 1997 [1922]: 42).

Bibliography

Amine, A. and Sitz, L. (2007) Emergence et structuration des communautés de marques en ligne. *Décisions Marketing*, 46, April–June: 63–75.
Araujo, L., Finch, J. and Kjellberg, H. (eds) (2010) *Reconnecting Marketing to Markets*, Oxford: Oxford University Press.
Bass, F. (1969) A new product growth model for consumer durables. *Management Science*, 15(5): 215–227.

Berger, J. (2013) *Contagious: Why Things Catch On*, New York: Simon and Schuster.

Beuscart, J.S. and Mellet, K. (2008) Business models of the Web 2.0: Advertising or the tale of two stories. *Communications and Strategies*, November, pp. 165–182.

boyd, d. and Ellison, N. (2007) Social network sites: Definition, history and scholarship. *Journal of Computer-Mediated Communication*, 13(1): 210–230.

Brooks, R. (1957) Word-of-mouth in selling new products. *Journal of Marketing*, 22(2): 154–161.

Callon, M. (1986) Some elements of a sociology of translation: Domestication of the scallops and the fishermen of St Brieuc Bay. In J. Law (ed.), *Power, Action and Belief: A New Sociology of Knowledge*, London: Routledge and Kegan Paul, pp. 196–233.

Callon, M. (ed.) (1998) *The Laws of the Markets*, Oxford: Blackwell.

Cardon, D. (2010) *La démocratie Internet: Promesses et limites*, Paris: Seuil.

Coleman, J., Katz, E. and Menzel, H. (1966) *Medical Innovation: A Diffusion Study*, Indianapolis: Bobbs-Merrill.

Cova, B. and Cova, V. (2001) *Alternatives marketing: réponses marketing aux nouveaux consommateurs*, Paris: Dunod.

Ewen, S. (1996) *PR! A Social History of Spin*, New York: Basic Books.

Gladwell, M. (2000) *The Tipping Point: How Little Things Can Make a Big Difference*, Boston, MA: Little, Brown and Company.

Jenkins, H., Ford, S. and Green, J. (2013) *Spreadable Media: Creating Value and Meaning in a Networked Culture*, New York: New York University Press.

Keller, E. and Berry, J. (2003) *The Influentials: One American in Ten Tells the Other Nine How to Vote, Where to Eat and What to Buy*, New York: Free Press.

Latour, B. and Lépinay, A. (2009) *The Science of Passionate Interests: An Introduction to Gabriel Tarde's Economic Anthropology*, Chicago, IL: University of Chicago Press.

Lippman, W. (1997 [1922]). *Public Opinion*, New Brunswick, NJ: Transaction Publishers.

Mellet, K. (2009) Aux sources du marketing viral. *Réseaux*, 27(157–8): 267–292.

Muniz, A. and O'Guinn, T. (2001) Brand community. *Journal of Consumer Research*, 27(4): 412–432.

Rogers, E. (1962) *Diffusion of Innovations*, New York: Free Press.

Sernovitz, A. (2006) *Word of Mouth Marketing: How Smart Companies Get People Talking*, Chicago, IL: Kaplan Publishing.

Wasik, B. (2009) *And Then There's This: How Stories Live and Die in Viral Culture*, New York: Viking.

Watts, D. and Dodds, P. (2007) Influentials, networks and public opinion formation. *Journal of Consumer Research*, 34(4): 441–458.

4 Interfacing attachments

The multivalence of brands

Carolin Gerlitz

In late 2003, the brand management team of the global cosmetic brand Dove responded to a managerial request to achieve higher sales targets by setting in motion a campaign against beauty and body norms in the media industry. Dove's reaction to the increased pressure to sell more was an interesting move, as it suggests that economic value can be achieved by associating Dove with a social issue. Rather than lowering the price, making specific promotional offers, improving the quality of their products, or altering the packaging to sell less for the same price, the brand's management team decided to create attachments with a societal cause. From 2003, this approach was realised through various campaigns, cooperations and increasingly participatory and co-creative approaches (Cova et al., 2011; Foster, 2011). First by commissioning an academic report on female bodily experience and the role of media, then through a series of advertising campaigns (most notably the 'Real Women Campaign'), events, and competitions. In cooperation with charities, such as Beat UK, Dove developed body consciousness workshops for schools, youth centres and parents, allowing the brand to become the subject of intimate conversations on bodily experience and beauty pressures.

Contemporary brands like Dove are usually characterised by a multiplicity of attachments. These attachments include, yet move beyond, the attachment of consumers to the brand through its immersion into their own lives (Callon et al., 2002), by involving external stakeholders, such as non-governmental organisations, as partners of campaigns, but also by creating specific associations between the brand, societal issues, such as body norms, and by making the brand part of media debates. Attachment, in this context, comes with different qualities and is, as the chapter sets out to show, closely connected to questions of valuation – the broader set of social, cultural or political values – and valorisation – the making of economic surplus (Vatin, 2013). What is of value in relation to the campaign differs across the various actors involved: the company sets out to increase its profits, non-governmental organisations campaign for their issues and consumers care about their relations towards media, bodies, family and friends. A specific assembly emerges, in which attachments, valuation and valorisation are entangled in specific and often asymmetrical ways.

Dove stands in line with a multiplicity of brands that seek to enable attachments with societal, cultural or political issues. In the last two decades, promotional culture has been highly influenced by the idea that brands or even products can be associated with a belief, a cause, an issue or an ideology. Brand managers argue (Gibbons, 2003) that by establishing connections with issues, it becomes possible for brands to create attachments across various levels: between the brand and a set of issue-related values, between brands and issue-interested consumers, and between consumers who are being connected to both issues and brands. Taking a cue from Callon and others (2002), who suggest that the qualities of goods do not reside in the goods themselves but in their capacities to generate associations, qualifications and attachments, sociological scholarship has explored the role of brands in organising attachments, both through company-centric modes of brand management, but also in relation to participatory forms of branding, which rely on consumer involvement (for an overview, see Dujarier, 2016). Brands are considered to operate through their incompleteness of attachment (Lury, 2004, 2009), through thriving on existing social attachments and formations (Arvidsson, 2006), as well as operating beyond commercial sectors (Moor, 2007).

This chapter sets out to explore the dynamics of multilayered attachment in contemporary branding practices, in which economic value production increasingly arises from non-economic activities, that is social, affective or cultural practices. Particular attention will be given to the specific assembly of attachment and the agential role of brands, consumers and other stakeholders. Second, the chapter focuses on the relation between attachments, the diverse registers of value they speak to, including social, cultural and political value, as well as their capacity to generate economic surplus. Tracing attachments, I suggest, offers a distinct perspective on the ways in which valuation and valorisation are entangled in contemporary branding.

In doing so, the chapter focuses on two brands which have attempted in very distinct ways to attach their branding endeavours to the issue of bodies and bodily experience: the cosmetics brand Dove and the US clothing company American Apparel. Dove, as outlined above, has come to be known for its 'Real Women Campaign' and its efforts to promote more diverse body norms in society and the media, with the help of various stakeholders. American Apparel has also drawn on the issue of body and beauty norms, but in a very different way. Their long-term visual aesthetic, established in 1999[1] and continuing until today, initially set out to differentiate itself from the digitally retouched conventions of fashion advertising. However, the company added a DIY pornographic aesthetic and an increasingly explicit sexuality to the mix, and it is this that it has been mainly recognised for. In both cases, the assembly of attachments cannot be regarded as the sole accomplishment of brand management, but is the subject of distributed and co-creative dynamics that require the involvement and participation of consumers and stakeholders. Dove and American Apparel have been chosen as they were among the first in their product category to draw on issues of body and beauty norms in (more or less) interventionist ways.

In focusing on cases that so heavily rely on consumer involvement, I am particularly interested in how brands on the one hand strategically seek to enact attachments, but also how attachments are subject to a 'happening' (Lury and Wakeford, 2012), that is a distributed, relational, dynamic, and ongoing accomplishment. From such a perspective, brands shall be approached as 'devices that are explicitly designed to compose and recompose the connections between market actors' (Deville, 2014: 4), while at the same time acknowledging that the accomplishment of such attachments and their valorisation is distributed across a wider set of stakeholders. In some cases, this accomplishment may be reducible to the strategic efforts of brands, but it is sometimes not, and therefore the focus shall be both on the making and the happening of attachments in branding.

Methodologically, the chapter accounts for such making and happening by offering a multiplicity of viewpoints on the two case studies. It assembles insights from four consumer focus groups held on the subjects of American Apparel and Dove, as well as a total of twenty-five consumer interviews about both brands. Additionally, it accounts for the activities of both brands and draws on various conversations with brand managers and cooperating partners.[2] The focus groups, interviews and conversations were conducted in London between 2010 and 2011.

Tracing attachments

Let me begin by scoping out some of the key attachments in the context of my case studies. At the beginning of my focus groups with consumers of American Apparel and/or Dove, participants were asked to create mind maps of the different associations they have about the respective brand. There was only one rule: 'No writing!'[3] In the case of Dove, a series of key figures emerged: participants' drawings were dominated by the colour blue, showing doves (the birds), clouds, sky, sea, water, but also soap bars, cream pots, women in white dresses or plain underwear, smiling women and women of different shapes (Figure 4.1).

When I asked my participants to narrate their drawings, they first focused on abstract attachments: for them Dove is associated with clarity, purity, healthy skin and 'taking care' of the body. On a more material level,

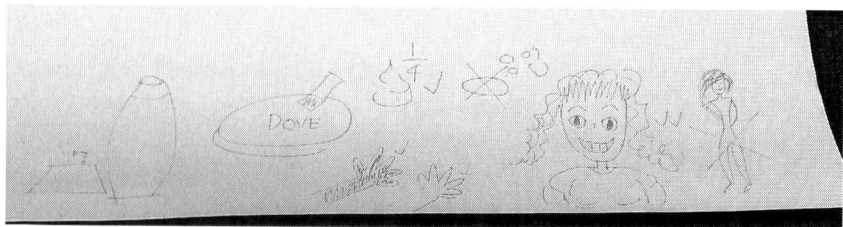

Figure 4.1a Associations with Dove. Drawings created during consumer focus groups

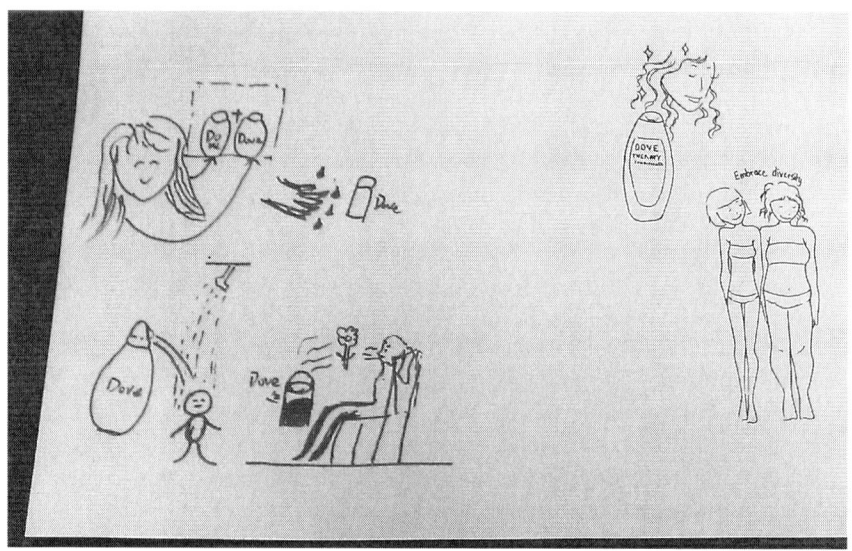

Figure 4.1b Associations with Dove. Drawings created during consumer focus groups

participants connected the brand mainly with its soap bar products, whilst being aware that Dove offers a wider range of products. Participants also often referred to Dove's so-called 'Real Women' campaign, initiated in 2005 as the first instance of the ongoing 'Campaign for Real Beauty'. The international campaign shows women of diverse body shapes, ages and skin colours, whilst offering tick boxes with options like 'grey or gorgeous', 'fat or fit', 'flawed or flawless', 'boy or babe'. Participants remember this campaign as 'iconic' or as 'introducing a new approach to bodies in advertising', suggesting that it was perceived to be distinct at the time (Gerlitz, 2012).[4]

During the individual interviews, further associations are addressed and the various social attachments forming around the brand came into focus. The initial contact with the brand mainly occurs at home and during childhood years, where Dove soap bars, shower gels and body lotion are often reported to feature as basic cosmetic essentials for the whole family. Their ongoing presence in family contexts enables consumers to develop a long-term relationship with these products, whilst at the same time attaching them to their family lives. As many of these initial attachments occurred before the launch of the 'Real Women' campaign, participants reported that the campaign functioned as a trigger of further attachments, for instance in debates between friends about body norms in media and bodily self-perception:

BK: Ahm, yeah, we might have spoken about it. It is kind of divided weirdly. A lot of girls were like, 'Oh, they don't look like I would wanna look! It doesn't seem glamorous, it does not seem, ahm, it doesn't seem like, it doesn't really appeal to me.' And other friends would kind of agree, and would be like, 'Yeah, I know what you mean.' One of my friends uses Dove a lot and she is definitely not a typical girl that you'd see maybe, she has really long ginger hair, and quite freckly and quite curvy and she has amazing skin and she uses Dove a lot and I think that appealed to her a lot because she did not feel she connected with any of the other cosmetics adverts around.

BK: Me and my friends often discuss what we see when we are flipping through a magazine or watching an advert and say 'Oh, no!... Oh no, you can see her hairline, it's not like that! They just edited like lots of hair out.' Yeah, we talk about stuff like that all the time.

This initial scoping of attachments in the case of Dove suggests that attachments between the brand and its consumers are not forged in the straightforward way envisioned by traditional forms of brand management, which seek to create consumer attachment by connecting brands to a core set of values and beliefs (Kornberger, 2010). Such accounts of branding have been gradually challenged, most notably by participatory or issue-based approaches towards branding (Cova et al., 2015; Zwick et al., 2008), which seek to attach the brand to an issue, in order for it to enter new relations, contexts and debates. In the case of Dove, the issue of body norms and its 'Real Women' campaign allowed the brand to become part of personal conversations between family and friends, inform consumers' own bodily relations, and enter media and educational discourses. These attachments connect consumers to brands by taking detours via the issue of media-defined beauty, personal bodily experience, existing relations and social practices. What emerges is a cascade of attachments, as one attachment (between consumers and issues) allows the ground to be laid for another (brands and issues/values or subsequently between consumers, brands and values). These attachments may be initiated by brand-management practices, but need to be completed and realised by consumers or the wider public, by first acknowledging, accepting and relating to the attachment between the brand and the issue, and later by integrating it into one's own routines, debates or relations.

Hence, attachments in branding are not only strategically 'made' by company activities, they are also (set out to be) a distributed accomplishment or a 'happening'. They are situated in the realm of the possible, as they need to be realised by a diverse set of actors (Lury and Wakeford, 2012). The brand, just as in Callon's account of the product, is an inherently unfinished object which requires completion through its various stakeholders: 'The product is thus a process, whereas the good corresponds to a state, to a result or, more precisely, to a moment in that never-ending process' (Callon in Barry and Slater, 2005: 31). Therefore, I suggest that the emergence of attachments should be understood as the interplay between strategic making and distributed happening. The notion of the happening which I deploy here draws attention to the eventive, emergent and distributed activities (Lury and Wakeford, 2012) of consumers, media and partners which are involved in the creation of attachments (Gerlitz, 2012). In the context of brands and their attachment, making and happening are mutually entangled: in order for new, cascading attachments to 'happen', brands need to initialise these processes through strategic making, however, strategic making is only successful if it elicits a subsequent happening.

To explore the interplay of making and happening attachments further, let me turn to the chapter's second case, the US clothing brand American Apparel. It was founded in 1989 in Los Angeles as a company for basic clothing. In the early 1990s American Apparel faced the need to differentiate from competitors who offered very similar products – mainly Hannes and Fruit of the Loom. The brand responded by developing its competitive distinctiveness at the level of its product offerings. As its competitors mainly produced loose-fit and unisex cuts, American Apparel started introducing clothes with a tight fit made of stretchy garments. This was perceived as product novelty for basic apparel at that time (Ritchie, 2002). Taking this as a cue to develop its differential positioning, the brand started to expand on this logic by bringing its products literally closer to the consumer's skin, allowing basic wear to appear sexier and more tightly fitting. Shortly thereafter, the company took this focus on body shapes and being sexy to develop a visual identity for which it is still known today. Since 1999, American Apparel has been pursuing a visual aesthetics that is inspired by DIY photography and hipster culture (N+1, 2010), as well as borrowing presentational formats from pornographic material. Similar to Dove, it also claimed to work with non-professional models who do not fully conform to professional beauty standards. In a promotional video, the company states: 'Our advertisements depict young people wearing our clothes in scenes that are devoid of a conventional pretence and staging. Instead of using models, we show the clothes on actual people. A refreshingly unmediated and innocent approach to advertisement' (American Apparel, 2012). Whilst its clothes move closer to consumers' skins, its visual aesthetic moves closer to private moments. Throughout their ads, lookbooks and in-store promotions, the company depicts private situations, often in bed,[5] or suggesting to be spontaneous snapshots of intimate scenes.[6] Models are largely slender and sometimes show sweat, body hair[7] or minor signs of cellulite, while make-up and hair styles are kept to a minimum.[8]

It was this investment in aesthetics that enabled American Apparel to lay the grounds for new attachments to happen, as the brand soon came to be integrated into the wider lifestyle of young metropolitan consumers interested in club and hipster culture:

CG: What made you buy their clothes for the first time?

GM: I don't know, I really like, I mean, I just met a lot of people who were buying it, like my friends, and I thought it was really cool although it was expensive. Yeah, because it was really entwined with the clubbing scene. So all of my friends, a lot of my friends that I knew were buying this stuff, so I had a try too.

This quote illustrates a consumer who discovered the brand after the making and happening of various attachments. This consumer observes how the brand increasingly became attached to areas of life that mattered to them, such as their friends, the local clubbing scene and its associated locations. It is via these cascading attachments that the brand gained value and relevance for consumers:

CG: Who are the people who would buy American Apparel?
RS: East London kids [Laughs]. I guess that there are also some younger kids as well but then again, it is not that cheap. I think, if you wanted to look like that you could probably do it, I mean, I don't know. I definitely think it is an East London trendy thing to wear. Like, because I live in East London. You definitely see a lot of American Apparel, particularly on young guys around Hoxton in pubs and stuff.
GM: Yeah. It was very associated with the party scene in Shoreditch. A lot of gay friends of my age were wearing a lot of American Apparel.

Here, a three-way relationship between the brand (or rather, its aesthetics), spaces and social formations emerges. The attachments consumers perceive in relation to hipster aesthetics are inextricably tied up with a distinct spatiality, more concretely with distinct locations in East London. However, in addition to appearing in the associated spaces, American Apparel products also need to be worn by influential people, enabling consumers to be drawn towards the brand, as its aesthetic is attached to the social formations they feel themselves attached to. The spaces that come to matter here exceed the spaces that have been designed by brands themselves (Moor, 2007), such as flagship stores or offices, and include clubs, bars and urban areas. What emerges is a proliferation of attachments which are relationally tied to each other, or, to put it in the words of Hearn, who explored relationally tied notions of reputation measure: 'the reputation we generate is simply a reputation for building the reputation of others, resulting in a seemingly endless circuit of exchange without foundation' (Hearn, 2010: 453).

Interfacing attachments

Such cascades of attachments bring up the question of the interfacing capacities of brands. In sociological accounts on brands (Lury, 2004), but also in marketing theory (Aaker and Joachimsthaler, 2002; Kapferer, 2008), the idea of the brand as interface figures centrally, but mainly refers to the ways in which brands make it possible for relations to be negotiated between companies and consumers or, in internal branding, between management and employees. Lury, for instance, addresses brands – with recourse to Manovich's new media theory – both as interfaces between actors and as platforms for action: 'a mode of organising activities in time and space' (2004: 1). Functioning akin to a frame (Callon, 1998; Goffman, 1986; see also Kessous, this volume), brands are understood to establish sets of values that inform internal and external processes and enable some actions whilst ruling out others. Due to changing environments of operation, or, as Lury calls it, the pressure to respond to feedback loops of information about markets and consumers, brands are required to remain dynamic and flexible. In this context, the logo is perceived as the materialisation of the interfacing capacities of the brand (Lury, 2004).

A different perspective on interfacing opens up when exploring the cascades of attachments emerging in the context of contemporary branding, as it is not necessarily the brand that operates as interface, but the brand is interfaced through its attachments itself. It is not merely the logo to which consumers of Dove or American Apparel are attached. They are attached to the specific issues, media debates and visual aesthetics to which the brand has formed attachments, by becoming embedded in style communities and spaces. And within these interfacing attachments, the brand is both present and not, both informing them whilst being itself informed. While Dove can be considered attached to its cause of beauty norms, neither the brand nor the issue are fully collapsed into the other. Attachments are both the outcome and the means of the interfacing capacities of branding, as initial attachments can operate as interfaces for the making and happening of further attachments – in the context of American Apparel, the attachment of the brand to its distinct aesthetic was needed for it to be attached to hipster culture and specific urban spaces.

Such cascading of attachments is also at stake inside organisations, as shall be shown with regards to the advent of Dove's 'Real Women' campaign. Before Dove started to attach its brand to the issue of beauty norms, the brand and product management team needed to establish an attachment to this idea in the first place. Brand consultant Martin Staniforth, who was involved in the early years of the campaign, pointed out that in order for the brand to start the 'Real Women' campaign, a series of preceding attachments were needed (Staniforth, 2011). In 2003, at the very beginning of the campaign, Dove asked sixty-seven female photographers to depict their perspectives on female beauty. Their input was used to create a mobile photo exhibition entitled 'Beyond Compare', which travelled around the world in 2004. Visitors were invited to comment upon and interact with the images displayed, as the objective was to explore potential consumers' affective involvement with, and attachment to, the issue of media beauty norms. Both consumers' responses and those of the media, according to Staniforth, were positive and supportive, with Dove therefore deciding to pursue the idea further. In 2004 the company commissioned 'The Real Truth about Beauty: A Global Report' (Etcoff et al., 2004), an academic research project carried out by members of the campaign's forthcoming advisory board, including the psychologist Nancy Etcoff and psychotherapist Susie Orbach. Through this report, Dove gained key argumentative elements for its campaign while at the same time showcasing its interest in the issue.

The translation of the report's insights into an actual branding campaign was not, however, a straightforward process. The advertising agency Ogilvy and Mather was hired and developed the initial idea for the 'Real Women' campaign, suggesting that Dove should create a critical commentary on media beauty standards by being among the first companies to show diverse female bodies in their ads (Staniforth, 2011). The brand management team responded reluctantly at first, so Ogilvy and Mather drew on the managers' very own relations to attach them to their campaign idea. The agency produced a video featuring interviews with the managers' and consultants' young daughters, asking them how they feel about their bodies, whether they think they are beautiful and how they experience bodies presented in the media. The movie depicted their responses, and showed that the girls have highly media-informed beauty ideals, are critical about their bodies, have to deal with insecurities and feel attracted to media beauty ideals. Being exposed to their daughters' experience of beauty pressure, the members of the management team signed off the campaign, according to Staniforth (2011), and further developed their own attachment towards it. Existing family attachments were utilised to inform and affect brand management and therefore the becoming of the campaign itself. The attachment of Unilever staff to the campaign remains an ongoing concern within the company: as cooperating partner Susan Ringwood from the charity Beat UK explains (2010), every time a new member joins the rotating brand management team, they have to follow an internal engagement programme, involving the conduct of workshops related to the cause.

In the particular approach followed by Dove, existing attachments, such as an interest in the societal issue of body norms, as well as personal attachments of the management (to their daughters and their experiences) were utilised by the agency to mobilise yet another different attachment – that of the management to the relevance of the issue of media beauty pressure and subsequently the launch of the 'Real Women' campaign. Similar cascades of attachments were relevant to Dove's endeavour to become involved in school and youth education. Brands usually face a series of obstacles when seeking to directly address children in school or youth in educational environments. Therefore, Dove took a detour of attachments by cooperating with national non-governmental organisations focusing on body or eating disorder-related issues. However, to convincingly attach the brand to this issue and to gain organisations like Beat UK as a cooperating partner, Dove needed to demonstrate that it had a long-term interest in the cause, which it managed by creating academic attachments via its global beauty report, according to Ringwood. In the UK, Dove approached Beat UK and jointly initiated the so-called 'Self Esteem Fund' through which the brand started to develop workshop materials that teachers, youth workers or parents can use. As the objectives and values educational institutions and brands follow are often non-aligned, schools and youth centres need to remain promotion-free and focus on pedagogic objectives, whilst brands obviously aim for the production of surplus value, Dove had to establish a series of cascading attachments. Through the interfacing attachments, the educational workshops contributed to the distinct valuation regimes of the different actors involved.

Partible, non-exclusive attachments

In the work of Callon et al. (2002), attaching a consumer to a brand required the same consumer to be detached from the brand's competitors. When attaching a brand to the issue of beauty norms, however, this issue neither gets detached from all its other attachments, nor does the attachment between the brand and the issue remain exclusive – the attachment of issues, qualities, aesthetics or communities does not require exclusivity as envisioned by Callon. If a brand comes to be attached to personal conversations or educational workshops, these attachments may add to the conversations or education, but do not replace them or collapse into them. Similarly, when attaching a brand to urban hipster communities, this attachment is also non-exclusive, as the style is inherently composed of other spatial, social and aesthetic attachments. Drawing on Strathern (1988), brand attachments can be understood as partible in their non-exclusivity, as what is attached to the brand is not necessarily detached from its original context but remains connected to it. Attachments are not replaced, they are added, and they can create value both for their original contexts and for the brand. What is being attached to brands is partible if it remains of value for the detached (the youth, the hipster culture), whilst also being valuable for brands (Foster, 2011). Interestingly, it also works the other way around, when consumers acquire branded products and seek to attach the brand into their own life world. Consumers cannot acquire the actual brand, but can only take part in its value or 'rent' it by deploying its products, aesthetics or by getting involved in its campaigns (Foster, 2011). Brands emerge as unalienable in a twofold sense, as consumers cannot acquire the brand as such, but only its partial actualisation in products or services, while companies at the same time cannot contain and control the value of the brand themselves, as it partly resides with consumers. Subsequently, consumers' discussions of branded products or immersion of them into everyday life practices add value to both brands and the consumer: whilst consumers gain social or cultural value from this attachment, brands also potentially gain economic value as their social value may contribute to building reputation or driving sales. Both sides can participate in value making, but under different conditions, as not all actors can realise all forms of value – for instance, consumers cannot translate the social value a brand brings them into an economic value in the same way the brand can.

Approaching brands as assemblages of partible attachments opens up the question of how these attachments endure and change in their non-exclusivity. If attachments are organised around partibility and non-exclusivity, how are their boundaries negotiated? Here, the case of American Apparel becomes relevant again. Whilst the brand seeks to address 'young urban metropolitan adults' (American Apparel, 2012), conversations with consumers show that this is neither a homogenous nor a stable attachment:

PK: One of my friends in Stockholm works in American Apparel... but she is actually... too cool for American Apparel. I have never seen her wearing

American Apparel. I don't think she does because she is actually a bit above that, because she is very, very fashionable... but... they sort of use cool people to... ahm... ahm, I don't know... to make, to make the brand cooler.

CG: So you like going to the store?

PK: Yes. But I would be a bit intimidated if I would be a bit less cool than I am [laughs].

CG: Do you think some people get intimidated?

PK: I think so yeah. I think everyone could go to H&M. But I don't... ahm... I don't think... everyone would go to American Apparel.

This quote shows that attachment to hipster culture is organised around one's capacity to be cool, that is performing and informing a certain style and being recognised as such. However, not everyone attached to hipsterish aesthetics connects to all others that are attached to it or to American Apparel with a similar intensity. The above quotation describes that certain people of the overall social formation are 'too cool', whilst others are 'not cool enough'. Both of these groups might not necessarily be consumers of American Apparel, yet both are crucial for the dynamics of hipster culture that the brand seeks to attach itself to. An interesting process of boundary making is at stake here, in which American Apparel's attachment to hipsterism remains partial and partible, as the brand is not embraced by those considered 'too cool' whilst the brand also does not enable users to 'become cool'. Rather, 'being cool' specifies a requirement and operates as a form of internal boundary making, both within hipsterism and American Apparel.

Diffracting attachments

The partibility of attachments is connected to the interplay between making and happening attachments. American Apparel can only strategically set up its attachments to hipster aesthetics. To become attached to these, it needs to be taken up and integrated by relevant consumers into their own contexts. In this process, the attachment is established, yet also altered, adjusted and personalised. Put differently, the happening of attachments creates a process of diffraction, in which it is partibly connected to other contexts, practices and relations, over and over again.

Let's engage further with American Apparel to explore the diffraction of attachments. The brand developed its key aesthetic around 2001/2002 and since then has developed yet not changed its underlying aesthetic concept. With the growing popularity of the brand, consumers have started to incorporate and re-enact this aesthetic, often independent of campaign activities. An example: of the 700 results I retrieved in 2011 on Flickr for the query 'American Apparel ad', only around 10 per cent feature original American Apparel ads or pictures of billboards. The rest were private images (Figure 4.2) that are remakes of the brand's ad (40 per cent), or pictures which resemble its ads,

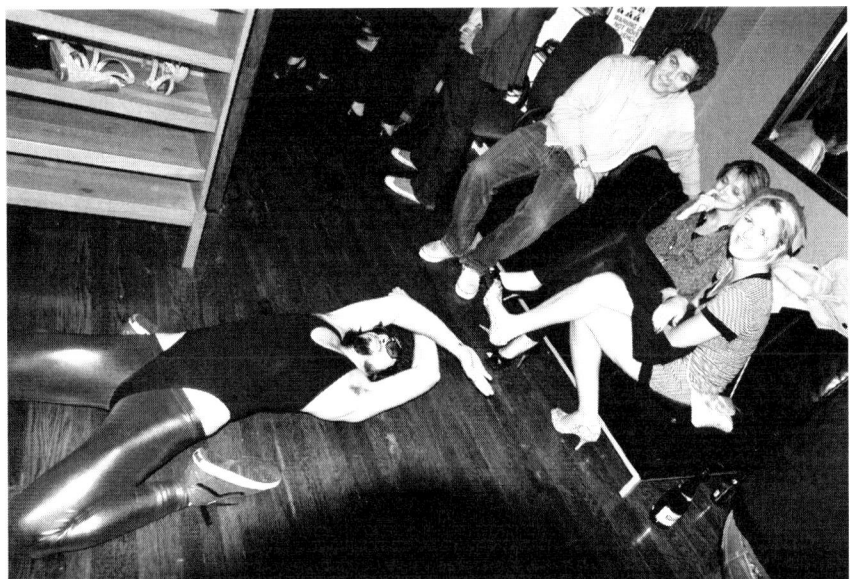

Figure 4.2a

Figure 4.2b Flickr results for 'American Apparel ad'. Top picture by user Jared eber-
hardt, caption "AMERICAN APPAREL AD SHOOT - ALLIE
WARD'S BDAY" (CC BY-SA 2.0) ; Bottom picture by user 70s Van
lover, caption "kind of looks like an american apparel ad" (CC BY 2.0).

with people adding comments like 'Looks like an American Apparel Ad' (35 per cent). When re-enacting the style of the ads or producing imagery that looks very similar to it, web users introduce a variation in the look of the brand whilst maintaining its recognisability. In doing so, the aesthetics of the brand impacts on the activities of these users, while their activities impact on the brand itself as well.

Attachments that include the incorporation of brands into consumers' life worlds or the inclusion of styles into their own aesthetic self-presentation render these attachments not only partible, but also fractal, as the attached aesthetic remains recognisable while at the same time being altered through consumers' interpretations. In the case of American Apparel, the brand's aesthetic is repeated, circulated, altered, adjusted, expanded by its consumers and these immersions into life worlds create diffractive patterns of attachment. From such a perspective, what constitutes a brand are not only its qualities but its capacities and incompleteness which in turn are involved in creating partible, diffracting attachments: 'In such practices of repetition, the making of an edge or a boundary (the limit of a part/whole, which itself can be part of a continuing series as a serialization of whole/part/whole and so on) sometimes introduces a patterning – a texture of interference (Gell 1998) – of similarity and difference' (Day et al., 2014: 145).

In the process of breaking apart whilst remaining the same, the multiplicity of attachments does not sum up to a total or comparable whole, but remains non-equivalent and non-comparable – various actors, such as consumers, stakeholders, media and partners, are invited to participate in the making and happening of attachments, but their participation does happen on equal grounds, as not all can realise all possible forms of value. Furthermore, due to its diffractive character, it is difficult to account for the multiplicity of attachments forged as a whole. Consumers and brand managers can never fully experience or account for the totality of partible attachments at stake in branding. Further, the different ways in which brands get attached to debates, issues, aesthetics and modes of self-presentation are not commensurable, that is they do not translate into a common measure (Espeland and Stevens, 1998). For consumers, experiencing American Apparel as being attached to specific forms of hipsterish aesthetics enables them to connect to their own peers, locations and modes of self-presentation. For American Apparel, meanwhile, this attachment bears brand and financial value. For the online photo platforms used to post one's American Apparel outfits, the value generated is traffic, interaction and thus ultimately revenue. In the last section of the chapter, I will explore this non-equivalence of valorisation of attachments further.

The multivalence of consumer attachment

The attachments made and happening around brands have been addressed as interfacing, partible, diffractive and non-equivalent. This non-equivalence emerges due to the multiple value registers to which these attachments contribute. Addressing Dove's 'Real Women' campaign in personal conversations, for instance, creates social and relational value for consumers, enables self-reflection for individuals and creates long-term economic value for the brand, as it is attached to a desired societal issue and can therefore consolidate its differential position. Within these entanglements, social, cultural and economic values get attached to – yet not collapsed into – each other. As these attachments are difficult to frame in terms of equivalence (Mackenzie, 2008) or commensuration (Espeland and Stevens, 1998), they may be considered multivalent (Marres, 2011). Multivalent actions, Marres argues, can operate and contribute to multiple axes of value. Such accountability has been considered as central to brands by Lury and Moor (2010), as brands establish the very values they are evaluated against. In this context, 'brand valuation techniques extend the chain of comparisons upon which its metrology depends, so that it includes relations that extend in many (differently organised and heterogeneous) directions simultaneously' (2010: 22). When school teachers draw on Dove's branded materials for educational purposes, they seek to teach pupils about media beauty norms, but they also contribute to creating attachments between Dove and the issue under discussion and hence between the pupils and Dove.

Marres develops the notion of multivalence in contrast to equivalence, highlighting how activities which can be evaluated alongside multiple axes produce related – yet not exactly comparable – forms of value. In her particular case of devices for carbon accounting, Marres contends that these 'devices facilitate a mode of co-articulation of participation that is more comprehensive than that of "involvement made easy": they enable the organisation of spaces of multi-valent action, in which a routine act like making tea is at once a technical, economic, and ethical act' (2011: 13).

In the context of American Apparel, wearing a piece of branded clothing in a particular style, in specific locations, is at the same time a social, aesthetic and economically valuable act. Becoming a part of debates, educational environments, social interactions, communities, bodily becoming and peer relations allows brands to bring together societal, educational, cultural and economic activities and to partibly connect them to their own becoming. Multivalence hence refers to the capacity to create continuity between social activities or bodily becoming and the brand without dissolving each into one another. The different attachments made and happening in relation to brands do not add up to a coherent account of the brand, yet they are connected by its invariance. They are closely tied up with the brand's capacity to be recombined, but can still be associated with the same set of values, aesthetics or causes, that is they remain invariant under deformation (Lury et al., 2012). And it is precisely the fact that consumer attachments cannot be subsumed directly into economic value, that they cannot be made entirely equivalent and comparable with each other, that allows brands to build diffracting attachments and participate in everyday life. The multivalence of attachments points to the asymmetric modes of participation in value that brands enable.

Brands rely on the interfacing of various attachments in order to enable the valuation of themselves alongside value axes that are relevant to the multiple actors involved, whilst allowing the company to valorise these attachments economically.

This chapter has shown that attempts at issue-driven and co-creative branding through the making and happening of attachments allow brands to become part of social relations, intimate conversations, societal causes and/or aesthetics. These attachments are relationally connected, interface towards new attachments, but remain partible and non-exclusive. In order for attachments to endure, they need to be realised over and over again, they need to be continued in their happening. It is in this context that brands can increasingly derive economic value from non-economic attachments and activities, by diffracting into social life whilst remaining invariant. Brands and their attachments are valuable for consumers as a part of their own life world, and most importantly, this mode of valuation does not necessarily result into a form of economic valorisation, that is the extraction of economic surplus (Vatin, 2013), as so far it is mainly the brand owners who can realise the financial value of these attachments. Brands and their attachments hence operate at a limit point, as they are set up as diffracting entities, made to be taken on by their own happening, whilst only allowing for asymmetric access to their multiple axes of value.

Notes

1 An archive of American Apparel's advertising campaigns can be found here: www.americanapparel.net/presscenter/adarchive/.
2 Including campaign partners, such as the organisation Beat UK, former brand advisers and store assistants.
3 This opening exercise was chosen to trigger more free-form and open-ended associations with the brands. Using visual methods rather than written forms of brainstorming would allow the drawn associations to be discussed afterwards and returned to throughout the conversation.
4 For an overview of the campaign, see here: www.adforum.com/creative-work/ad/pla yer/56475/wrinkled-wonderful/dove.
5 Such as www.americanapparel.net/presscenter/adarchive/Ad.html?i=2666.
6 www.americanapparel.net/presscenter/adarchive/Ad.html?i=2459.
7 www.americanapparel.net/presscenter/adarchive/Ad.html?i=2830.
8 www.americanapparel.net/presscenter/adarchive/Ad.html?i=2491.

Bibliography

Aaker, D.A. and Joachimsthaler, E. (2002) *Brand Leadership*, New York: London, Simon and Schuster.

American Apparel (2012) *Advertising*. www.americanapparel.net/advertising (accessed 1 August 2012).

Arvidsson, A. (2006) *Brands: Meaning and Value in Media Culture*, London: Routledge.

Barry, A. and Slater, D. (2005) *The Technical Economy*, New York: Routledge.

Callon, M. (1998) An essay on framing and overflowing: Economic externalities revisited by sociology. In M. Callon (ed.), *The Laws of the Market*, Oxford: Blackwell, pp. 244–269.

Callon, M., Meadel, C., Rabeharisoa, V. and Meadel, C. (2002) The economy of qualities. *Economy and Society*, 31(2): 194–217.

Cova, B., Dalli, D. and Zwick, D. (2011) Critical perspectives on consumers' role as 'producers': Broadening the debate on value co-creation in marketing processes. *Marketing Theory*, 11(3): 231–241.

Cova, B., Pace, S. and Skalen, P. (2015) Brand volunteering: Value co-creation with unpaid consumers. *Marketing Theory*, 14(4): 465–485.

Day, S., Lury, C. and Wakeford, N. (2014) Number ecologies: Numbers and numbering practices. *Distinktion: Scandinavian Journal of Social Theory*, 15(2): 123–154.

Deville, J. (2014) *Lived Economies of Default: Consumer Credit, Debt Collection and the Capture of Affect*, London: Routledge.

Dujarier, M.-A. (2016) The three sociological types of consumer work. *Journal of Consumer Culture*, 16(2): 555–571.

Espeland, W.N. and Stevens, M.L. (1998) Commensuration as a social process. *Annual Review of Sociology*, 24(1): 313–343.

Etcoff, N., Orbach, S., Scott, J. and D'Agostino, H. (2004) *The Real Truth about Beauty: A Global Report*. www.clubofamsterdam.com/contentarticles/52 Beauty/dove_white_paper_final.pdf (accessed 1 September 2016).

Foster, R.J. (2011) The uses of use value: Marketing, value creation, and the exigencies of consumption work. In D. Zwick and J. Cayla (eds), *Inside Marketing Practices, Ideologies, Devices*, Oxford: Oxford University Press, pp. 42–57.

Gerlitz, C. (2012) *Brands and Continuous Economies*, PhD thesis, Goldsmiths, University of London.

Gibbons, G. (2003) The social value of brands. In R. Clifton (ed.), *Brands and Branding*, London: Economist Books, pp. 45–60.

Goffman, E. (1986) *Frame Analysis: An Essay on the Organization of Experience*, Boston, MA: Northeastern University Press.

Hearn, A. (2010) Structuring feeling: Web 2.0, online ranking and rating, and the digital 'reputation' economy. *Ephemera*, 10(3/4): 421–438.

Kapferer, J.-N. (2008) *The New Strategic Brand Management: Creating and Sustaining Brand Equity Long Term*, London: Kogan Page.

Kornberger, M. (2010) *Brand Society: How Brands Transform Management and Lifestyle*, Cambridge: Cambridge University Press.

Lury, C. (2004) *Brands. The Logos of the Global Economy*, London: Routledge.

Lury, C. (2009) Brand as assemblage. *Journal of Cultural Economy*, 2(1–2): 67–82.

Lury, C. and Moor, L. (2010) Brand valuation and topological culture. In M. Aronczyk and D. Powers (eds), *Blowing Up the Brand*, New York: Peter Lang, pp. 29–52.

Lury, C. and Wakeford, N. (2012) *Inventive Methods: The Happening of the Social*, New York: Routledge.

Lury, C., Parisi, L. and Terranova, T. (2012) Introduction: The becoming topological of culture. *Theory, Culture and Society*, 29(4–5): 3–35.

Mackenzie, D. (2008) Making things the same: Gases, emission rights and the politics of carbon markets. *Accounting, Organizations and Society*, 1(6): 440–455.

Marres, N. (2011) The costs of public involvement: Everyday devices of carbon accounting and the materialisation of participation. *Economy and Society*, 40(4): 1–31.

Moor, L. (2007) *The Rise of Brands*, Oxford: Berg.

N+1. (2010) *What Was the Hipster? A Sociological Investigation*, New York: HarperCollins.

Ringwood, S. (2010) Interview with Susan Ringwood, CEO of the charity Beat UK.

Ritchie, E. (2002) Dov Charney takes on the garment industry with his American Apparel. *Los Angeles Downtown News*, 7 October.

Skeggs, B. (2014) Values beyond value? Is anything beyond the logic of capital? *British Journal of Sociology*, 65(1): 1–20.

Staniforth, M. (2011) Interview with Martin Staniforth.

Strathern, M. (1988) *The Gender of the Gift: Problems with Women and Problems with Society in Melanesia*, Berkeley: University of California Press.

Vatin, F. (2013) Valuation as evaluating and valorizing. *Valuation Studies*, 1(1): 31–50.

Zwick, D., Bonsu, S.K. and Darmody, A. (2008) Putting consumers to work: 'Co-creation' and new marketing govern-mentality. *Journal of Consumer Culture*, 8(2): 163–196.

5 'You are a *Star customer*, please hold the line…'

CRM and the sociotechnical inscriptions of market attachment

Alexandre Mallard

Introduction

That market exchange involves some sort of attachment between the stake-holders engaged in transactions has given rise to controversial discussions among scholars of economic practices.[1] While early political economy implied the idea that market exchange would promote the development of peaceful relationships between people – see the influence of the *doux commerce* thesis in the writings of eighteenth-century philosophers, from Montesquieu to Hume to Smith (Hirschman, 1982) – neoclassical economics has been inclined to prescribe the complete absence of social bonds for the smooth running of transactions and the achievement of market equilibrium. Sociologists have variously observed this belief within modern economic thought (Fourcade and Healy, 2007), with one of the ambitions being to develop a conception of market attachment that goes beyond the way personal relationships are configured. Indeed, sociology has traditionally considered market relations through notions such as the 'social tie' and 'embeddedness' but many relational configurations in the economy cannot be solely described using these analytical tools (Cochoy, this volume). The infrastructures and processes implemented by companies to organise, automate and rationalise their relations with clients obviously constitute a domain of interest from this perspective: the very fact that there exists a professional area of expertise and a set of technical tools devoted to 'Customer Relationship Management' (CRM) should attract the curiosity of sociologists studying market attachments. In this chapter, I propose to investigate the modalities of market attachment involved in CRM, drawing on an analysis of its implementation in the particular context of a call centre.

I will pursue two objectives here. The first is to examine the sociotechnical and organisational resources involved in the construction of market attachments. In the contemporary world, market relationships can take many different forms (Cochoy, 2012): just compare the relation between a household and a service provider (for instance for the provision of gas or electricity), between a user and a brand, between a consumer and a techno-organisational infrastructure of distribution like a supermarket. As soon as one focuses on market relationships beyond the interpersonal context *per se*, there is a vast and heterogeneous array of entities to take into account. I will consider attachment as the dynamic process – the process of 'attaching' – through which the sociotechnical and organisational entities supporting this kind of relationship emerge.

The second objective is to develop an analysis of market attachment that takes into account its ambivalent character. There are many different ways to be attached in the market – many different ways in which 'the market will have us', to echo Liz McFall and Joe Deville (this volume). Let me dichotomise things for the sake of simplicity. One can be attached in the sense of being bound, trussed-up or chained, e.g. unwillingly held back in a relationship that is imposed by contingent circumstances or by the power relations of a given situation. An entrepreneur may thus be attached to a service provider on whom he is dependent. But one can also be attached in the sense of being voluntarily involved in a relationship characterised by its singularity, its inscription in time along a shared history, its active character and its associated production of values (Hennion, 2007, 2015). A consumer may be attached to the corner shop because the opening hours, the products offered and the proximity enable easy shopping for dinner when coming back from work late at night: the regularity of the practice, the convenience of circumstances, the irreducibility of proximity, all contribute to this singular attachment. In this chapter, I propose the hypothesis that this opposition between, on the one hand, an *instrumental* conception of the relationship and, on the other hand, a conception that insists on its *active and open-ended* character, is a fruitful way to characterise the ambivalence of market attachments and to explore their expressions in various situations.

For the pursuit of both objectives, the case of call centres is a radical one. Call centres occupy a significant place in contemporary consumption: we use them to buy train tickets, to set up car insurance contracts, to handle telephone services and so forth. As compared with other contexts of market exchange (the interaction with a corner shop merchant, in a supermarket, etc.), the relationship that takes place in a call centre interaction has an extreme configuration: it is highly anonymous (the consumer never or rarely speaks twice to the same person), highly mediated by technology (communication networks and information systems intervene in the relationship) and conspicuously rationalised (one usually feels that the dialogue with a call centre operator is heavily framed by time constraints). The complaints of consumers who have had a bad experience with call centres illustrate the vicissitudes of a relationship that is marked by technical intricacies, organisational constraints and commercial cunning. They refer to Interactive Voice Response (IVR)[2] systems, those user unfriendly automated voice server systems, the endless waiting times while listening to haunting music on hold before talking to the right person, an impersonal touch in the dialogue with employees reading pre-written scripts. Very few of these consumers would consider that there is any human feeling in the call centre employee's discussion. The attachment at stake here, if any, clearly looks instrumental.

Yet professionals of call centre design and management make substantial efforts to improve the quality of customer service, drawing notably on CRM tools. My contention is that the study of these efforts offers a fruitful opportunity for exploring the dynamics of market attachment in all its dimensions: not, or not only, as an intention to increase the degree of instrumental constraint on the customer, but also as an attempt to open up a space for the production of active relationships. In order to flesh out this idea, I will outline the case of a project that I had the chance to follow, involving the reorganisation of call centre units in a large company which aimed to implement a system of differentiation in its customer service provision. I will show that the complex techno-organisational work that took place during this reorganisation supported a rich and plural conception of the market relationship. This approach suggests that one of the issues at stake in the construction of market attachment is the articulation and adjustment of the various relational dimensions involved, in the organisational realm and in the associated sociotechnical processes.

A CRM system to implement customer differentiation in call centres

The 'Star Customer' project

At the beginning of the 2000s, the French telecommunication operator 'Global Telecom'[3] – abbreviated as 'GT' – considered implementing commercial differentiation in the customer service provided by its call centres. As a large international organisation employing more than 200,000 people in France and other countries, GT relied extensively on call centres for its commercial activities. In 2001, it launched a project named 'Star Customer', whose main purpose[4] was to offer a type of customer service that would differ according to the consumers' attitude towards the company: the idea was, for instance, to reward those customers who were the most faithful to the company, to grant extra attention and energy to those who consumed the highest amount of services, etc. In an era of market development where the loyalty of customers was an ever greater area of concern, the question of their attachment to the company appeared important, and customer differentiation was seen as a way to develop customer relationships in order to counter the rise of 'unfaithful' behaviours.

The Star Customer project – which I will call the 'SC project' for the sake of simplicity – had a great deal of scope within GT. It concerned call centres providing services for all the mobile phone, fixed phone and internet product lines sold by the group. Customers would use these call centres for routine service operations such as subscribing to new mobile packages, getting information about the price of an internet service, cancelling a landline contract, etc. Although it focused only on the activities of call centres, the project touched upon a variety of marketing, commercial and organisational issues at stake in CRM. These ranged from the definition of characteristics of consumers, to the organisation of call centres, to the staging of differentiated commercial interaction scenarios, to the management of phone operators, etc. Designed as a large-scale experiment, it required the implementation of specific organisational and technical devices in a dozen or so call centre units, and envisioned a possible generalisation of the system across the whole group.

A large number of actors inside and outside the company were mobilised in the analysis and experimentation associated with the SC project. I was engaged in this collective work, being commissioned to a consultancy project intended to provide the project managers with insights on the so-called 'sociological dimension' of the implementation process. This quite loose mission statement gave me the opportunity to carry out a survey in cooperation with two sociological colleagues, Valérie Beaudouin and Christine Guilbert. We conducted qualitative interviews with phone operators, managers, marketers and engineers working in the eight call centre units involved in the project, and analysed phone interactions between operators and clients.[5]

The SC project intended to bring changes in the call centres that were typical of the evolutions of the CRM in large commercial organisations at the turn of the 2000s and that scholars of the domain have identified under the heading of 'mass customisation' (Taylor and Bain, 1999; Frenkel, 2005). In this conceptualisation, CRM appears as a system that enables the call centre worker to read off a computer screen the information about the customer that is stored in the service provider's database. But our field survey suggested that the project aimed to do a bit more than that. It relied on a combination of specific organisational provisions and technological innovations known as Computer Telephony Integration (CTI), a series of devices that enabled new modalities of interconnection between telephone networks and corporate information systems. According to both the presentation slideshows circulating around the project and the managers' accounts, the aim was to introduce a small revolution in how customer service was treated. Let me briefly sketch the sociotechnical scenarios of these changes, as far as we were able to gather them over the course of the survey.

The basis of the system was the possibility of allocating customers to a call centre employee suited to their particular needs, based on a process of segmentation. For each customer present in the GT commercial database, a segment was calculated using data on former consumption practices and specific marketing algorithms. The call centre unit was divided into several sub-units, each devoted to a different segment, where employees were trained in providing differentiated answers, from both a technical and interactional point of view. When a customer would call the service, the incoming phone number was detected by the CTI system and used as a search term in the database. The customer record was retrieved and the call was routed to the relevant sub-unit not only in accordance with the motive declared to the IVR system by the customer ('To buy a new service, please press 1', 'To obtain information on your account, please press 2', 'To cancel a contract, please press 3', etc.), as is usual in call centre interactions, but also by taking into account the segmentation. The overall result was that mutual anonymity could be replaced by a singularised relationship that integrated customer desire (via the call motive) and identity (via the segmentation).

Call centre research and the analysis of market attachment

Using the distinction proposed by Barbara Gutek in her analysis of service provision in the modern era, one can say that the link between the customer and the call centre employee as it was conceived of in the SC project was typically a pseudo-relationship (Gutek, 1995):[6] both actors are in a situation of mutual anonymity with 'something more' between them. How is it possible to analyse this 'something more' and to qualify the particular relationship at stake? Looking at research on call centres in the fields of organisation studies, management, marketing and sociology (Russel, 2008), this question refers to three analytical dimensions.

The first concerns the role of the client in the dynamics of service provision. Existing research on call centres tends to underexamine this aspect, as Marek Korczynski noted in his article on the 'mystery customer' (Korczynski, 2009). A large portion of the studies on call centres investigate their mode of orga- nisation rather than the relationships with customers that they institute. The titles of early publications on call centres – for instance the reference to the assembly line in Taylor and Bain's (1999) seminal paper, or the reference to the 'modern factory' in the paper by Buscatto (2002) – testify to an interest more in organisational than commercial or economic issues. This remains largely true for recent research: sociologists interested in call centres have investigated such issues as the emergence of new forms of Taylorisation associated with this regime of productivity, the development of surveillance at work (Ball and Margulis, 2011), the construction of work cooperation in call centre units, the modality of emotional labour at stake in telephone interac- tion (Jenkins et al., 2010) and the specific forms of trade union mobilisation in this professional context (Taylor and Bain, 1999). In all these studies, the way in which the management of the customer relationship involves specific market devices is a very indirect concern. By contrast, it seems impossible to understand the changes brought by the SC project in the call centre without examining the way it modifies the very definition of the customer.

The second aspect concerns the technical devices involved. Call centre research quite rarely enters into the technical questions implied in the custo- mer relationship. To a certain extent, one could say that many researchers in this domain carry out their surveys with the quite restricted definition of the 'technological content' of the call centre CRM process that I have evoked above. While the definition is not in itself incorrect and may be largely suffi- cient for investigating managerial and human resource concerns, the sketchy character of its construction prevents any thorough examination of the tech- nical and organisational mediations at stake in the production of specific market attachments. Most of the time, technology is, beyond these rudimentary elements, relegated to being part of the 'context' of activity, with the analysis focusing on managerial action, organisational routines and human resource prescriptions. This second limitation of existing research, when combined with the first, has the consequence that the customer is usually apprehended independently from the sociotechnical processes enacting his/her presence – in other words, it ignores the performative processes at stake in any customer relationship situation.

Third, existing research tells us very little about the dynamic processes involved in the sociotechnical construction of the call centre as a stable device that, in a sense, 'sticks to the market'. This lack of a sufficiently dynamic perspective evokes a methodological issue that has long been well known in the field of the sociology of technology (Akrich, 1992): in order to grasp the social implications of a particular technology, one shouldn't describe it in a static way, but rather scrutinise dynamic configurations – for instance the historical trajectory of a project, or a situation of innovation. This makes it possible to follow the mutual shaping of technology and its uses. In spite of a few notable exceptions (Licoppe, 2002; Russel, 2007), this dimension is not really present in existing research. As I will show, looking at the construction of customer relations in the SC project in a dynamic way provides a key for understanding the construction of market attachments.

The plural sociotechnical inscriptions of the customer relationship

To address this issue, I will examine the plural sociotechnical inscriptions of the relationship that the SC project was designed to establish between the customer and GT. This perspective, which is informed by a pragmatist understanding of the notion of relation,[7] takes a stance opposite to Barbara Gutek's analysis when she mobilises the concept of 'pseudo-relationship': the present view supports the idea that what is at stake here is not the substitution of a (interpersonal) relationship, but a plurality of (sociotechnical) relationships that have to be adjusted and articulated.

Four conceptions of the relationship

In the course of the field study, we asked the various practitioners to tell us what processes in the customer relationship-management process were to be impacted by the SC project. We were thus able to identify four different areas of practice where the notion of relationship was involved in one sense or another and where its sociotechnical inscription was to be modified. I propose to name these contrasting conceptions as follows: conversation, acquaint-anceship, liaison and availability. Here I will only briefly qualify these four conceptions and the associated sociotechnical processes. I will pay particular attention to the way in which the customer is each time involved in this component of CRM via a specific actant.

Shaping commercial dialogue: relation as conversation

Each of the four modalities of relationship can be associated with a specific category of professionals that we interviewed as part of the research. The first modality, which I propose to label 'relation as conversation', represents the perspective of call centre employees themselves: undoubtedly, their work is based on a specific art of talking to the customer. This art can be observed in traditional, face-to-face market interactions (see Callon, this volume). It involves: politeness and the use of particular language conventions; compliance with an asymmetric interactional order where the customer appears as the important stakeholder ('the client as king'); a capacity to provide answers that at the same time deliver customer 'satisfaction' and remain compatible with the company's commercial objectives; an ability to interweave the diagnosis of customer requests and the promotion of new transactions; an ability to close a conversation at the right moment for the sake of productivity in the sales process (Vargha, 2011; Kessous and Mallard, 2014). To this generic ordering of commercial conversations, call centre interaction adds some peculiarities: bodily performance is absent and replaced by vocal activity; the employee is heavily assisted by information technology (he or she can usually read on-screen information that the customer doesn't have and is sometimes also provided with particular sentences to pronounce in given circumstances, etc.). To the extent that the production of commercial conversations is largely a collective construction, the sociotechnical inscription of this relationship involves other actors working in the back office: coaches, trainers, team leaders, designers of the scripts that guide commercial interaction, managers who set the incentives that orient salespersons towards the promotion of certain products or services, etc. Depending on the situation, the actant 'customer' can be endowed with very different skills: s/he can be defined as a talkative person, as a disciplined speaker, as a calculating or emotional individual, etc. In the SC project, this relational modality was characterised by the fact that in the shaping of commercial conversations, the customer segment intervened as a primary parameter for differentiating between contrasted actants and their specific interactional patterns: the conversation with the customer was intended to depend largely on the segment.

Indexing the customer in the database: relation as acquaintanceship

In call centres using CRM systems, customers are understood in the sales situation in relation to (they are *indexed by*) information present in the database that has been constituted over the course of earlier commercial processes. I propose to use the notion of acquaintanceship, a near translation of the French word *interconnaissance*, as a term for the conception of the relationship underlying this form of organisation. The idea here is that call centre actors should be in a position to mobilise knowledge about customers in order to get familiar with (understand, anticipate, penetrate, develop, elaborate on, etc.) their needs and expectations. This knowledge can potentially be used for various purposes: for instance, it can serve to shape the commercial conversation but can also determine who should answer the calls. The sociotechnical inscription of this relational modality involves the set of actors, data, devices and processes that are necessary to enact such an indexing, e.g. calculating information about the customer and delivering it to the appropriate actors. A customary concern here is the relevance of information likely to provide customer knowledge and to generate familiarity about needs and expectations in the associated situations.

As I explained above, customer indexing in the SC project notably involved a specific task of segmentation.[8] It was taken on by marketers and experts of GT's customer database. Each customer in the database was characterised by the products and services s/he had bought from the operator – subscriptions to landline, mobile and internet services over a given period and the associated levels of consumption – as well as various other data concerning commercial processes that had been engaged. On the basis of this information, the commercial database was divided into a limited number of groups representing different market segments. Segments were identified with names that cannot be listed in detail here, but that were akin to standard labels in marketing culture, such as 'Stars' (customers with the potential for high levels of consumption), 'VIP' ('Very Important Person', for customers who have some sort of public influence), 'Moderate' (customers with a middling potential), 'Bad Payers' (customers having repeated payment issues), 'Winback' (customers that are transferring part of their consumption to an alternative operator, and that should be cared for in order to convince them to stay at GT), etc. It is on the basis of this set of standardised identities provided by the segmentation that the SC project proposed to index the actant 'customer' in the database.

Programming the routing of calls: relation as liaison

A third modality of relationship, which I propose to name 'liaison', concerns the establishment of an encounter between the customer and the commercial organisation. Encountering is a distributed process, requiring that both stakeholders symmetrically carry out the practical operations that enable them to meet and initiate interaction. Commercial organisations spend a lot of time and energy trying to shape this process on their side: at stake is not only the 'capture' of customers in stores and over the telephone, but also encouraging them to choose the right channel for their particular requirement (visiting the retail store, dialling the right telephone number, sending letters and emails to the right service, pressing the right key in the dialogue with an IVR system, etc.), passing a customer smoothly and efficiently from one interlocutor to another, etc. In call centre relationships, the sociotechnical inscription of the liaison mainly concerns the processes of call reception, routing and redirection. The software governing these operations is generally set and managed

by marketers and information system engineers and, in spite of its importance, has been largely ignored by social scientists. As I have explained above,
the originality of the liaison in the SC project is that it articulated two different actants: the customer as indexed in the commercial database through
his or her segment and the customer as currently calling and expressing a
desire as being recorded by the IVR system ('Are you calling to take out a
new service?', 'Do you want to a contract?', 'To get information?' etc.).

Planning commercial manpower: relation as availability

A fourth modality of relation concerns its temporality. I propose to address
this through the dimension of availability. Under what conditions is the call
centre available to the customer? When is it ready to take a call in order to
perform the customer relationship? The sociotechnical inscription of this
dimension involves the planning of call centre employees' work. It is one of
the main professional prerogatives of call centre managers: they have to
guarantee that enough people will be present in the call centre at any moment
in order to ensure a customer waiting time that complies with service com-
mitments that have been entered into. For this, call centre managers have to
adjust two different temporalities: the frequency and duration of customer
calls and the organisation of employees' working activities. Our field investigation showed that this work, roughly speaking, requires the matching of
information given by two different instruments: on the one hand, the call
centre schedule, showing the working hours of each employee; on the other
hand, the load curve, showing how many customers are contacting the call
centre at any given time. A central operation in the sociotechnical inscription
of availability is the estimation of the number of employees that are necessary
at any time, taking into account the number of customers expected and the average duration of conversations. Legal issues intervene in this planning activity,
since employees' work schedules are largely framed by arrangements defined
in their employment contracts, leaving only a small margin of adjustment for
managers in their day-to-day negotiations. The actant 'customer' appears here
in a particular way: s/he is one of the numerous people that have contacted
the call centre at a given moment and helped define the position of a dot on
the load curve. As we will see later, in the SC project, this task of planning
commercial manpower took on a new dimension: the issue was not only
determining how many people should be present in the call centre, but also
organising their distribution across the different sub-units corresponding to
the customer segments.

Instrumentality and open-endedness in the production of attachments

The reader might feel that the terms chosen to define the dimensions of relationship have a positive undertone, insisting on the active and open-ended
dimension of attachments at stake. One may even take those terms as

describing the features of relationship in a realm other than the market – the realm of friendship ties for instance: 'my friend' is typically someone who is available for me, has an acquaintanceship with my concerns, is ready to establish a liaison and enter into conversation with me. Those terms may be used to evoke what a market organisation is searching for when it tries to develop an open-ended and active relationship with customers. However, a customer relationship is very different from a friendship, and some more instrumental dimensions enter into account in the attachments at stake. Qualifying what comes under instrumentality or open-endedness is a quite difficult analytic task. In the scope of the present reflection, I will only provide some brief suggestions and examples illustrating how these issues concretely manifest in the field – and illustrating also that they would need further and more systematic examination.

From conversation to information exchange, manipulation or inauthenticity

Let me take first the case of commercial conversations. There are different ways to fold them into an instrumental expression. One is to eradicate every trace of humanity through the restricted use of standardised and fixed interactional scripts: the concern is no longer with the conversation but instead for a pure exchange of information which excludes the possibility of opening the dialogue to any unforeseen issues. Another is to shift from the art of seduction (which might be acceptable in certain contexts) to the art of manipulation. Note that manipulation can be the result of an individual practice (for instance when a salesperson decides on his/her own to cheat a customer) or of an institutional or organisational arrangement (for instance when interactional scripts are designed so as to compel the client to take a decision). Note also that the border between open-endedness and instrumentality can be hard to trace here: in a commercial conversation, a sales pitch is acceptable but a lie is not.

There is still another way to swing between instrumentality and open-endedness in commercial conversations: concerning the authenticity of the relationship. In play here are for example the games of identity that shape conversations. How should call centre employees introduce themselves: by using their real name, or a fake name, or a standardised and impersonal identity (Kessous and Mallard, 2014)? More generally, the whole debate around the meaning of the 'emotional labour' that is at stake in the call centre, and in service work in general (Hochschild, 1983; Jenkins et al., 2010), directly addresses this issue: depending on the conception, performing emotional labour can be considered as a way to deepen the interaction with customers or to cheat them.

Customer acquaintanceship: the construction of singularity at the risk of surveillance?

The ambition to use in the market interaction knowledge that has been produced from the customer's past consumption corresponds quite closely to the ideal of promoting singularity in the relationship: it is an attempt to weave a common history between the customer and the provider. This is actually the basis of the principle of 'mass customisation' that supports call centre inter-action in general. Yet the tensions between the instrumental and open-ended character of the relationship clearly appear when considering the tenuous frontier between a desire for acquaintanceship and the will for surveillance. I had the opportunity to see a situation in the SC project where this frontier was under discussion. Indeed, in one of the call centres, employees were asked to record in the database information that might appear during their com-mercial conversations and that could be useful in the future. This request was justified as being motivated by 'improving the quality of customer records' or 'better knowing the customer so as to better address his expectations'. Dif-ferent categories of information could be listed by GT as 'useful': the elec-tronic devices present in the household, the size of the apartment, the number and ages of the children, etc. Our survey showed that, depending on the kind of information and on the way the gathering of it was concretely organised (Should the customer be explicitly informed? Should the employee ask tar-geted questions or just note information that emerged from the flow of con-versation?), employees would feel more or less embarrassed about the practice: sometimes, they might feel that they were doing an ordinary job of data collection and generating value for the service, and sometimes that they were spying on customers and intruding into their private life.

From liaison to intrusion or capture

In general, it seems that the relationship remains open-ended and active when the process of liaison can be perceived by the customer as a simple encounter, e.g. as a situation where the devices that it mobilises are symmetrically dis-tributed on the side of both the customer and the organisation. If there is a feeling of asymmetry or a saturation of these devices, then the liaison becomes purely instrumental. This might be the case, for instance, when advertising (a major agent of liaison, as I explained above) becomes intrusive and irrelevant to the context in which it is perceived. It might also be the case when chan-nels of communication form constrained trajectories or exclude particular opportunities. A case in point, one that can make the difference between an attachment being positive or negative, relates to the capacity of an IVR system to offer the customer relevant alternatives. The relationship may feel particularly instrumental when the system proposes options that do not match the customers' real concerns.

Negotiating the attachments of availability: making time a more flexible constraint

Let me finally comment, very briefly, on the dimension of availability. At first glance, the most open-ended relationship is achieved when the service is instantaneously and permanently accessible for all customers. However, achieving such an ambition is very costly for the provider – and for the customer, who usually pays for it, directly or indirectly. It is probably also unnecessary since customers tend not to need permanent access to the service and can accept a certain lack of instantaneity. Conversely, an instrumental situation is when the provider imposes its own criteria of availability on the customer, without any possibility of adjustment. It therefore seems to me that open-ended and active attachments are achieved when availability is not unilaterally limited and when it is made wholly negotiable. In call centres, this may be a matter of making their relation to time more flexible and easier to handle for the customer. All the devices and practices oriented in this direction might contribute to this: clear public information about the call centre's opening hours and, possibly, about periods of peak demand; information about expected waiting times when employees are all busy; providing alternative options for accessing the service when there is a lack of availability; the possibility of being called back, etc.

Market attachment and the art of dynamic implementation

Each of these four dimensions constitutes a way of apprehending customer relationships that corresponds to a particular viewpoint within the commercial organisation. Of course, none of the devices and processes described here, given that they were designed at the beginning of the SC project, mechanically leads to the existence of the customer relationship. The sociotechnical scripts underlying each of these modalities are tested in the implementation of CRM and the customer is performed as the relationship targeting him or her progressively takes shape. Conversational patterns generate unexpected customer reactions, leading in turn to the adaptation of conversations; the initial marketing definition of segments is enriched and changed as call centre activity produces new information concerning them; call routing procedures are adjusted in order to take into account the changing flows of demands; the shape of the call load curve is transformed as the call centre's capacity grows and waiting times decrease, etc. It is in the course of many technical and organisational adjustments of this sort that attachment between customers and the call centre emerges and is consolidated. These adjustments are particularly interesting when they combine several of the modalities described above, because it is here that the relationship becomes stronger and more coherent. I will now enter more detail into three examples of these adjustments that were particularly visible in the SC project.

Adjusting conversation and acquaintanceship to improve market interaction

A first series of adjustments relates to the link between the 'customer-in-the-conversation' and the 'customer-in-the-database'. It questions the articulation between CRM as the management of conversations and as the indexing of customer information. Indeed, an important task for the call centre employees is to go back and forth between what they read on the screen and what they hear on the phone, as well as performing the interpretative work that enables their combination in order to deliver the particular service. This kind of interpretive activity raises specific issues that depend notably on the kind of information stored in the database.

Marie Benedetto-Meyer has studied an interesting case where customers are characterised in the database by a score calculated on the basis of former consumption practices in order to indicate their sensitivity to new products. Her analysis shows that different professionals in the commercial organisation in question, including its call centre employees, reconstruct the meaning of the score in a specific way, in spite of the efforts of the dataminers who have built the indicator to circumscribe a specific and stable interpretation (Benedetto-Meyer, 2014). In the case of the SC project, many adjustments concerned the identity of customers, relating to the definition of the different groups in the segmentation. Before the reorganisation, call centre employees had followed a training session that presented the features of the customer segments with which they were to be confronted. They had to become familiar with the way the information system would qualify customers. But real work situations proved to be slightly different from what they had learnt during training: the stereotypes that had been presented and the related commercial expectations were not immediately prominent in their own experiences.

An emblematic example concerns the 'Star' segment. The SC project segmentation had been elaborated according to a method of estimating customer value, taking into account the amount of services consumed, of which customers in the 'Star' segment consumed a high volume. Call centre employees were told that customers in this segment had a specific sociodemographic composition (many of them were men in their forties or fifties, who held positions of responsibility at work and had a family with children) and high expectations both about matters of service and of their telecommunication products. However, experience showed that a number of customers in this segment had a totally different profile:

> In the Star segment, we have numerous customers who do have a large bill, but who are also in the course of a payment incident. Our problem is to know whether these customers should be attracted and retained or not. Are they in the 'Star' segment just because they had a large bill at a given moment, but do not really have the commercial potential of a genuine large customer?
>
> (Call centre employee)

Here, it seems that employees' experiences contradicted the marketers' hypothesis, that the clients who consumed a high level of services would also be likely to be interested in innovative products and services. This is a case where, to some extent, the statistical work that has been done upstream from the call centre is insufficient or incomplete, leading to a flawed representation of the market with erroneous categories of customers. But in many other situations, the gaps between the company's expectations and employees' experiences reflected the fact that there is no simple way to give practical or sociological meaning to aggregates fabricated by statistical work in a manner that can be helpful for a conversation with a customer.

Thus, during the early period of the SC project, a whole series of adjustments took place in both the call centre and the CRM system. These processes – through which the customer in the database, the customer holding a conversation and the call centre employee become ever more tightly attached to one another – are typically of two different kinds. On the one hand, the discrepancies that are brought to the fore during commercial conversations can give rise to new knowledge that is formalised and reinjected into the information system in order to improve the quality of informational indexing. On the other hand, call centre employees produce, individually and collectively, new meanings, conventions and narratives that, at this level, enable them both to articulate the different versions of the customers with which they are confronted and to make sense of the varieties of information at their disposal for the conduct of the commercial conversation. Experience suggests that the second process is much more common than the first: it is quite rare that new knowledge produced in the course of service work is collected, transformed and reutilised by marketers in the construction of their market models. From this point of view, the production of knowledge in commercial organisations still largely conforms to a hierarchical scheme.

Tuning conversation, liaison and availability to meet the demand

The second interesting dimension of adjustments bears on the routing of telephone calls. As I explained above, one of the strengths of the SC project was to match each customer to a specific employee, depending on the desires expressed by the customer on the IVR interface but also according to his/her market profile, as indicated by the segment. But the ability to deal with profiles in such a customised way requires the call flows to be anticipated well, not only for the whole population of consumers but also for each of the segments, in order to keep the waiting times within a normal range.

In the early period of implementation of the SC project, it appeared obvious that adaptations were necessary in the routing of calls. For instance, at certain moments, the traffic for one of the segments greatly exceeded the number of employees present in the corresponding call centre sub-unit. In this case, the software had been programmed to redirect the excess calls to other employees who were present in the call centre but specialised in another segment. This was a way to address customer demand without creating an overly long waiting time, but it clearly had a reduced commercial efficiency and delivered a quality of service that was lower than proposed by the differentiation approach. There were also anomalies the other way round. Thus, for instance, in one of the call centre units, an employee was allocated to the 'Moderate' customer segment, corresponding to limited needs in terms of their telecommunication products and, as a result, to quite short average conversation times. But the call flow for this segment had been a little over-estimated. As a consequence, the employee spent a large part of her day waiting for the telephone to ring, which really is a rare situation in a call centre.

These examples show that the adjustments in play question the articulation between conversation, liaison and availability: the proper functioning of the system requires an adequacy between the average duration of the conversation within each segment, the dispatching of employees to the different sub-units and the associated call routing strategies. Since this delicate equilibrium between the differentiated supply and demand of telephone conversations cannot at any moment be fully obtained, an amount of flexibility is necessary. This is usually achieved through 'overflow strategies' that are programmed in the software governing call routing: when a call centre sub-unit is over-run, calls are rerouted to employees with available working time, as in the case evoked above. Overflow strategies may be complex to define since they are usually not symmetrical. Thus, in the SC project, it was common for employees who specialised in a given segment to be able to deal with the demands of other segments, but the contrary was not true. For instance, customers of the 'Moderate' segment could be treated by employees who specialised in the 'Star' segment, because this segment requires extended competences, but the opposite may not be straightforward.

The field study showed that in such situations two kinds of adjustment could take place, which, in implementing customer differentiation, operated according to two different temporalities. A short-term adjustment consisted in the reintroduction of human choice in the routing of calls, a process that was originally governed by a software algorithm: the call centre supervisor would independently monitor the ongoing traffic and, in the case of overflows, define ad hoc strategies on the basis of a personal knowledge of the skills of the different employees. In the long term, a more complex adjustment could be considered, one that required the production of previously unavailable but now refined knowledge: a load curve differentiated by segments. Indeed, the call centre manager already had a good knowledge of the load curve for the whole population of customers, but he ignored how the flow was distributed among the segments in each time period. Since the segments had been designed in order to target distinctive behaviours and expectations, they also corresponded to distinctive practices for calling customer services: for instance 'Star' customers would often call after working hours while 'Moderate' customers would rather tend to call during the day. A load curve differentiated by segments would enable a better estimation of the quantity of staff and a better definition of the overflow strategies necessary in different periods of the day and the week, thereby addressing demand more efficiently.

Recalibrating sales incentives to adapt to a new relationship

A third series of adjustments in the SC project touched upon the incentives and motivation policies involved in managing the sales process. It played on the articulations between conversation, acquaintanceship and availability. In call centres, sales employees are generally paid on the basis of their capacity to meet commercial objectives. This can be calculated using various indicators: the number of products sold in a given category, the number of customers handled per day, the amount of new information concerning customers entered into the corporate information system, etc. Each reorganisation in a call centre affects the calculation of incentives: since a new mode of organisation changes employees' activities, it also changes the values of indicators, and the amount of money finally paid.

The SC project is a case in point. Many of the call centre employees we met expressed concerns about this issue. The implementation of customer differentiation by the project generated difficulties in how incentives were redefined. Some employees complained that they would earn less money than before, which appeared particularly paradoxical given that they had been recruited to the SC project on the basis of their high-level selling skills, skills that were necessary for the differentiation of customers and for their complex needs to be addressed: 'We do have an incentive but in the new system, the targets cannot be reached… We now get less money than before the customer differentiation project, this makes me nervous since they told me I was chosen because I was a good salesman' (a call centre employee).

Beyond this general complaint about calculative changes in the context of an organisational shake-up, more specific concerns were raised in the frame of the SC project. One of them related to the unevenness of the traffic in the early stages of the customer differentiation implementation, as I have evoked above: since the incentive largely depended on the number of clients dealt with by an employee, an irregular number of calls would have consequences on their salary. Another problem concerned the homogeneity of the indicators used by employees allocated to the different segments, and the risk of inequality that this could imply. Indeed, in the former system, each employee would handle a similar number of calls, with a comparable mix of different categories of customers, some of them having high needs while others had low needs. The amount of money paid would then really depend on the employee's performance, and not on the customers' features. In the new system, employees would by definition deal with a specific category of customers, and people doubted whether customers in the different segments would share the same interests for the same products – since, if not, this would result in differentiated incentives. Overall, a period of adjustment was necessary in order to better understand the commercial potential of the different categories of customers, and to determine how the incentives too had to be differentiated and recalibrated in order to enhance sales performance without generating iniquities among employees.

Conclusion

Attachments are very often considered from the perspective of the inter-personal relationship. CRM systems invite us to reflect on the processes that are necessary to attach the consumer not to a product or to a particular person but to a commercial organisation. In this chapter, I have shown that market attachments rest on a plurality of definitions of what makes the rela-tionship between the customer and the organisation. This perspective offers the opportunity to consider the ambivalence of market attachments as expressed in each of these conceptions of the relationship. It invites us to investigate the various devices, processes and organisational arrangements producing customer relationships that can be, depending on each particular situation, either more instrumental or more active and open-ended. The multifaceted dimension of the customer relationship reflects the plurality of actors involved in the construction of CRM, and it points to a series of pro-blems of coordination that are well known within commercial organisations: since these organisations are structured around the systematic investigation of customer identities and skills, they tend to multiply the number of protago-nists involved as well as the approaches that are mobilised, leading to the question of their harmonious and efficient functioning as a coherent entity. The study shows the importance of adjustments between knowledge produced in several interconnected domains: in the definition of 'good categories' of customers through segmentation, in the appropriation of this by call centre employees, in the identification of customers' expectations of the availability of a service, in the identification of employees' skills and in the definition of their rewards, etc. That the art of market attachment is a knowledgeable art may not be a surprise. What the study of CRM systems teaches us is the importance of this labour – of the collective production and coordination of knowledge – that is necessary for the relationship with the customer to appear.

Notes

1 I want to thank Joe Deville and Liz McFall for their suggestions on the writing of this chapter and for their help in the correction of the English. I also want to thank Antoine Hennion for a vivid discussion concerning the risks of a reckless use of the notion of attachment to describe market relations. All mistakes remaining in the text are mine.
2 An IVR system is an automatic device managing all the operations presented to the customer calling a call centre: a recorded or synthetic voice provides a series of messages explaining the content of the service, the customer is invited to press spe-cific keys on the phone to access given services, music is offered while the caller is on hold, the call is automatically routed to given service, etc.
3 All names of companies, projects, places and people used in this chapter are pseudonyms.
4 Another explicit purpose of the project was to federate and homogenise the custo-mer relationship carried out by the different services and subsidiaries of GT. This secondary purpose was slightly less important, and in spite of its potential interest, I won't examine this aspect in the present text.

5 We carried out in-depth qualitative interviews with twenty-five phone operators and fifteen managers, marketers and engineers, and recorded 130 customer–operator interactions. This empirical material was gathered according to prevailing ethical standards in the conduct of market research, guaranteeing notably the consent of employees of Global Telecom and the anonymity of all actors involved in the interviews and phone interactions. Fieldwork took place in call centres situated in Paris, Grenoble, Chambéry, Boulogne and Nantes.

6 Barbara Gutek (1995) distinguishes between three situations of commercial relationship in service provision: it is an 'encounter' when the customer and the service worker are in a situation of total anonymity and are not supposed to interact anymore after the transaction; it is on the contrary a 'relationship' when both actors know each other and interact on a regular basis; it can be called a 'pseudo-relationship' in various intermediary situations, for instance when the customer doesn't personally know the employee but knows very well the organisation of the service provider, or when the service worker has information concerning the customer that make it possible to take into account specific needs and demands.

7 See Hennion (2015) and the very inspiring reflection on the notion of relation in James (1905).

8 Alternative types of informational indexing are for instance scoring practices, qualifying customers in relation with given concerns, for example the appetite for a particular service. On the construction of scores and their use in sales situations, see Poon (2009) and Benedetto-Meyer (2014).

Bibliography

Akrich, M. (1992) The de-scription of technical objects. In W. Bijker and J. Law (eds), *Shaping Technology/Building Society Studies in Sociotechnical Change*, Cambridge, MA: MIT Press, pp. 205–224.

Ball, K.S. and Margulis, S.T. (2011) Electronic monitoring and surveillance in call centres: A framework for investigation. *New Technology, Work and Employment*, 26(2): 113–126.

Benedetto-Meyer, M. (2014) Du datamining aux outils de gestion: enjeux et usages des 'scores' dans la relation-client. In E. Kessous and A. Mallard (eds), *La Fabrique de la vente. Le travail commercial dans les telecommunication*, Paris: Presses des mines.

Buscatto, M. (2002) Les centres d'appels, usines modernes? Les rationalisations paradoxales de la relation téléphonique. *Sociologie du Travail*, 44(1): 99–118.

Cochoy, F. (2012) *Du lien marchand. Comment le marché fait société*, Toulouse: Presses Universitaires du Mirail.

Cochoy, F. (2014) *Aux origines du libre-service. Progressive Grocer (1922–1959)*, Lormont: Le bord de l'eau.

Fourcade, M. and Healy, K. (2007) Moral views of market society. *Annual Review of Sociology*, 33: 285–311.

Frenkel, S.J. (2005) Service workers in search of decent work. In S. Ackroyd, R. Batt, P. Thomson and P.S. Tolbert (eds), *The Oxford Handbook of Work and Organization*, Oxford: Oxford University Press, pp. 356–375.

Gutek, B.A. (1995) *The Dynamics of Service: Reflection on the Changing Nature of Customer/Provider Interactions*, San Francisco, CA: Jossey-Bass.

Hennion, A. (2007) Things that hold us together: Taste and sociology. *Cultural Sociology*, 1(1): 97–114.

Hennion, A. (2015) Enquêter sur nos attachements. Comment hériter de William James? *SociologieS*, Dossiers 'Pragmatisme et sciences sociales: explorations, enquêtes, experimentations'. https://sociologies.revues.org/4953.

Hirschman, A.O. (1982) Rival interpretations of market society: Civilizing, destructive, or feeble? *Journal of Economic Literature*, 20(4): 1463–1484.

Hochschild, A. (1983) *The Managed Heart*, Berkeley: University of California Press.

James, W. (1905) The thing and its relations. *Journal of Philosophy, Psychology and Scientific Methods*, 2(2): 29–41.

Jenkins, S., Delbridge, R. and Roberts, A. (2010) Emotional management in a mass customised call centre: Examining skill and knowledgeability in interactive service work. *Work, Employment and Society*, 24(3): 546–564.

Kessous, E. and Mallard, A. (2014) A la découverte du client. In E. Kessous and A. Mallard (eds), *La Fabrique de la vente. Le travail commercial dans les télécommunication*, Paris: Presses des mines.

Korczynski, M. (2009) The mystery customer: Continuing absences in the sociology of service work. *Sociology*, 43(5): 952–967.

Licoppe, C. (2002) L'évolution des centres d'appel téléphoniques des agences de voyage sur l'internet. Inscriptions sociotechniques de la coordination marchande. *Réseaux*, 114: 119–152.

Poon, M. (2009) Scorecards as devices for consumer credit: The case of Fair, Isaac & Company Incorporated. In F. Muniesa, Y. Millo and M. Callon (eds), *Market Devices*, Oxford: Blackwell, pp. 284–306.

Russel, B. (2007) 'You gotta lie to it': Software applications and the management of technological change in a call centre. *New Technology, Work and Employment*, 22(2): 132–145.

Russel, B. (2008) Call centers: A decade of research. *International Journal of Management Reviews*, 10(3): 195–219.

Taylor, P. and Bain, P. (1999) 'An assembly line in the head': Work and employee relations in the call centre. *Industrial Relations Journal*, 30(2): 101–117.

Vargha, Z. (2011) From long-term savings to instant mortgages: Financial demonstration and the role of interaction in markets. *Organization*, 18(2): 215–235.

6 The market will have you

The arts of market attachment in a digital economy

Liz McFall and Joe Deville

Introduction

> Click stream: an enormous, imperfect recreation of a man's brain. Digital DNA. You are the numbers, John. Accessible in a million ways, all ones and zeros. Where you go, what you do there, questions asked, money spent, the brand of beer you drink. You are on show John, in an infinite number of ways. The most visible person imaginable. And right now someone is watching.
>
> (K.D., 2014: 257)

What can it possibly mean to say that the market will have you? Accustomed as we are to hearing about the havoc markets wreak upon social institutions, communities and individuals, it could perhaps signal the thuggishness of markets as in 'h' dropped, the market 'is gonna 'ave you'.[1] There is of course a whole tradition in economic sociology and anthropology from Polanyi onwards, of seeing what markets do this way. But since we are concerned, in this collection, with seeing how market exchange *produces*, rather than dissolves or proceeds from, social ties (see Cochoy in this volume), that is not the path we are taking.

Another possibility is that 'having us' signals the dystopian future that many commentators think is almost upon us. This is the future that K.D. is envisioning in the extract from the novel *Headless* above, one in which markets use their new toolkits to produce digital doppelgangers, doubles or DNA replicas to predict, place, pre-order and even purchase things without any action on our part. This is the same vision of accessibility, surveillance and modelling referenced famously in Spielberg's 2002 depiction in *Minority Report* of a 2054 obsessed with prediction and saturated with scanners that identify, monitor and target consumers.[2] With Amazon in 2015 patenting 'anticipatory shipping', a logistics system designed to ship products before they are purchased, and with a catalogue of 'smart' technologies from face-recognising advertising billboards to self-refilling refrigerators already in existence, not to mention the conventional use of data mining and digital customer relationship-management strategies across a variety of domains, these visions can even seem a bit conservative. Since Savage and Borrows published their prescient analysis of the challenges posed by digital transactional data in 2007, there has been a proliferation in the means of analysis of what sovereignty over what is now known as 'Big Data' means for social science, for citizens and for consumers (Savage and Burrows, 2007, 2009; Burrows and Savage, 2014). There are now at least seven academic journals with 'big data' in their title (none of them in more than their third volume); Microsoft, Google, Facebook, Apple and Intel all have research facilities employing social scientists; digital methods, digital humanities and social science appointments and departments are springing up at universities everywhere and funders have announced a series of programmes designed to sponsor research in the area. Data science in 2017 is hip.

What all this might mean for market attachment, whether it does indeed signal a step-change in commercial capabilities to access, to know, even to 'have' their customers, is one of our concerns here. In the last decade, the capacity of the transactional data routinely gathered through retailers' loyalty schemes and users' online behaviour, to cluster associations between products, and between products and customers, has been causally linked to commercial efficacy.[3] The big four, Apple, Amazon, Google and Facebook are, in this view, what they are, in large part because of their success in orchestrating these associations. This included, for example, wrangling with data associations to figure out the probability that purchasing X means that shopper Y will purchase Z next. Such is the potency of such successful strategies, some claim, that we are conditioned not only to buy certain things, but to buy at particular times, in response to particular sorts of offer, in particular volumes and for occasions defined not by *a priori* social ties but through commercial signals that certain relationships should matter enough to mark with a gift.[4]

The digital toolkits and vast data-sets behind such strategies are certainly new and they certainly aim to foster relationships with customers that might lead to stable attachments. Yet, amidst all the hype about the power of big data, the consequences of who has the means to access, own, manage and control it, the epistemological and ontological possibilities of being able to simultaneously derive breadth and depth, quantitative and qualitative, insights from the same data set, there has been little concrete, historically informed discussion of what exactly it is about market attachment that these changes change. Critics raise big questions about surveillance, privacy, dignity, rights and exploitation as Google, Apple, Facebook, etc. own and enclose more and more of 'our' data (c.f. Lanier, 2013; Lyon, 2014; Ritzer and Jurgenson, 2010). This kind of challenge to techno-utopianism, as Bill Maurer (2015) has recently argued, is appealing. And yet it leaves out some really big questions about the nature of the data and the associations produced in digital networks. What if, Maurer ponders, instead of an era of enclosure and accumulation, this is one of assisted reproduction in which new beings and new kinds of relations are being created? Questions about relations, rather than ownership per se, then might become what matters most.

We tackle these questions in this chapter in a number of related steps. First we consider what relations, and more particularly 'having', means in the context of markets. Using as a departure point the forgotten, then remembered, sociologist Gabriel Tarde's central provocation that what we are, our identities, are not a matter of 'being' but of 'having', we explore the idea that markets can only exist through this 'having'. The art of markets lies in how having – data, relations, associations, ties, 'us' – is accomplished practically. It is possible, as Bruno Latour and Vincent Lepinay (2009) have argued, that Tarde is a sociologist whose time has come, finally, more than a century after his death. The current general prevalence of digitisation now at last provides the conditions to test his initial hypotheses that qualitative quantification is possible. This chimes with the critical trend that sees digitisation as pumping up the domain corporations have over us. Yet, if this *is* what is changing, this is an historical change that needs, well, to be historicised. Our next step then is to consider the question of relations in markets historically. From the emblematic device of Customer Relationship Management (CRM) we move to explore how central relationship management has been to marketing over time. Marketing, as Tadajewski (2009, 2015) has demonstrated, has a more subtle and varied history of relational strategies than the presentist preoccupations with marketing innovations allow. The equivalence between relationality and marketing is captured in Tarde's account through the theme of conversation, which is scored as the necessary connective between buyers and sellers. Conversation *devises* market attachments by providing a channel through which sellers can talk, listen and respond to their customers.

We test this idea further, in the next section, by looking at how marketing conversations were conducted in two consumer finance product cases: the industrial life assurance company, Prudential Assurance, and the payday loan company, Wonga. The two cases are very different but share the challenge of targeting the lower, 'bottom of the pyramid' end of the consumer finance market. Prudential grew rapidly in the late nineteenth century by catering for the appetite for small life assurance policies among the people Charles Masterman (1902) once characterised as the 'silent poor' as a mark of how little policymakers understood about their lives. How Prudential managed to get into conversation with the silent poor is a powerful exemplar of market attachments being devised. More than a century later, Wonga began targeting a similarly low end of the consumer finance market with online payday loans. At Wonga, exemplary digital data techniques including website optimisation strategies and algorithms combining thousands of data points were being used, the company claimed, to enable them to listen to their customers and target their product offers accordingly.

While Prudential's business model endured for over 150 years, it took around five years for trouble to set in at Wonga. This of course suggests nothing in general about the efficacy of digital means of market attachment but it does throw the spotlight on the other things that can get in the way even when advanced quanti-quali means of 'having' the customer – the new magic epistemologies – are in play. We close by considering the limits of epistemological modelling in a context of proliferant, superabundant data for accomplishing market attachment.

On having: the question of relationships in marketing

Gabriel Tarde's economic sensibility is easier to follow when it is located in the right historical intellectual context. This was a moment in which Charles Darwin's account of evolution as the incidental by-product, not the goal, of material struggle in a world characterised by 'chance, change and difference' (Menand, 2001: 123) was having a profound impact across social thought. Darwin – among many other things – supplied a way of thinking about individuals and the relations and interactions between them rather than types or essences. By developing systems for analysing probabilities, relations and functions rather than causes, categories and purposes, Darwin sponsored the kind of relational, radically empirical disposition that can be found in Tarde's thinking. If the idea of natural selection offered an explanation of how organisms with certain characteristics are *randomly* favoured in certain environments for adaptation and survival – such that species evolve because they must struggle and not the other way around – then relations, interactions, adaptations *are* existence.

This concern with relations, rather than being or essence, is what places 'having' as the core of existence for Tarde. 'Possession,' he wrote, 'is the universal fact, and there is no better term than that of "acquisition" to express the formation and the growth of any being' (in Latour, 2002: 130). Entities are defined by their properties and by how they come to possess them. This avidity, this acquisitiveness, carries no moral stain – it simply expresses the process by which all entities – including buyers and sellers, users and providers, products and markets – come into existence. As in chemistry, avidity concerns the generative nature of multiple bond interactions, or the ways that what an entity *is*, is entirely, radically, contingent on the relations formed around it. There is not, in nature or in markets, any being, essence or property except that defined by dint of these relations. Tarde's Darwinian naturalising of economic activity elevates it 'to the level of proliferation, multiplication, and invention, which will make it possible to explain the *content* of goods and not only the *form* of exchange' (Latour and Lepinay, 2009: 46).

Just as Latour (1991) argued of innovation in his classic discussion of the path that led to the technological and mass market establishment of the Kodak camera in the nineteenth century, the path taken is one in which all actors, all entities, evolve together, becoming themselves through the associations forged round them. It is the length of the chain of associations that makes things real. As Latour puts it, 'reality is thus paid for by continual extension in the syntagm (AND)' (1991: 118). The word (AND) here always signals another relation, that there is more to come and more to become. Step by step, relation by relation, markets owe their existence and their survival to this extension. The idea of interdependence is pushed to its furthest in Tarde's thought to reveal individual identities, acts and authorships as apparitions – everything is collaboration and imitation in a world that 'could not exist or change or advance a single step unless it possessed an untold store of blind routine and slavish imitation which was constantly being added to by successive generations' (1962 [1903]: 75).

One of the primary factors of production in this imitative, relational economy is conversation:

> Conversation is eminently interesting to the economist. There is no economic relationship between men that is not first accompanied by an exchange of words, whether verbal, written, printed, telegraphed or telephoned... how do these needs for production and consumption – for sale and purchase – which have just been mutually satisfied by a trade concluded thanks to conversation arise? Most often, thanks again to conversations, which had spread the idea of a new product to buy or to produce from one interlocutor to another, and, along with this idea, had spread trust in the qualities of the product or in its forthcoming output, and finally the desire to consume it or to manufacture it.
>
> (Tarde in Latour and Lepinay, 2009: 49)

It is because of the relational and contagious character of imitation that conversation is so important to market exchange. Through conversations desire, belief and trust in products spread, from one person to another, and through them, the efforts of marketing managers can be amplified. Following the babble of multiple lines of market-relevant conversation in the era in which Tarde was writing might sound like an exercise in the impossible. Yet, as we describe below, there were practical marketing techniques, even then, that companies used to 'listen in' to their customers. The existence of such techniques suggests that we pause before accepting wholesale the plausible arguments that it is only the present context of ubiquitous computing, viral marketing, social media and sentiment analysis that, at last, offers effective means of quantifying chatter, moods and inclinations (c.f. Latour and Lepinay, 2009).

Thinking about markets as long, multistranded chains of relations has implications for how they are defined. Instead of imagining markets primarily as a space, arena or a forum, of whatever kind, in which buyers and sellers confront one another, they can be thought of as a distribution across a crowd of actors and intermediaries: suppliers, researchers, publicists, publishers, etc. (c.f. Cochoy, 1998; Musselin and Paradeise, 2005; McFall, 2014b). A whole crowd plays parts in making markets move. What buyers/consumers do *with* products, what sellers/producers do to find this out and then what they do *to* products in response, is the understated loop that practically defines markets. All markets can be thought of as employing 'devices', in the sense proposed by Muniesa et al. (2007), that contribute to this looping of feedback within long, multistranded chains. The core task is to provide a mechanism for generating and transferring information from one place to another with the aim of producing particular sorts of action.

In the last two decades, through its combination of digital technologies and relationship marketing techniques, one device has made a particularly strong claim to this territory: CRM systems developed in parallel with online retailing. They employ a dynamic mixture of the principles of relationship marketing, the 'transactional data' accumulated through sales records, online searches and/or retailer loyalty schemes and data management software. Through this mixture CRM proffers a solution to the problem of knowing, or having, distant, potentially anonymous customers through its apparently extraordinary surveillance capacities (see Mallard, this volume). CRM users are promised the capacity to 'identify customers by attribute and behaviour; distinguish between them by profit contribution; facilitate better decisions on product design and promotion; target customers as individuals and as segments; as well as measuring promotional effectiveness and return on investment' (Knox et al., 2010: 340; see also Beckett, 2012; Felgate et al., 2012). Through digitisation, especially in the user-generated Web 2.0, CRM, it is claimed, accelerates the blurring of production and consumption into 'prosumption' (Ritzer and Jurgenson, 2010). But is CRM really having this sort of structurally transformative impact on markets and the production/consumption relation?

In the particular context of the last two decades CRM has set out to solve some of the particular contemporary forms taken by the market relationship problem. CRM promises to demassify or 'mass personalise' consumers (c.f. Vargha, 2010) into individual profiles and deploy feedback technologies that automate consumption and modify marketing systems. Different sorts of outcome do emerge from CRM systems and this is because of their location in a distinct field of possibilities addressing the particular market problems presented by mass, relatively anonymous, geographically distributed online exchange.

But market problems are always relational problems. One doesn't need to turn to Tarde's idiosyncratic economic psychology to find recognition of this. There is plenty of historical evidence documenting practitioners who equated the problem of marketing with that of relationships. Mark Tadajewski (2008) identifies the emergence of 'relationship marketing' as a distinct concept in the 1970s but questions whether it amounts to anything more than a 'remarketing' of the marketing concept that has been in circulation as far back as the seventeenth century. In a series of articles Tadajewski (2008, 2009, 2015) has fleshed out this argument with empirical descriptions of the role of relationships in the marketing philosophies and strategies adopted by practitioners from Daniel Defoe to John Wanamaker and in twentieth-century industrial marketing. These accounts describe a set of ideas about the way to manage relationships in order to increase profitability and customer goodwill that was 'driven by practitioners and academics who were influenced by government regulators and the legal complexities of their day' (Tadajewski, 2009: 31).

From the interwar years, crowd psychology and propaganda theory, after the model of Edward Bernays, began to be deployed to meet the new challenges of relating to customers in the context of mass production

(Schwarzkopf, 2009a, 2009b). After the war, emphasis shifted in some quarters to using psychological sciences and motivation research to get to know consumers and their desires even better than they knew themselves (Deville, 2015; Nixon, 2009; Miller and Rose, 1997). Since then a long succession of techniques have been used to socioeconomically, anthropologically and psycho-sociodemographically render consumers knowable using everything from government statistics to semiotic analysis to residential neighbourhood profiling in patented methods like PRIZM in the US and ACORN and MOSAIC in the UK (Burrows and Gane, 2006). These techniques are all about building stable market attachments.

Some time ago now Hennion et al. (1989: 204) argued that within organisations 'the big opposition between the product and the market' is not dissolved by breaking down barriers but, conversely, by multiplying them in order to 'localise and organise' a series of small-scale face-to-face, bilateral encounters (see also Callon, 2015). Barriers in the form of fields, sectors, areas, divisions or departments transform the abstract problem of production and consumption into the more or less manageable, organisational process that – in practice – it always is. This characterisation applies even in digital marketing, despite the defining lack of physical co-presence of 'producers' and 'consumers', since the market encounter is never just between the buyer who clicks and the seller who lists, but between a prolific and distributed series of specialist participants. This series, not a single magical intermediary or system, is what accomplishes exchange transactions. It is the series that puts 'us' *in* the market. Desire happens then, when we:

> have in front of us not a strange object, but an object that already contains us since we have been incorporated in it by a thousand techniques from the moment of its production; and it is to be ourselves but the simple addition of the objects through which we are defined. The product traces out the consumers, the consumers the product: the familiarity of the couple has replaced the otherness of the confrontation between the reality of things and the illusions of desire.
>
> (Hennion et al., 1989: 208)

This formulation softens the contrast between the solutions of digital marketing – whether they deploy CRM, crowdsourcing or social media – and traditional marketing. It is both banal and important to remember that the core work undertaken by CRM is different – but not all that different – from that of the archetypal grocer in listening, remembering, reacting and responding to what their customers say and do in face-to-face interactions.

What, then, does a comparison between the work of digitally mediated technologies of market attachment and some of their fleshier forebears afford? This is the question we pursue in the remainder of the chapter through a brief discussion of the marketing work of Prudential Assurance Company and the payday lender Wonga. These two UK-based companies, despite the temporal distance that separates them and despite the quite different sets of techniques and technologies they employ, share a common concern with soliciting and securing the attachment of sets of customers often struggling to stay afloat in the economic margins of society.

In conversation with the silent poor

Prudential Assurance

> And we are very silent, so very silent that no one to this hour knows what we think on any subject or why we think it.
>
> (Masterman, 1902)

When Charles Masterman wrote these lines he meant to signal his exasperation at how little policymakers understood the lives of the new, urban industrial poor. Around the same time, one sector of the financial services industry was experiencing phenomenal growth by selling a product to precisely this group. Industrial life assurance was a form of small-sum life assurance that began to be traded in the 1840s.[5] It was named after its target market amongst the 'industrious' classes, those whose income was wholly dependent on their own labours. By the end of the century millions upon millions of policies had been sold. At the industry's peak in the 1940s, there were over 100 million industrial life policies in force in Britain. Table 6.1 offers a snapshot of the rapid growth of the sector in the last decade of the nineteenth century. The undisputed industry leader was Prudential Assurance Company, established in 1848 and which, by 1900, was three to four times, depending on which measure is used, the size of its nearest rivals. By 1890, in premium income terms, Prudential was not only the largest company in the industrial sector but the largest British life company overall. In 1870 Prudential sold 670,000 industrial life policies and in 1891 they sold 10 million.[6]

Just how quickly the industry, and Prudential's particular stake in it, became colossal is remarkable. Policies were being sold in implausible volumes because multiple small policies were routinely bought on the same life. This was only possible because of the peculiar character of industrial life assurance products. Life insurance contracts since the Life Assurance Act of 1774 were required to meet the legal standards of a demonstrable 'insurable interest' in the life of the person insured.[7] This legislation was designed as a response to the notorious practice in early life insurance of using policies effectively as bets on the duration of other lives (Clark, 1999). This meant that the multiple policies on other people's lives – the so-called 'life of another' policies issued in industrial assurance on relatives like dependent children, but also aunts, uncles and grandparents – were technically illegal. The illegality of the sector's core product was tolerated because of the small sums involved and because they were spent on funerals that might otherwise be charged against the public purse. Industrial life assurance was effectively

Table 6.1 Industrial Life Assurance Associations (1890–1902)

Associations	Founded	Income		Funds	
		1902	*1890*	*1902*	*1890*
Companies		£	£	£	£
British Legal, Limited	1863	142,000	51,000	187,000	97,000
British Workman's, Limited	1866	822,000	275,000	927,000	109,000
Citizens, Limited	1886	176,000	–	316,000	–
London, Edinburgh, and Glasgow, Limited	1881	376,000	187,000	259,000	28,000
London and Manchester, Limited	1869	202,000	77,000	250,000	40,000
Methodist and General, Limited	1867	200,000	–	154,000	–
Pearl, Limited	1864	953,000	264,000	1,109,000	238,000
Prudential, Limited	1848	5,691,000	3,518,000	19,616,000	7,912,000
Refuge, Limited	1864	1,204,000	598,000	733,000	236,000
Wesleyan and General	1841	549,000	201,000	649,000	223,000
Totals of companies		10,315,000	5,171,000	24,200,000	8,883,000
Societies					
Liverpool Victoria Legal	1843	791,000	403,000	1,966,000	684,000
Royal Liver	1850	615,000	405,000	2,071,000	1,104,000
Royal London	1861	668,000	190,000	1,104,000	272,000
Scottish Legal	1852	220,000	103,000	528,000	265,000
Totals of societies		2,289,000	1,101,000	5,669,000	2,325,000
Totals of companies and societies		12,604,000	6,272,000	28,869,000	11,208,000

Source: Adapted from *Economist*, 1904.

death assurance – small policies taken to cover funeral expenses. Even where policymakers were sympathetic (and many weren't) to the poor's impulse to save for death, the funeral insurance industry had a dreadful reputation. It sold products that were repeatedly condemned by policymakers and reformers across the political spectrum as inappropriate, expensive, legally 'grey' and morally hazardous.

The exasperation with the industry, and the 'feckless' poor who invested in it, led to decades of political controversies and legislative restraints. It wasn't just the percentage of income spent, or even its final motivation, that provoked outrage: it was the structure of the whole system. Industrial life assurance was built around a system of agents who acted to sell the product then collect weekly premiums on the doorstep. Weekly collection was eye-wateringly expensive to deliver, and for several decades an average of around 50 per cent of premium receipts went on administrative expenses. This stoked an argument that the poor were paying far too much for a product they shouldn't want that did little to promote the qualities of thrift that they should. By collecting door to door, agents became the source of discipline that ensured cash-strapped customers paid the regular, weekly premiums required to service their policies.

This made agents the core devices in the distribution and promotion of industrial life assurance, but their role went deeper still. Through weekly collections, agents literally got 'inside' households. They acquired a foothold and a standing that helped defend the high price of the industrial version of life assurance. As the offices caught on to the significance of agents, they were carefully organised and cultivated as ideal representatives, an inoffensive fit in any home, and the industry's central motif, repeatedly activated through advertising, sales promotion, merchandising, etc. Agents were devisers – they did not just take the product to the market, they were expected to prospect, cultivate and nurture their markets, even to become themselves part of what was being traded. At stake was the quality of the relation, the capacity for an ostensibly distant, potentially impersonal organisation to become entwined with the intimate affairs of the domestic and the everyday. To achieve this meant acting as a fully fledged system, receiving and transmitting information but also responding and adjusting their performance and the products they presented.

This was not work that agents could have managed acting by themselves. Although much of their work was conducted 'in the field' and without direct supervision, agents were always the local bearers of a vast, bureaucratic organisation, division and specialisation. They distributed the market attachment work of a series of other actors – accountants, managers, actuaries, mortality tables, medical officers, statisticians, data processors, tabulators, superintendents, publicity experts, clerks and many more. Collectively, this crowd of specialists configured and reconfigured products in line with the aggregated feedback that agents gathered in an attempt to ensure that the products incorporated customer (and seller) experience.

The art of market attachment here rested on Prudential's capacity to orchestrate countless situated conversations with the – clearly not quite so – silent poor. These organised conversations spread ideas about how products could fit into people's lives, solve their problems and stabilise their relationships. Customers had their agents, and agents had their customers but the relationships and conversations they shared were arranged in ways that allowed the Prudential to 'have' its market. How does this compare with Wonga's efforts to have their customers?

Wonga: a morality tale?

For those unfamiliar with it, Wonga is now the largest of the array of so-called 'payday lenders' that have multiplied in the UK in recent years, occupying around 30 to 40 per cent of the market (Bachelor, 2014). Payday loans or, to use the industry nomenclature, short-term loans, are high cost, unsecured consumer credit products, usually repayable within around a month (hence the name 'payday'). Wonga, like many others, also allows borrowers to set far shorter repayment periods – as short as a single day in their case. Alongside its primary operation in the UK, it has expanded its reach to include Canada, Poland, South Africa and Spain. Following regulatory changes that came into force in 2015, the cost of the loans payday lenders operating in the UK can offer has been capped (Financial Conduct Authority, 2015). Wonga, like most of its rivals, now provides loans at an annual percentage rate (APR) of just over 1,500% interest, although it prefers to frame this in terms of the lower, non-compound flat or 'fixed' annual rate (292%). Before the introduction of this cap, Wonga had attracted huge notoriety as one of the fastest growing lenders in the sector despite blatantly aggressive pricing. With a prominently advertised APR of 4,214% in 2010, its rates eventually rose closer to 6,000% APR, around double the cost of those of its (still expensive) direct competitors.[8] As a point of comparison with the credit card market, British borrowers with a poor credit history can expect to pay interest between 30 and 40% APR (MoneySavingExpert, 2015).

It is Wonga's historically exceptionally high cost and high profile rather than the company's size that seems to be the main reason for the intensity of the criticism it has faced in recent years, whether from politicians, advocacy groups or members of the public. Its ascent to the top of the UK payday lending tree is relatively recent; for much of its history, in terms of market share it sat behind Dollar Financial, which runs the Money Shop network and now occupies around a quarter of the UK market. Wonga rose to public attention initially as an online-only lender offering a peculiar justification that algorithmic analysis and data-led pricing lay behind its capacity to combine high customer satisfaction and the huge interest rates that were prominently displayed on its website.[9] Wonga, Maija Palmer reported in the *Financial Times* in 2009:

> is pushing innovation in this market, harnessing technology to create a faster, slicker, more foolproof service. The online service is entirely automated and available 24 hours a day. Once a user has entered their details, the system pulls in about 1,500 data points to build a picture of their credit history. If accepted, the money can be in a borrower's bank account within the hour, even at 2am.[10]

This initially admiring reception turned relentlessly hostile as interest rates rose and began to be obfuscated in distracting television adverts.[11] A long-standing feature of Wonga's advertising was a cast of raucous rubber-faced puppets that were accused of having an inappropriate capacity to appeal to children (Collinson, 2013) and a levity that misrepresented the character of their loans. In 2014 the Advertising Standards Authority banned Wonga from using an advertisement that failed to disclose their 5,853% interest rate (Osborne, 2014).

Most damaging of all, both reputationally and financially, was the line taken on the company by the Financial Conduct Authority, the UK's newly formed regulatory body with oversight over consumer finance. In 2014, it first ordered an estimated £2.6 million compensation to be paid to customers for unfair debt-collection practices (Financial Conduct Authority, 2014a), before compelling Wonga to write off 330,000 loans because of apparent failures to correctly assess the affordability of its products to certain borrowers (we will return to both of these actions shortly) (Financial Conduct Authority, 2014b). The effect of such scandals has been to push Wonga into unprecedented territory. After nearly a decade of unrelenting ascendancy, the company is struggling. In 2015, it made a pre-tax loss of £80.2 million, more than doubling the previous year's previously unprecedented losses, driven both by the effects of the introduction of the interest rate cap and a fall in the number of loans issued (Osborne, 2016). One response to such issues has been to try to rebrand the company as 'transparent and responsible' – which has included revamping the website, ditching the controversial puppets and displaying more flexibility towards late-paying customers (Anon, 2015).

It is tempting to tell Wonga's story to date as a morality tale about the relations between state and commerce, whereby rapacious capitalists meet their just desserts at the hands of a newly invigorated regulator willing to listen to, and act on, public criticism. There is another story to be told here though, one that takes more account of the party that has been largely absent in this tale: Masterman's 'silent poor'. Where exactly do they figure? Who is listening to them, taking account of them (in all senses of that word) and how exactly? What sort of relations, to return to our chapter's starting point, are at stake? Through this we can begin to tie down some of the practical and ethical ambiguities in the everyday work of market attachment.

Wonga: the art of listening?

Wonga's relationship to the British state is not as straightforward as it might seem. A telling example is its appearance before the influential Public Accounts Committee in 2013. Chaired by Member of Parliament, Margaret Hodge, the committee became known for its ability to respond to a public impulse to see high-profile, apparently untouchable corporations humbled; a particular success was the committee's forceful interrogation of the tax-avoidance practices of Amazon, Google and Starbucks in 2012.[12] A similar outcome was anticipated when the committee summoned Wonga as a witness in its investigation of the regulation of consumer credit. The course this encounter took and the report that ensued, however, reveal the degree to which the committee misunderstood Wonga, its customers and its business model, fundamentally limiting their ability to hold Wonga to account.

It is clear from the various lines of questioning that many in the committee took, that they were working on the assumption that Wonga's growth could be traced to its status as the most exploitative lender within a generally exploitative industry. Concern was expressed not just about the high cost of its loans but about its overall customer treatment. These were detailed discussions but one example, an exchange between the Committee and Wonga representative Henry Raine, on the question of loan 'rollovers', offers a flavour:

CHAIR [HODGE]: The business model depends on people paying you back on time.

HENRY RAINE: That is right, and we turn down some two thirds of applicants.

FIONA MACTAGGART: But don't you make your money on repeat loans? Don't you make much more money when someone has a repeat loan and a further repeat loan? I am confused, because that seems to be where the very high percentage of your income comes from.

HENRY RAINE: Just to be clear, people paying us back on time does not only mean that people are paying us back on the first loan. It means we credit-check them again and people can have another loan with us when they have repaid.

CHAIR: So they do not pay you back on time. You roll over the loan.

HENRY RAINE: No, we don't. In terms of roll-overs – if I can just briefly explain, because this is an interesting area.

(Public Accounts Committee, 2013: ev1–2)

As Raine begins to patiently explain here, there is a major distinction between a rollover – effectively an extension on a loan – and what is here termed a repeated loan. The latter refers to a customer returning at some future point to borrow again. As Raine discloses, it is this latter scenario that is the basis for Wonga's business model, not the former. In fact, in the resulting report, the committee recommended that Wonga's practice of limiting rollovers to a maximum of three occasions 'is adopted across all lenders' (Public Accounts Committee, 2013: 12; in due course, however, the Financial Conduct Authority (FCA) would in fact ban all loan rollovers).

Given its profile, it is easy to see why Wonga was chosen to stand as the representative of the UK payday lending industry.[13] Yet in many ways it was a poor choice: Wonga's business model is quite distinct from those of its competitors. Whereas Wonga operates exclusively online, its nearest rival, Dollar Financial, attracts much of its customers through its high street network of Money Shop outlets. The long tail that makes up the rest of the market is where the murky practices that the committee was hoping to expose with Wonga are more likely to be found. This particular arm of the state apparatus was, it seems, befuddled by exactly how Wonga went about the business of 'attaching' (or 'having') its market.

This is not to downplay the issues identified by the FCA, a different and more powerful state institution. The FCA's actions, which are often presented as the victory of the state over an over-reaching and aberrant domain of the market, also missed some vital context. Wonga were, for instance, censured by the FCA for their debt-collection practices. These involved Wonga issuing letters purporting to be from law firms that proved to be fictitious. This was done in a conscious effort to mislead debtors into thinking that their case had reached a serious point in the collections process. Yet what the FCA failed until recently to acknowledge is that this practice was also common in the mainstream UK retail banking and consumer credit industry (c.f. Deville, 2015). Wonga's attempt to copy a collections practice developed in the standard sector backfired because it had not anticipated the degree of attention that would be focused on its corner of the industry. With regards to affordability assessments, whatever its failings, Wonga paid probably more attention than its rivals to establishing borrowers' ability to repay (see Deville and van der Velden, 2016). Wonga are more or less unique in the UK payday lending market[14] in the effort they put into credit assessment. This has involved the development of an assessment model that blends conventional credit scoring by Callcredit, a third-party credit bureau, with analysis of thousands of alternate data points. Key to this has been the attempt to exploit the data that actual and potential customers 'leak' about themselves when accessing Wonga's website. This could be as mundane as their choice of browser, their screen resolution settings, or it could involve clues about user location derived from the IP address, or even traits inferred from browsing habits. At its peak the company claimed that its algorithmic analysis of all these data points allowed it to make 'objective and unprejudiced' lending decisions:[15]

> Once a customer has decided on the size of a loan, he is taken through a series of questions. Within about 15 minutes, Wonga has retained around 30 pieces of simple information about a potential borrower. And, from those pieces of information, Wonga has found it can access a further 6,000 to 8,000 online data points that relate to the applicant.[16]

Wonga won't disclose precisely what data points they use or how but responsive web optimisation design strategies that alter details of an 'offer' depending on how a user behaves on the page are an increasingly common feature of Web 2.0 marketing strategies.[17] The company certainly invested in its user interface, making it simpler and more user friendly than many of its rivals. Given the digital trackers that can be detected operating in the background of its site (Deville and van der Velden, 2016), it is highly likely that Wonga, like many established e-commerce sites, is routinely monitoring this usability to make the customer's route to borrowing and managing loans as smooth as possible. It has therefore very much engaged in the development of the digital marketing toolkits that an ever expanding list of companies are using to better have – and hold onto – their customers. Digital tools like these have begun to supersede the 'man at the door', in organising, gathering and ana-lysing the intimate domestic information that is required to market financial services to the (relatively) silent poor.[18]

Wonga's particular approach to credit risk assessment appears for now to be under threat in the UK. The FCA's recent action included an agreement by Wonga that a 'Skilled Person… will review the new lending decision plat-form' (Financial Conduct Authority, 2014b). On the one hand, this does not rule out the possibility of Wonga maintaining at least part of its unique approach to risk assessment. On the other, perhaps it will struggle to demonstrate that some of its more outlandish methods and data sources have a place in the landscape of UK credit assessment.

Despite these new requirements and all the controversies surrounding Wonga, one aspect of the company's business model merits more careful attention than it has yet had. This concerns how Wonga positioned *the char-acter of the relation* between itself and its remote customers as the key to profitability and set digital experiments to work on configuring it. Setting aside the ethical trouble that non-standard lending raises, Wonga achieved something remarkable: amongst a section of the population with constrained financial means, it became the UK's largest payday lender over the course of a period in which it was simultaneously by far the most expensive. There is a long-standing tendency to assume the poor lack the financial skills or 'rationality' to make decisions in their own best interests (McFall, 2014a) and one does not have to dig too hard at payday lending critiques to detect this sentiment. Yet the uncomfortable fact that loomed over the Public Accounts Committee discussion was that Wonga thrived off of borrowers returning repeatedly. Given that it had competitors offering similar products at much lower cost, the continuing appeal of Wonga is worth thinking carefully about. It is easy – and common enough – to dismiss borrowers as foolish, desperate or both and lenders as manipulative, unethical or both. There is truth in all these claims but there is also something more systemic at play. Wonga, like all non-standard financial services providers, at least for a time has devised suc-cessful means of listening and responding to those quiet borrowers, on whose behalf critics (and sociologists) so often speak.

Epilogue: conversation as data

> The central problematic of human affairs is not dealing with scarcity, but dealing with excess.
>
> (Abbott, 2014: 1)

Listening in financial services, historically, might be categorised after Zelizer (2005) as 'relational work'. The human agents of industrial assurance cer-tainly had their conversational skills cultivated. It would be a mistake, however, to reduce the historical shift in the relational form from Prudential to Wonga as the succession of proximate, human relations by remote, digital ones. Prudential agents certainly conducted human, person-to-person conversations but these conversations were bureaucratically and technically organised on a much larger scale than any at Wonga. The mass processing of millions of pieces of data in advance of automation in insurance companies has been well documented (c.f. Campbell-Kelly, 1992; Yates, 2005) but what this implies about the way market attachment is – perforce has to be – underpinned by infrastructure deserves more thought.

Figures 6.1 and 6.2 offer a glimpse into how agents' conversations with their customers were organised through relational data infrastructures. Figure 6.1 shows a specimen of two of the key data files used in life insurance, the Agency Register and the District Life Register. The Agency Register, a heavy foolscap book, had to be carried by agents working in the field at all times. It records details of the individual lives insured through a particular agent and the premium contributions received. The District Life Register abstracts key elements of the Agency Register data and repeats it to be stored at district level. Figure 6.2 shows how some of this locally gathered data, the original proposals, were stored at head office. The salient point here is that the front-end human conversation between agent and customer (or 'life') had its own data double in manual registers and archived files. These data doubles informed both how Prudential priced its risks centrally and how agents sold

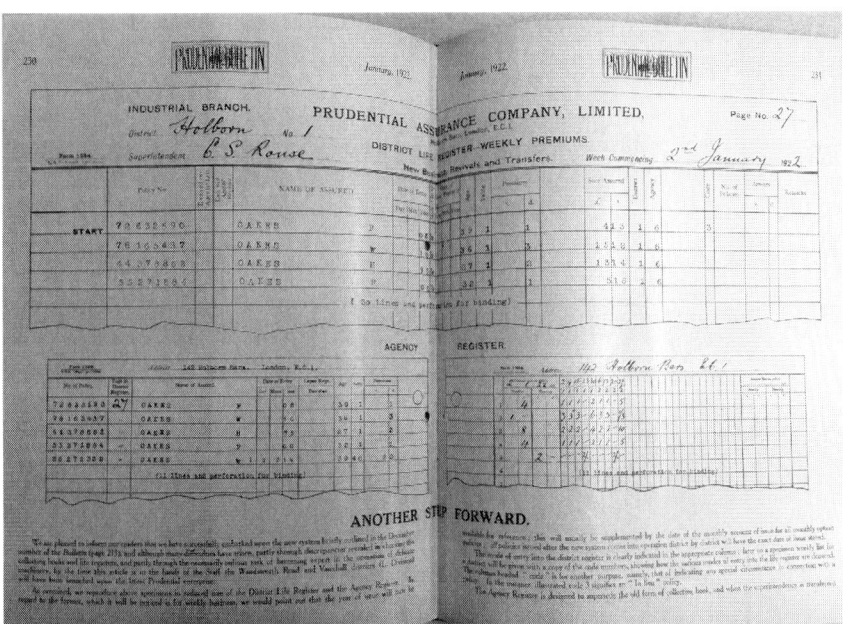

Figure 6.1 Manual data infrastructures at Prudential Assurance, *Prudential Bulletin*, 1922

Industrial Branch Proposals.

Figure 6.2 Manual data infrastructures at Prudential Assurance, *Prudential Bulletin*, 1922

insurance products to their repeat customers locally. For instance, a long-term weekly customer with no premium arrears recorded might be seen as a good prospect for a larger, monthly paid policy offering a better return.

Structurally, this is similar to how data relations were used to price risk at Wonga. Details about precisely what algorithms and data points Wonga use are unavailable but the company have conceded that relational data analysis lies at the foundation of their lending practices:

> The crux of the algorithm is less about the individual pieces of data – your postcode, the colour of your car, how large your mortgage is – but how these pieces of information relate to one another. Crucially, the data points are stacked against the other pieces of information gleaned from past Wonga clients.[19]

At both Prudential and Wonga a range of qualitative and quantitative data were gathered, stored, combined and analysed to inform the product offer. Offering the right product in the right form at the right time – whether money collected on the doorstep every week or money deposited in the bank account within minutes – was central in both companies to their capacity to stably attach or 'have' their markets through repeat custom. Listening and talking to customers was a necessary part of this but at neither company was conversation sufficient. Marketing strategy cannot be made out of data or analysis alone – judgement and decisions still have to be made and this is where questions about the efficacy of digital market attachment get interesting.

The glaring difference between Prudential and Wonga is that the conversation with customers at the latter was conducted by digital means. While at its peak, Prudential was processing millions of tiny weekly transactions, from the hands of millions of customers, through those of tens of thousands of agents, to hundreds of districts and finally back to one central head office, this is still not the scale or the level at which 'big data' operates. Scale, as boyd and Crawford (2012: 663) explain, is not really what drives the epistemological fascination with big data so much as 'the capacity to search, aggregate, and cross-reference large data sets'. On these counts, even the reciprocal exchange between life insurance and pre-computer machinery like punched cards and tabulators designed to cope with massive data sets in the first half of the twentieth century (Yates, 2005) falls short. Big data, in boyd and Crawford's terms, concerns the interplay between technology and analysis that underpins a mythological 'belief that large data sets can generate insights that were previously impossible, with the aura of truth, objectivity and accuracy' (2012: 663). It is precisely this kind of mythology that can be detected in Wonga's founder and former chief executive Errol Damelin's assertion that algorithmic analysis of all those thousands of data points allowed the company to make 'objective and unprejudiced' lending decisions that would be safe even in a market with a high default rate. Damelin's claims may – or may not – have been a hubristic over-reach but it is clear that Wonga's eventual troubles would not have been solved by any amount or combination of data, technology or analysis. At root, the trouble with Wonga was the judgement that its regulators, critics and eventually its market would tolerate its business model.

Andrew Abbott's (2014) careful dissection of the problem of excess nails this tension. Excess, overload, superabundant quantities of anything – here specifically data and information – either paralyses or in some other way impedes production. Abbott refers back to Eric Leifer's reflection that skill actually resides in arranging things so that you never have to engage in the impossibilism of making a 'rational' choice from 'the excess of information and the infinite excess of possible futures' (2014: 23). This bind is precisely what is at work in the cognitively conflicted market research industry's efforts to alternately query, orchestrate and legitimate the role of data or information in what can ultimately be 'known' about markets (Cochoy, 2012; Schwarzkopf, 2015):

> Clearly, while this industry no doubt produces genuine service solutions that help companies work more efficiently, it is also an industry that *structurally* hinges on inducing doubt and managerial ignorance: the more of the latter, the more data are needed. This, in turn, means that the problem of market research data is an agnotological one, a problem

bound up closely with ignorance management, the social creation of persistent states of not-knowing, and of never knowing enough.

(Schwarzkopf, 2015: 4)

One of the services that commissioned market research provided at Prudential in the late 1960s was data confirming a pattern of decline in the industrial assurance market that the company's internal sales information had been demonstrating for years. The commission report concluded that 'in terms of consumer perceptions of the company certain definition inhibitions... will require a major calculated action by the Prudential to overcome' (Prudential Assurance Archive, 1970: 1.3). The report offered more data about the factors underlying this decline but what neither it, nor the company, could do on the basis of this data was work out what form the 'major calculated action' required should take. The company was not paralysed by this data, it tried a range of variously fated alternate ventures, but none that were sufficient to prevent long-term decline. Industrial assurance in the UK no longer 'had' its customers, listening to them only revealed some of the reasons why. Things worked out differently at Wonga but there too all the millions of data points the company gathered offered no protection against the tide of public and regulatory critique.

So where, then, does this leave the question of what it means to say 'the market will have you'? In both the formalist and substantivist terms used to analyse economies and markets (Çalışkan and Callon, 2009) it will always be possible to conclude that en masse, overall and in the end markets 'have' us; they do violence to us. One of the problems with this that our bottom-of-the pyramid cases raise though, is that if markets have us, do us in or do us over, we are complicit in this. In repeat custom, over decades at Prudential and over a shorter period at Wonga, people came back. There are of course ways that this return can be explained. Powerful, manipulative, deceitful companies; ignorant, irrational or desperate consumers, but such explanations often involve critics speaking on behalf of, rather than in conversation with, market participants. As the awkward exchanges with Wonga at the Public Accounts Committee demonstrate it is not only the poor who can sometimes be silent in critical and regulatory conversations.

Another of the possibilities we started with was that 'having us' was a reference to the technological breakthrough that big, digital data represents. Digital DNA, doppelgangers or data doubles make us accessible to the market in unprecedented ways. There are, however, long historical precedents to these attempts to build, know, have and hold onto customer relationships. In the case of Prudential, the quality of the relationship was essential to a marketing strategy that turned on the capacity of agents to be admitted into the intimate, domestic affairs of households. This in turn was underpinned by a data infrastructure that allowed the company to convert relationships and transactions into data that could inform product, promotion and pricing offers. In very different ways, our cases both illustrate a simultaneous use of breadth and depth, quantitative and qualitative market data. Prudential combined qualitative means of engagement through their human agents with manual data infrastructures and Wonga combined qualitative and quantitative data points and algorithms to work out who their customers were and, especially, what they might do next. There is an irreducible element of future-casting mystery in the relationship between data showing what consumers have done, even in the immediate past, and what they might do next. What it is that allows the market to 'have' us, that turns a product into 'the thing' that enables us, becomes us, that already in someway *is* us, before slowly, or sometimes suddenly, it is not – is not wholly explainable. The epistemological chutzpah of big data is that it will solve this mystery to allow markets to imperfectly, but more finally, have us. It can't and it won't.

Notes

1 This is a parochial reference to the emblematic gangster slang associated with the East End of London, 'we're gonna 'ave you' is an explicit threat of violence to come.
2 K.D.'s novel is part of conceptual artists Goldin and Senneby's *Headless* project, www.goldinsenneby.com/gs/?p=116. On *Minority Report* see Knox et al. (2010).
3 See for instance Lace (2005); Zwick and Pridmore (2011); Pridmore and Lyon (2011). Beckett (2012) offers a measured review.
4 Beckett (2012) for instance describes how relatively new shopping customs like gift buying for teachers at the end of the school year have become normalised with the help of supermarket CRM and loyalty schemes, while Felgate et al. (2012) note how Tesco supermarket's Clubcard scheme established a new promotional logic of 'buying on offer'.
5 Life assurance, rather than life insurance, was the term initially adopted, particularly in the UK. 'Assurance' refers to insurance against an event that *would* happen, i.e. eventual death as distinct from an event that *might* happen, e.g. theft or death within a given period. Increasingly the term life insurance is generally used but the industry still employs the technical distinction.
6 Prudential Assurance Company annual reports.
7 A wife, for instance, had an insurable interest in the life of her husband as she would likely be dependent upon him for income.
8 BBC News, 2012a; Osborne, 2014.
9 www.wired.co.uk/magazine/archive/2011/06/features/wonga?page=all.
10 www.ft.com/cms/s/0/be7ead42-48c3-11de-8870-00144feabdc0.html#axzz3zDzrwQEO.
11 www.theguardian.com/media/pda/2008/jul/23/elevatorpitchwongafixestha; www.theguardian.com/money/2013/oct/09/wonga-ad-banned-payday-lender; www.theguardian.com/money/2013/nov/05/payday-lenders-accused-grooming-children-ads.
12 BBC News, 2012b.
13 The only other company called was Provident, which offers a quite different credit product; c.f. McFall, 2017.
14 Although not globally.
15 See note 8.
16 www.wired.co.uk/magazine/archive/2011/06/features/wonga/viewall.
17 See Mellet in this collection. Kreiss (2012) provides a compelling account of the use of web optimisation strategies in US electoral politics.
18 Although it is notable that while industrial life assurance products largely disappeared in the UK more than two decades ago, doorstep credit as sold by

Provident Financial continues to have a significant share of the non-standard credit market; c.f. McFall (2017).
19 See Shaw (2011).

Bibliography

Abbott, A. (2014) The problem of excess. *Sociological Theory*, 32(1), 1–26. http://doi.org/10.1177/0735275114523419.

Anon (2015) Wonga rebrands as 'transparent and responsible' lender after hiring Fold7. *Campaign*. www.marketingmagazine.co.uk/article/1347610/wonga-rebrands-transparent-responsible-lender-hiring-fold7.

Araujo, L., Finch, J. and Kjellberg, H. (eds) (2010) *Reconnecting Marketing to Markets*, Oxford: Oxford University Press.

Bachelor, L. (2014) Payday lenders should wipe out loans in wake of Wonga ruling, experts say. *Guardian*. www.theguardian.com/money/2014/oct/03/payday-lenders-repay-loans-wonga.

BBC News (2012a). Wonga what makes moneylender tick? 11 May. www.bbc.co.uk/news/business-18019272 (accessed 3 February 2016).

BBC News (2012b). Starbucks, Google and Amazon grilled over tax avoidance. 12 November. http://www.bbc.co.uk/news/business-20288077 (accessed 3 February 2016).

Beckett, A. (2012) Governing the consumer: Technologies of consumption. *Consumption Markets and Culture*, 15(1): 1–18.

boyd, d. and Crawford, K. (2012) Critical questions for big data. *Information, Communication and Society*, 15(5): 662–679. http://doi.org/10.1080/1369118X.2012.678878.

Burrows, R. and Gane, N. (2006) Geodemographics, software and class. *Sociology*, 40(5): 793–812.

Burrows, R. and Savage, M. (2014) After the crisis? Big data and the methodological challenges of empirical sociology, *Big Data and Society*, 1, 1.

Çalışkan, K. and Callon, M. (2009) Economization, part 1: Shifting attention from the economy towards processes of economization. *Economy and Society*, 38(3): 369–398.

Callon, M. (2015) Revisiting marketization: from interface-markets to market-agencements. *Consumption Markets and Culture*, 19(1): 17–37.

Campbell-Kelly, M. (1992) Large-scale data processing in the Prudential, 1850–1930. *Accounting, Business and Financial History*, 2(2): 117–140.

Clark, G. (1999) *Betting on Lives: The Culture of Life Insurance in England 1695–1775*, Manchester: Manchester University Press.

Cochoy, F. (1998) Another discipline for the market economy: Marketing as a performative knowledge and know-how for capitalism. In M. Callon (ed.), *The Laws of the Markets*, Oxford: Blackwell, pp. 194–221.

Cochoy, F. (2012) La sociologie economique relationniste. In F. Cochoy (ed.), *Du Lien Marchand: Comment Le Marché Fait Société. Essai(s) de Sociologie Économique Relationniste*, Toulouse: Presses Universitaires du Mirail, pp. 19–54.

Collinson, P. (2013) Payday lenders accused of 'grooming' children with catchy ads. *Guardian*. www.theguardian.com/money/2013/nov/05/payday-lenders-accused-grooming-children-ads.

Deville, J. (2015) *Lived Economies of Default: Consumer Credit, Debt Collection and the Capture of Affect*, London: Routledge.

Deville, J. and van der Velden, L. (2016) Seeing the invisible algorithm: The practical politics of tracking the credit trackers. In L. Amoore and V. Piotukh (eds), *Algorithmic Life: Calculative Devices in the Age of Big Data*, London: Routledge, pp. 90–109.

Economist (1904) Industrial assurance. 24 September, 1538–159.

Felgate, M., Fearne, A. and Di Falco, S. (2012) Using supermarket loyalty card data to analyse the impact of promotions. *International Journal of Market Research*, 54(2): 221–240.

Financial Conduct Authority (2014a). Wonga to pay redress for unfair debt collection practices. www.fca.org.uk/news/wonga-redress-unfair-debt-collection-practices.

Financial Conduct Authority (2014b). Wonga to make major changes to affordability criteria following discussions with the FCA. www.fca.org.uk/news/wonga-major-cha nges-to-affordability-criteria.

Financial Conduct Authority (2015) FCA confirms price cap rules for payday lenders. www.fca.org.uk/news/fca-confirms-price-cap-rules-for-payday-lenders.

Hennion, A., Meadel, C. and Bowker, G. (1989) The artisans of desire: The mediation of advertising between product and consumer. *Sociological Theory*, 7(2): 191–209.

Humby, C., Hunt, T. and Phillips, T. (2006) *Scoring Points: How Tesco Continues to Win Customer Loyalty*, London: Kogan Page.

K.D. (2014) *Headless*, Berlin: Sternberg Press.

Knox, H., O'Doherty, D., Vurdubakis, T. and Westrup, C. (2010) The devil and customer relationship management. *Journal of Cultural Economy*, 3(3): 339–359.

Kreiss, D. (2012) *Taking Our Country Back: The Crafting of Networked Politics from Howard Dean to Barack Obama*, New York: Oxford University Press.

Lace, S. (ed.) (2005) *The Glass Consumer: Life in a Surveillance Society*, Bristol: Policy Press.

Lanier, J. (2013) *Who Owns the Future*, London: Penguin.

Latour, B. (1991) Technology is society made durable. In J. Law (ed.), *The Sociology of Monsters*, London: Routledge, pp. 103–131.

Latour, B. (2002) Gabriel Tarde and the end of the social. In P. Joyce (ed.), *The Social in Question*. London: Routledge, pp. 117–132.

Latour, B. and Lepinay, V.A. (2009) *The Science of Passionate Interests: An Introduction to Gabriel Tarde's Economic Anthropology*, Chicago, IL: Prickly Paradigm Press.

Lyon, D. (2014) Surveillance, Snowden, and Big Data: Capacities, consequences, critique. *Big Data and Society*, 1(2): 1–13.

Masterman, C. (1902) *From the Abyss of Its Inhabitants by One of Them*, London: R.B. Johnson.

Maurer, B. (2015) Principles of ascent and alliance for big data. In T. Boellstorff and B. Maurer (eds), *Data, Now Bigger and Better!* Chicago, IL: Prickly Paradigm Press, pp. 67–86.

McFall, L. (2014a). *Devising Consumption: Cultural Economies of Insurance, Credit and Spending*, London: Routledge.

McFall, L. (2014b). The problem of cultural intermediaries in the economy of qualities. In J. Maguire and J. Matthews (eds), *The Cultural Intermediaries Reader*, London: Sage, pp. 42–51.

McFall, L. (2017) What's in a name? Provident, the People's Bank and the regulation of brand identity. In I. Ertürk and D. Gabor (eds), *The Routledge Companion to Banking Regulation and Reform*, Abingdon: Routledge, pp. 55–74.

Menand, L. (2001) *The Metaphysical Club*, New York: Farrar, Straus, and Giroux.

Miller, P. and Rose, N. (1997) Mobilizing the consumer: Assembling the subject of consumption. *Theory, Culture and Society*, 14(1): 1–36.

MoneySavingExpert (2015) Credit cards for bad credit. www.moneysavingexpert.com/credit-cards/bad-credit-credit-cards.

Muniesa, F., Millo, Y. and Callon, M. (2007) An introduction to market devices. In M. Callon, Y. Millo and M. Callon (eds), *Market Devices*, Oxford: Wiley-Blackwell, pp. 1–12.

Musselin, C. and Paradeise, C. (2005) Quality: A debate, *Sociologie du Travail*, 47: S89–S123.

Nixon, S. (2009) Understanding ordinary women: Advertising, consumer research and mass consumption in Britain, 1948–67. *Journal of Cultural Economy*, 2(3): 301–323.

Osborne, H. (2014) Wonga banned from using ad that didn't mention 5.853% interest rate. *Guardian*. www.theguardian.com/business/2014/oct/08/wonga-banned-tv-ad-interest-rate.

Osborne, H. (2016) Wonga losses more than double. *Guardian*. www.theguardian.com/business/2016/may/04/wonga-losses-more-than-double-payday-loans.

Palmer, M. (2009) Wonga drives web loan innovation. *Financial Times*, 9 May.

Pridmore, J. and Lyon, D. (2011) Marketing as surveillance: Assembling consumers as brands. In D. Zwick and J. Cayla (eds), *Inside Marketing: Practices, Ideologies, Devices*, Oxford: Oxford University Press, pp. 115–136.

Prudential Assurance Archive (1970) Consumer attitudes to insurance and insurance companies: A report from the Attitude Research Programme. Prudential Archive, High Holborn, London.

Public Accounts Committee (2013) Regulating consumer credit. www.publications.parliament.uk/pa/cm201314/cmselect/cmpubacc/165/165.pdf.

Ritzer, G. and Jurgenson, N. (2010) Production, consumption, prosumption: The nature of capitalism in the age of the digital 'prosumer'. *Journal of Consumer Culture*, 10(1): 13–36.

Savage, M. and Burrows, R. (2007) The coming crisis of empirical sociology. *Sociology*, 41(5): 885–899.

Savage, M. and Burrows, R. (2009) Some further reflections on the coming crisis of empirical sociology. *Sociology*, 43(4): 762–772.

Schwarzkopf, S. (2009a). Discovering the consumer: Market research, product innovation, and the creation of brand loyalty in Britain and the United States in the interwar years. *Journal of Macromarketing*, 29(1): 8–20.

Schwarzkopf, S. (2009b). What was advertising? The invention, rise, demise, and disappearance of advertising concepts in nineteenth- and twentieth-century Europe and America. *Business and Economic History On-Line*, 7: 1–27.

Schwarzkopf, S. (2015) Data overflow and sacred ignorance: An agnotological account of organizing in the market and consumer research industry. Conference paper. doi: 10.13140/RG.2.1.4694.3849

Shaw, W. (2011) Cash machine: Could Wonga transform personal finance? *Wired*, 5 May. www.wired.co.uk/magazine/archive/2011/06/features/wonga/viewall.

Shove, E. and Araujo, L. (2010) Consumption, materiality and markets. In L. Araujo, J. Finch and H. Kjellberg (eds), *Reconnecting Marketing to Markets*, Oxford: Oxford University Press, pp. 13–28.

Simkin, L. and Dibb, S. (2013) Social media's impact on market segmentation and CRM. *Journal of Strategic Marketing*, 21(5): 391–393.

Tadajewski, M. (2008) Relationship marketing at Wanamaker's in the nineteenth and early twentieth centuries. *Journal of Macromarketing*, 28(2): 169–182.

Tadajewski, M. (2009) The foundations of relationship marketing: Reciprocity and trade relations. *Marketing Theory*, 9(1): 9–38.

Tadajewski, M. (2015) The complete English tradesman: Business relations, trust, and honesty or 'let's rethink the history of relationship marketing'. *Journal of Historical Research in Marketing*, 7(3): 407–422.

Tadajewski, M. and Saren, M. (2008) The past is a foreign country: Amnesia and marketing theory. *Marketing Theory*, 8(4): 323–338.

Tarde, G. (1962) *The Laws of Imitation*, trans. E.W.C Parsons, Gloucester, MA: Peter Smith.

Vargha, Z. (2010) Technologies of persuasion: Personal selling and the making of markets is consumer finance. PhD thesis, Columbia University.

Vargha, Z. (2011) From long-term savings to instant mortgages: Financial demonstration and the role of interaction in markets. *Organization*, 18(2): 215–235.

Yates, J. (2005) *Structuring the Information Age: Life Insurance and Technology in the Twentieth Century*. Baltimore, MD: Johns Hopkin University Press.

Zelizer, V.A. (2005) *The Purchase of Intimacy*, Princeton, NJ: Princeton University Press.

Zwick, D. and Pridmore, J. (2011) Marketing and the rise of commercial consumer surveillance. *Surveillance and Society*, 8(3): 269–277.

7 'My story has ~~no~~ strings attached'
Credit cards, market devices and a stone guest

José Ossandón

Introduction: seeing like a credit card

The title of this article comes from an advertisement I first encountered a couple of years ago outside a store located on the campus of the University of California, Irvine (Figure 7.1). The text of the campaign was: 'My story has no strings attached. With no late fees and no penalty rate, the Citi Simplicity Card keeps life simple.' This slogan connects the two main conceptual and methodological challenges the chapter tries to unfold.

First, 'Citi Simplicity Card keeps life simple'. This sentence informs potential customers they can relax because there are no late fees or penalty rates that they should be concerned about. But, at the same time, by highlighting that it is simplicity that makes this product unique, the campaign implies that customers should not necessarily expect pleasant surprises when dealing with credit cards. The starting point seems to be that credit cards are

Figure 7.1 City Simplicity advertisement, Irvine, CA
Source: photo by the author.

opaque economic goods. And, no doubt, they are. Credit cards are certainly opaque for consumers trying to understand interest rates and fees, not to mention the complicated markets where their personal data and debt are securitised and exchanged. At the same time, although credit issuers certainly have a better grasp of fees, interest rates and the secondary markets of data and debt, cards, as will be explained in some detail in the following sections, are not simply transparent objects for them. Credit issuers gather massive amounts of data, but this data is limited to what can be digitally traced, credit cards also play crucial parts in secondary economies that cannot be observed by credit issuers' own data collection devices.

In grappling with the opaqueness of credit cards, this chapter combines stories gathered at two different fieldwork sites. On the one hand, by using credit card statements as financial diaries and in-depth interviews, the chapter reconstructs and maps credit transactions carried out by the inhabitants of twelve households in low-income areas in Santiago, Chile. On the other hand, based on forty in-depth interviews with senior executives and regulators (most of them risk managers of department stores and banks and executives from other institutions, such as debt-collection companies, regulatory bodies and industry associations), it points to the particular risks faced by, and marketing strategies of, consumer credit lenders in Chile.[1] These two kinds of material are not combined to obtain a privileged, panoramic point of view on the subject of interest. Rather, it is only through the study of the practices of credit card users that I can observe the blindness of data managers and, vice versa, it is only through the study of data-management practices that I can see what the card users cannot see. Mine, therefore, is a second-order observation (Esposito, 2014; Frankel, 2014; Ossandón, 2014a; Stark, 2014) of observations performed from two different positions in domestic finance. But, perhaps more importantly, it is by combining the information collected in these different sites that I, as a researcher, can deal with the opaqueness of credit cards as economic objects.

The methodological approach followed here, in this sense, might fit with the type of anthropology recently defended by Bill Maurer and colleagues. In their words: 'This kind of anthropological analysis stands in relation to its objects not as sign to signifier (in which the goal is an adequate description of the world), but as itself a channel that brings other relations into focus as objects of joint attention' (Maurer et al., 2013: 56, discussing Kockelman, 2010).

In this case, the objects of joint attention are credit cards. And cards are not observed from one point of view, but rather from different sites. From each site, different relations are brought forward, calling also for different questions and concepts. The sections of this chapter address the different questions encountered in this process of joint attention.

Second, 'the strings attached'. A page on the online Wiktionary connects the expression 'No strings attached' with this strange story:

> In ancient times, documents that were written on parchment had strings that were used to tie them shut, after they were rolled up. The Babylonian

Talmud in Tractate Bava Metzi'a mentions an example of a man who gives his wife a get (bill of divorce) with a string attached, but holds on to the string, so that he can snatch it back (apparently because he is unwilling to actually give her a divorce). According to Jewish law, this is not a valid divorce, because the man has not properly delivered the get, by freely giving it to his wife.

(Wiktionary, 2015)

Now, note the next quotation taken from Michel Serres' *The Natural Contract*:

The bond is doubtless the first quasi-object suited to making our relations visible and concrete; the real chains of obligation, which are light and unburdensome within a space, weigh us down at its edges... All in all, its triple tress links me to forms, to things, and to others, and thus initiates me into abstraction, the world, and society. Through its channel pass information, forces, and laws. In a cord can be found all the objective and collective attributes of Hermes.

(Serres, 1995: 107–8)

The story from the Talmud does not refer only to the hidden conditions of a particular contract, nor does it refer to the particular relations with those goods that captivate or even capture us, which have been associated with the term 'attachment' (Latour, 2013; Hennion, 2015; Deville, 2014) in the recent social studies of markets. Strings or bonds or cords, as Serres explains, connect things and people, they produce collectives. The same, or so it is argued here, can be said about credit cards. Cards are not only opaque, technically black-boxed 'market devices' (Muniesa et al., 2007), but they are also economic objects that assemble new, though not always easy to grasp, collectives. This chapter uses the metaphor of strings attached to refer to the collectives assembled with credit cards.

Another term explored by Serres (2007), which fits nicely with the issues analysed here, is that of the parasite. His book *The Parasite* is about observation and the observation of observations. The host cannot see the uninvited guests or parasite. But the guests cannot see if they have been observed by someone else. Only an 'excluded third', one that is neither host nor guest, can observe their relation. But the excluded third can also become a parasite, and so on. The logic of money (and so credit cards, we can argue) is also parasitical (Serres, 2007). Not only can money and cards be exchanged with almost everything, but using them usually comes with a cost. As parasites, they transform what they mediate. They separate, they make things and people into objects of calculation, but they also connect, produce new circuits, populations, collectives. Thanks to Serres, we already understand this. This chapter describes *how* this happens. It narrates a journey that followed some of the hidden strings attached to credit cards and, by doing so, mapped some of the parts played by cards in the multiple collectives they have been helping to assemble.[2]

Luisa

Luisa (not her real name, a pseudonym as are all other informants' names in this chapter) is a 54-year-old housewife who lives in the municipality of La Pintana, south of Santiago. Seven others live in her household: her husband Patrick, her children Nacho, Paty and Andrea, her son-in-law Rafael and her grandchildren Camila and Cristian. Luisa also has a fourth daughter Katia, who lives with her husband Rodrigo in the same neighbourhood. Luisa's husband works as a freelance painter sporadically, and he earns on average Ch$150,000 (US$312) a month. In addition to housework, Luisa manages a *kiosco* or small shop in her home, which earns her between Ch$20–30,000 a month. Andrea and her husband work and take care of their own expenses. Paty, in turn, is unemployed and so receives help from her parents to cover her expenses and those of her daughter. Nacho is studying nursing with the support of a state-guaranteed loan and recently has begun to receive his first income as an occasional construction worker.

Luisa has a savings account, an emergency fund of Ch$40,000 cobbled together with money from the kiosk in the BancoEstado, a state-owned financial institution. Since Luisa and her husband have informal jobs, neither has access to checking accounts or bank loans. Luisa is, however, an active participant in three informal financial institutions, two *pollas* (rotating savings organisations) and a *caja común* ('common fund') that functions as a Christmas savings club. The *caja* can also be used as a source of credit, but under certain restrictions. Loans must be repaid with interest, there are fines for late payments and, if a member misses her quota for three consecutive dates, she is removed from the group and the money she has contributed up to that point is not returned to her.

Like many other Chileans, Luisa also has access to loans facilitated by retail companies and their credit cards. As I have summarised elsewhere:

> While loans provided by banks and other institutions have increased in the last years (Morales and Yáñez 2006), the most impressive expansion has been in department store credit. In a country with a population of about 17 million, the amount of bank credit cards increased from 1,310,325 in 1993 to 4,499,627 in 2007, while retail credit cards expanded from 1,350,000 to 19,273,919 in the same period (Montero and Tarziján 2010). In other words, there are more than four retail cards per bank card in Chile (while this rate is 0.9 in the USA; 1.5 in Brazil; 0.25 in Colombia and 0.4 in Mexico; Montero and Tarziján 2010); and store card transactions almost triplicate those of bank cards (SBFI 2010). Furthermore, in today's Chile, retail cards are not merely used to get instalment credit, but they can also be used as credit cards in a growing network of associated stores and as medium to get 'cash advances' and other personal loans.
>
> (Ossandón, 2014c: 430)

According to the 2011–12 Chile Central Bank's Finance Survey, 58 per cent of Chilean households owe consumer credit debt, 23 per cent hold unsecured loans from banks and 45 per cent hold unsecured loans from retailers (Banco Central, 2013). These numbers are unevenly distributed, as the richer households have equal access to banks and department store credit, while those with lower incomes have access primarily to credit issued by department stores and supermarkets.

Ten years ago, Luisa acquired her first credit card in the department store La Polar and a few years later ended up with cards from the department stores Paris, Corona, Tricot, Fashion Park and the pharmacy chain Salcobrand. Two years ago, however, after feeling that her debts were spiralling out of control, she closed the Tricot, Fashion Park and Salcobrand cards and, a year before our conversation, a loan renegotiation ended with La Polar blocking her card; currently, she only holds cards from Paris and Corona.

Luisa uses these store cards in various ways. For example, between September 2011 and February 2012, she used the Paris card to purchase two pairs of sneakers for her son, a cell phone for herself and merchandise in a supermarket which is part of the same business group as the store and where this card is also accepted. Each purchase was paid for in six instalments. She also used the Corona card for a cash advance. But Luisa did not use her cards only for her own purchases. For example, Luisa lent her Paris card nine times to her daughter Andrea – three times for instalment purchases of merchandise, another five times to purchase goods in the shop and once for a cash advance consisting of six instalments of 15,000 pesos each. In addition, Luisa lent her card from La Polar to her daughter Andrea to buy a refrigerator; and her Corona card for an advance of ten instalments of 10,000 pesos. Luisa has also lent her La Polar card to her daughter Katya for a cash advance and for a furniture purchase, and the Corona card to her daughter Paty to buy an iron in ten instalments. On two other occasions, moreover, Luisa's son-in-law Rafael used her Corona card, once to buy himself sneakers and another time to buy a cell phone for his son.

In our study of the financial practices of twelve households in three municipalities in low-income sectors of Santiago, we encountered many similar stories. Obviously, we anticipated that, just as it is common for Chileans to lend health insurance vouchers to one another, it would likewise be expected that they also lend retail credit cards to one another. What we did not expect was the degree of pervasiveness and complexity of such practices of borrowing and lending of retail store credit cards. Thus, in every home we visited, we encountered such lending and borrowing organised in complex ways. Card lending came to constitute one of the main objects of our inquiry.

The sociology of card lending

It is not difficult to associate the practice of borrower-to-borrower card lending with the basic principles of the New Economic Sociology, as formulated three decades ago by Mark Granovetter (1985). At first glance, credit cards might appear to be an individual thing, owned and managed by the person whose name is on the card, but a closer observation of card lending reveals a parallel and collective circuit of debt – that is, a social network. Still, how and what might we see were we to examine the lending of credit cards as a network? What are the nodes and types of relations? How to classify the types of actors involved?

As explained in further detail elsewhere (Ossandón et al., forthcoming), we pursued an experimental path to understanding such lending networks. Instead of working directly with relational data visualisation software, we decided to embrace the flexibility afforded by using our own hands. Figure 7.2[3] visualises the case of Luisa. The figure is split in four rows. Pins in rows 1, 3 and 4 represent people. The two pins in the first row, from up to down, represent Luisa and her husband, the seven pins in the third row represent Luisa's daughters, son and their partners and the two pins below Luisa's grandchildren. The three larger pins in the second row represent retail store cards. In this case, Luisa is the only one that 'owns' cards – one from Paris, one from Corona and another from La Polar. The yarn threads represent uses of a card involving some form of credit, and they connect the person that receives the loan of the card with the credit card used for the transaction. As can be seen, Luisa has used her three cards for personal transactions, but the same cards have also been used by her daughters and sons-in-law. We completed similar exercises with the other eleven households.

After several attempts, the images displayed here have left us satisfied as a good way of visualising our data (Ossandón et al., forthcoming), but the central question remains unanswered. As has already been said, credit card lending practices produce networks. But what kind of collective or social formation are we talking about? One possible answer could be that card lending

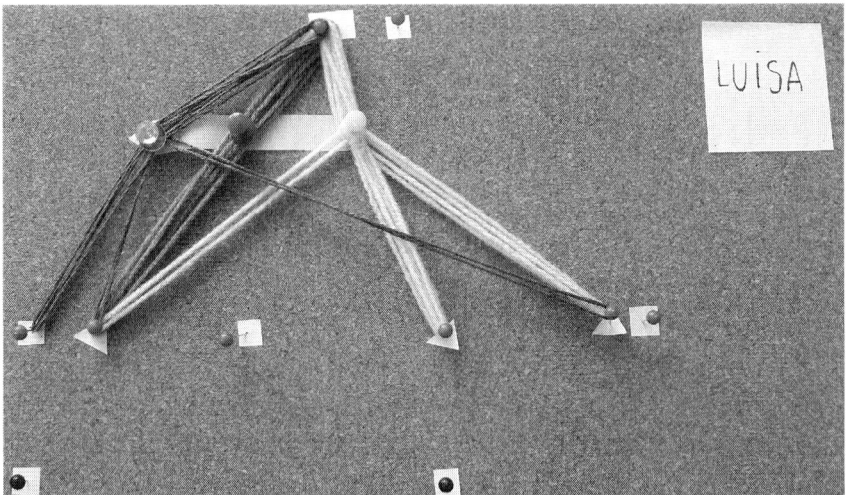

Figure 7.2 Luisa's card transactions
Source: © José Ossandón.

reflects existing collectives such as the nuclear family (Figure 7.3). As is evident in the case of Luisa, however, card lending can span different family units living together in the same residence. A second option could be the family or extended kinship network. Luisa not only lends her cards to her family members living in the same property, but also to her daughter Paty, who lives in another house. In several of the cases studied, however, we found card lending extending beyond the family to friends and neighbours. The case shown in Figure 7.4, of two homes connected through two friends, is instructive in this respect.

A more suitable starting point is Julia Elyachar's (2010) notion of 'phatic labour'. *Phatic* she draws from Malinowski's remark that communication is not only used 'for the purpose of conveying any information in particular' (p. 453) but for the sake of communicating itself, and *labour* she uses in Marx's sense. 'Phatic labour' thus refers to the work of producing new 'social infrastructures

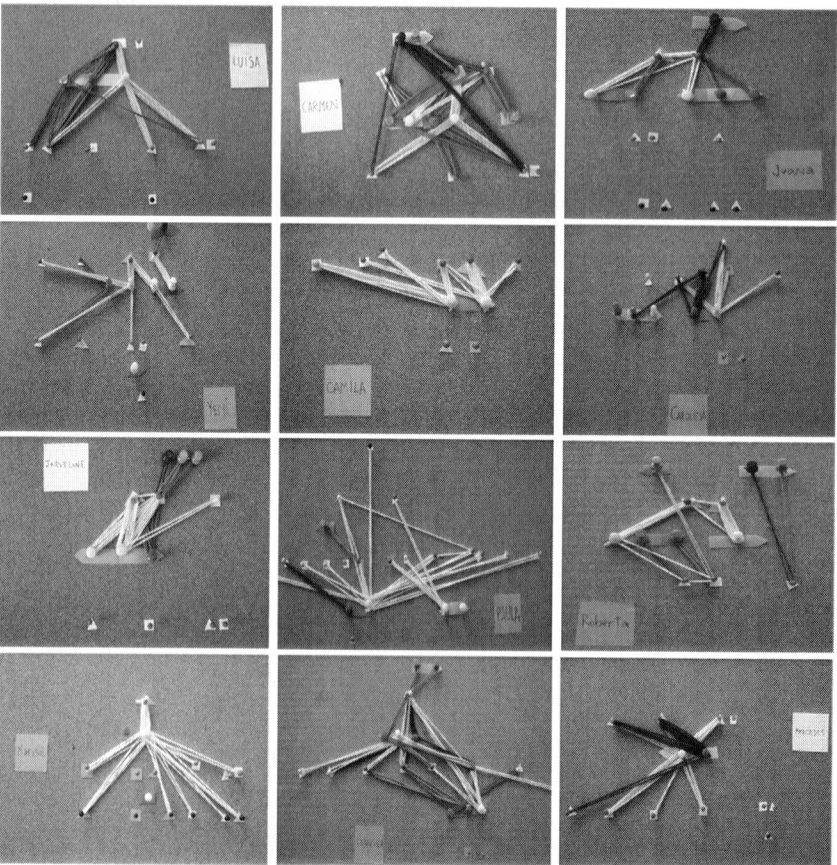

Figure 7.3 Visualisation of card-lending networks
Source: © José Ossandón.

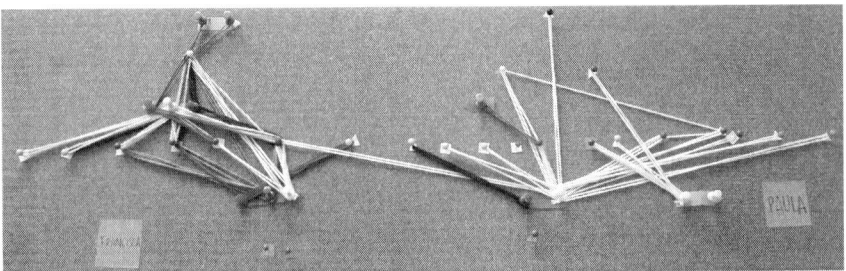

Figure 7.4 Francisca and Paula's transactions
Source: © José Ossandón.

of communicative channels' (p. 120) by (especially female) inhabitants from poor countries that also become crucial economic resources as recognised by non-governmental organisations and micro lenders. It could be argued that card lending travels along and reinforces the phatic channels produced by everyday forms of communication. But what is being lent? What is the medium of these channels?

Viviana Zelizer's (2010) notion of 'commercial circuits' helps here. Zelizer's circuits are webs of economic transfers among a delimited group of actors, who bestow upon these transactions a shared meaning, a clear line of belonging, and make use of a particular medium of payment. Each of these networks of credit card lending functions as a commercial circuit that frames or connects to existing collectives – neighbourhoods, families or households – but that also has its own emergent character and forms of inclusion and exclusion. Indeed, an important part of the interviews revolved around the edges or boundaries drawn when a commitment is broken and how the limits of these circuits can be re-established. Moreover, such circuits entail a system of parallel calculations, which are in fact often written and drawn in the margins of the monthly bill (Ossandón et al., forthcoming). People do not lend money to each other. Rather, what is lent, or even exchanged, is the capacity to borrow and go into debt. The medium in this circuit is the credit limit of the different cards involved.

The credit limit, however, is an economic object that is delimited elsewhere. Accordingly, to understand how it works, it is important to move to a different site – to the stores from where credit is issued – and to its own characters – risk managers and their algorithms.

Sowing consumers with retail credit

Consumer credit is what is known as an unsecured form of lending; no collateral or guarantee is set aside to back the debt. This does not mean these loans are made under conditions of pure uncertainty. Banks in Chile for instance use 'structural' social data (such as information about income, job contract and patrimony) to screen in and out their customers. Retailers use this kind of information, too, but for them it is more important to screen customers via their credit behaviour. If a customer's credit is well managed and debts are paid on time, retailers will increase the credit limit assigned to a card. I have explained this process in more detail elsewhere (see Box 7.1).

Box 7.1 Sowing consumers with retail credit in Chile (taken from Ossandón, 2014c: 440–4)

The process can start, for instance, when someone is about to buy any item and, if he/she is not already a customer of that specific store, this person will be asked whether he/she would like to participate in a contest, with the only requisite to provide the client's ID number. This number will be automatically cross-checked with the information collected by some of the available commercial bureaus… If the client is not registered as defaulter, a store card will be offered to him/her. To get the card, though, the customer will have to provide some extra information: particularly, place of residence and to press a fingerprint detector. The address is georeferenced (to locate, for instance, areas of the city that are considered not 'good' for debt collection) and the fingerprint is connected with 'Previred', a side business of the private pension funds that provides provisional information… The sales person will probably also do what is known as 'to turn the customer's wallet inside out', that is, to check whether the potential client has other credit cards or, in other words, has been screened by another institution, for instance, the stricter banks. The collected information will be contrasted with the store's statistical models and the case will be associated to a specific category, score and its correlated credit limit. All in less than five minutes.

Here is the main difference between banks and stores. Chilean banks do not only take much longer to evaluate a new client, but they will not open a credit account for a customer without income or another type of collateral. Stores, on the other hand, tend to exclude only those that have previously defaulted or are associated to very specific risk patterns (for instance, considering place of residence). Instead, what stores do with those customers that lack collateral or have a low income is to grant them a very small credit line (i.e. US$100 or less). Certainly, risk managers know that this is a risky operation. In fact, they assume that an important number of the new customers will default. However, they see these losses as marketing expenses, the price paid for attracting new card holders. They are more interested in starting a long relationship with those that will not default.

This is when the second moment of the credit process starts. After screening, the most important information about cardholders is not their income or any other external source, but instead their commercial behaviour: what do they do (and do they not do) with their cards. Depending on this behaviour the credit limit varies. For instance: if the customer of the example does not only accept the card that was offered to him/her, but uses it and pays the instalments back on time, he/she will be granted a credit ceiling update, which will be extended again in case the 'good' pattern continues. The limit for these extensions will be the ceilings of the particular category in the matrix where the customer has been located... It is this form of management that is known as 'to sow':

> Try to imagine this: we could spend 10 or 15 thousand trying to capture new customers, so instead, why not try a quick transaction at the cash register. We offer them something, let's say $30,000 [US$60] in credit, and, let's be extreme, half of them fail. With these small credits we have only spent $15,000 on each. You can say, but 50% is a risk rate that no-one can afford, but you can, with micro-credits you can. This is why it is known as 'to sow', because when you sow you spread many seeds, but seeds are small, and we want them to become big plants, and some of these seeds blossom and others die, but that part that dies, dies with small credits, with these others, what we call 'green buds', the idea is to grant them bigger credits to make them properly profitable.
>
> (Interview 3, risk manager, department store, own translation)

What replaces collateral in department stores' consumer credit products in Chile is individual behaviour. The more a card is used 'correctly' (i.e. debts are paid on due time), the more secure that customer will be seen by a store's risk-management systems, and accordingly a higher credit limit will be granted to him or her. This picture, however, is questioned by the commercial circuits described above. It might be instead that store-issued credit works invisibly as a case of what Biggart and Castanias (2001) named 'collateralized social relations'. Like in micro finance, credit card loans would be backed by social relations that make repayment more likely. It is in this sense that what has been presented so far can be read along the already traditional lines of the Granovetterian New Economic Sociology. The language of behavioural scoring, wrongly, describes credit card lending in undersocialised terms, when it is instead embedded in social networks. But, are retailers really blind to collectives?

Let's go back to the circuits of card lending visualised in the previous section. They are a kind of network, but they are not about just any network. In the technical terminology of social network analysis, these are '2-Mode networks', since the actors are connected not directly to each other, but through nodes of a different kind. Specifically, what we have here are people connected to each other through their use of a common card. The cards, in turn, are not just any node. They are 'market devices' (or what Latour (2013) recently termed 'value meters') inserted in a sociotechnical assemblage oriented towards collecting transactional data (Savage and Burrows, 2007). Unlike traditional commercial exchange, whose mode of payment is cash and for which there is no record besides the receipt, every transaction carried out with a card is recorded, as the bills we receive at the end of each month stubbornly remind us. This information is central to the operation of department store credit, which statistically evaluates the behaviour of each customer. Retailers, or the retailers' algorithms, observe the information traced by credit cards in terms of risk. Risk works by pooling, assembling statistical populations. To use a term popularised by Deleuze: risk management is about *dividuals* not individuals (Deleuze, 2006; Langley, 2014). It is at this level that the metaphor of sowing used in the department store industry in Chile works (see Box 7.1). A garden is composed of many seeds and many of them will never grow. An investment is valued not in terms of specific individuals but in terms of a population. As with insurance companies (Ossandón, 2014b), retailers are not blind to collectives: a key part of their business is to actually assemble a population, and the credit limit accessed by each customer is based on this invisible collective amongst whom risk is spread.

Retail-issued credit cards are not therefore part of just one but two different types of collective. They are part of circuits of card lending which are personalised, case-to-case social networks. And they are part also of statistical populations which are impersonal, digital, big data-based sociotechnical networks. Mechanical and organic solidarities: formal and informal economies coexisting in the same assemblage (Wilkis, 2014). Suddenly our case is not about explaining the economy by way of the social, but is instead a comparative analysis of two different social formations emerging with consumer credit. What is embedded in what? Concepts more suitable than those of the New Economic Sociology were developed by Michel Serres in his *The Parasite*. To conclude, let's then parasite *The Parasite*.

A stone guest whose host is already a parasite

> This is the good botanical model, and botany, as we shall soon see, is the queen of sciences and of all parasitic detours.
>
> (Serres, 2007: 111)

Credit cards are not just any kind of economic object. Credit cards are market devices that trace each single transaction. Credit cards can even be tools for 'gardening' (Cochoy, 2007). Sowing is the term used in Chile's retail industry to name the marketing strategy that consists of extending the credit limits of low-income customers depending on their payment behaviour. Data on previous transactions – behaviour – thus replaces collateral. But, credit cards are not only used by the persons whose name is in the cards. Some borrow cards, while others loan them or, more precisely, the cards' credit limit. Can social relations therefore be parasites on credit – uninvited guests whose host is already a parasite?

> The parasited one parasites the parasites. One of the first, he jumps to the last position. But the one in the last position wins this game. He has discovered the position of the philosopher.
>
> (Serres, 2007: 13)

Cards are strange objects that project a different social shadow depending from where you see them. Consumers can see their cards and the circuit of people that use them. As their credit limits grow they can also guess at the operation of the retailers' algorithms but consumers cannot see them, nor can they see the population, or the garden, in which they have been located. Risk managers, meanwhile, can trace and follow every single transaction carried out with the cards associated to their stores and can pool their users into statistical populations, but they cannot see the circuits of card lending which leave no digital trace.

Drawing on fieldwork carried out at two different sites, the site of domestic uses of credit cards and department stores' risk management, the current chapter reports my observation of these two different modes of observing and their respective forms of blindness. I am the excluded third party in this story, one who can observe both circuits and populations. But, am I alone?

> The only information that comes out of the black box is that there is a channel through which information passes. The only message that comes out of the path is that there is a path by which messages pass. A thread comes out of the box. The only thing that passes in the channel is the name of the channel.
>
> (Serres, 2007: 240)

No I am not. I am not the only excluded third party. Credit cards in Chilean stores were born as 'marketing devices' that aimed to ease the attachment between consumers and the goods being sold (Ossandón, 2014c). Later on, credit turned out to be a profitable business in its own right. It is in this sense that, in the retail industry (Trumbull, 2014), credit is sometimes seen as a dangerous parasite that can end up eating its host. But retail credit cards are not only about marketing and credit management. As with 'mobile money' in Africa (Maurer et al., 2013), retailers in Chile are also competing to provide the medium of payment for those whose income is not enough to consume without credit. It is not only about enhancing the purchase of particular goods or extending payment schedules to profit from the charging of interest, it is also about providing a particular channel of payment and charging fees for its use. From this perspective, it does not matter much whether the channel is a statistical population or a circuit of commerce. Both are good infrastructures for extending the use of department store cards as means of payment.

To paraphrase Latour's (2013: 426) playful use of the notion of embeddedness, payment does not lie on a single social bed, but on two at the same time. Payment networks parasite two different collectives to become a network of their own. The channel is not the conduit but the parasite. To make things still more complicated, payment is not the only channel in this story. The circuits of card lending are based on forms of *phatic labour* which create and transform their own communicative channels (Elyachar, 2010; Kockelman, 2010). Card lending is enabled by the risk-management practice known as sowing and it makes use of the retailers' payment networks, but it also crosses them. Credit card lending creates a new sort of financial activity based on the exchange of credit limit of cards issued by different companies which also makes possible a new kind of social infrastructure.

And here is where this journey finishes. Following the strings attached to credit cards we have found two different types of collective (population and circuits), two types of financial activity (card lending and consumer credit) and two different channels. Credit cards, however, remain opaque to us. But maybe it is because they are the ultimate parasite. 'The parasite is really a joker, or wild card, who takes on different values depending on its position in a system' (Kockelman, 2010: 412). And perhaps the best way to know about them is by describing the set of nodes they replace, in as many networks as they take part.

Acknowledgements

Earlier versions and portions of this text were posted on the blogs of the *Institute for Money, Technology and Financial Inclusion, Estudios de la Economía* and *Charisma: Consumer Market Studies*. The English version of one of these posts was kindly translated by Taylor Nelms and Smoki Musaraj. Discussions with Joe Deville, Bill Maurer, Liz McFall and Viviana Zelizer have been very helpful. I also thank for comments on presentations, blog posts and earlier versions of this document, Tomás Ariztía, Nicholas D'Avella, Christian Borch, Franck Cochoy, Ann-Christina Lange, John Law, Mariana Luzzi, Sean Mallin, Smoki Musaraj, Manuel Tironi and Tomás Undurraga. Last but not least, many thanks for the time and help given by those that kindly accepted to be interviewed for this project.

Notes

1 Interviews with executives were conducted in two stages: between October 2010 and January 2011, and between September and December 2011. The information collected in the interviews has been complemented with a review of secondary documents and participant observation during the main annual convention of the Chilean credit and debt-collection industry in 2010. This work was funded by Chile's National Fund for Scientific and Technological Development (Project 11090375). Felipe González, Camila Peralta and Felipe Ubeira provided important assistance in the process of collecting the information. Fieldwork with users of credit cards was carried out in 2011 and 2012 and was funded by the Institute for Money, Technology and Financial Inclusion at the University of California, Irvine. The research team of this latter project was led by the author of the current chapter and counted on the collaboration of Tomás Ariztía, Macarena Barros and Camila Peralta. Further information about the methods and results of each project can be found in Ossandón (2014c) and Ossandón et al. (forthcoming). The later piece is a methodological reflection that directly complements the current chapter.

2 The chapter, therefore, does not try to solve the discussion about whether credit cards are part of socially embedded or disembedded transactions. Think for instance about the heated debate a decade ago between Daniel Miller (2005) and

Michel Callon (2005). Are credit cards parts of perfect commodity exchanges, cut and detached from previous relations? Or, are they objects, like Zelizer's (1978) insurance, that instead of cutting us from others, help us to reinforce previously existing bonds? This chapter does not try to answer, as do Alya Guseva and Akos Rona-Tas (2001), whether it is possible to distinguish between arms' length and embedded credit card operations. Here I am more interested in the process of knitting or assembling collectives through the strings attached to credit cards.

3   For colour versions of these images, see a previous Working Paper version of this chapter available at: www.imtfi.uci.edu/files/blog_working_papers/2014-3_Ossa ndon_Working%20Paper%202.pdf.

Bibliography

Banco Central (2013) Encuesta Financiera de Hogares: Metodología y Principales Resultados EFH 2011–12. www.bcentral.cl/estadisticas-economicas/financiera- hoga res/pdf/Resultados_EFH_2011–12.pdf.

Biggart, N.W. and Castanias, R.P. (2001) Collateralized social relations: The social in economic calculation. *American Journal of Economics and Sociology*, 60(2): 471–500.

Callon, M. (2005) Why virtualism paves the way to political impotence. A reply to Daniel Miller's critique of The Laws of the Markets. *Economic Sociology: European Electronic Newsletter*, 6(2): 3–20.

Cochoy, F. (2007) A sociology of market-things: On tending the garden of choices in mass retailing. *Sociological Review*, 55(s2): 109–129.

Deleuze, G. (2006) Post-scriptum sobre las Sociedades de Control. *Polis. Revista Latinoamericana*, 13.

Deville, J. (2014) Consumer credit default and collections: The shifting ontologies of market attachment. *Consumption Markets and Culture*, 17(5): 468–490.

Elyachar, J. (2010) Phatic labor, infrastructure, and the question of empowerment in Cairo. *American Ethnologist*, 37(3): 452–464.

Esposito, E. (2014) Circularidades económicas y observación de segundo orden: La realidad de las calificaciones crediticias. *Revista Mad*, 30: 1–24.

Frankel, C. (2014) ¿Dentro o fuera? O: ¿Dejarías a un luhmanniano invertir tu dinero? *Revista Mad*, 30: 49–60.

Granovetter, M. (1985) Economic action and social structure: The problem of embeddedness. *American Journal of Sociology*, 91(3): 481–510.

Guseva, A. and Rona-Tas, A. (2001) Uncertainty, risk, and trust: Russian and American credit card markets compared. *American Sociological Review*, 66(5): 623–646.

Hennion, A. (2015) Paying attention: What is tasting wine about? In A.B. Antal, M. Hutter and D. Stark (eds), *Moments of Valuation: Exploring Sites of Dissonance*, Oxford: Oxford University Press, pp. 37–56.

Kockelman, P. (2010) Enemies, parasites, and noise: How to take up residence in a system without becoming a term in it. *Journal of Linguistic Anthropology*, 20(2): 406–421.

Langley, P. (2014) Equipping entrepreneurs: Consuming credit and credit scores. *Consumption Markets and Culture*, 17(5): 448–467.

Latour, B. (2013) *An Inquiry into Modes of Existence*, Cambridge, MA: Harvard University Press.

Maurer, B., Nelms, T.C. and Rea, S.C. (2013) 'Bridges to cash': Channelling agency in mobile money. *Journal of the Royal Anthropological Institute*, 19(1): 52–74.

Miller, D. (2005) Reply to Michel Callon. *Economic Sociology: Electronic Newsletter,* 6(3): 3–13.

Muniesa, F., Millo, Y. and Callon, M. (2007) An introduction to market devices. *Sociological Review,* 55(s2): 1–12.

Ossandón, J. (2014a). Enmarcando las redes de observaciones en la reciente sociología de las finanzas. *Revista Mad,* 30: 39–48.

Ossandón, J. (2014b). Reassembling and cutting the social with health insurance. *Journal of Cultural Economy,* 7(3): 291–307.

Ossandón, J. (2014c). Sowing consumers in the garden of mass retailing in Chile. *Consumption Markets and Culture,* 17(5): 429–447.

Ossandón, J., Ariztía, T., Barros, M. and Peralta, C. (forthcoming). Accounting in the margin: Financial ecologies in between big and small data. In B. Maurer, S. Musaraj and I. Small (eds), *Money at the Margins: Global Perspectives on Technology, Financial Inclusion & Design.*

Savage, M. and Burrows, R. (2007) The coming crisis of empirical sociology. *Sociology,* 41(5): 885–899.

Serres, M. (1995) *The Natural Contract,* Ann Arbor: University of Michigan Press.

Serres, M. (2007) *The Parasite,* Minneapolis: University of Minnesota Press.

Stark, D. (2014) Observando las finanzas como una red de observaciones: Un comentario a Esposito. *Revista Mad,* 30: 25–38.

Trumbull, G. (2014) *Consumer Lending in France and America Credit and Welfare,* Cambridge: Cambridge University Press.

Wiktionary.org (2015) *No Strings Attached.* https://en.wiktionary.org/wiki/no_strings_attached (accessed 9 September 2015).

Wilkis, A. (2014) Sociología del crédito y economía de las clases populares. *Revista Mexicana de Sociología,* 76(2): 225–252.

Zelizer, V.A. (1978) Human values and the market: The case of life insurance and death in 19th-century America. *American Journal of Sociology,* 84(5): 591–610.

Zelizer, V.A. (2010) *Economic Lives: How Culture Shapes the Economy,* Princeton, NJ: Princeton University Press.

8 From market relations to romantic ties

The tests of internet dating

Emmanuel Kessous

The way in which intimate relationships are evolving in contemporary societies is putting a greater strain on romantic projects. According to Allan Bloom, 'isolation, a sense of lack of profound contact with other human beings' is the syndrome of a prevalent form of contemporary discomfort. He argues that people no longer talk of love or friendship, but of romantic or friendly relationships, terms that he sees as signalling business ties, such as contracts, more than human attachments. 'This abstract term', he wrote about the relationship, 'puts citizenship, family, love and friendship under the same makeshift tent and abstracts from their very different foundations and demands' (Bloom, 1993: 14). Bloom furthermore pointed out that people multiply relations in the hope of obtaining particular advantages in an uncertain future. Paradoxically, this relational economy increases the pressure to maintain relationships. From a more progressive standpoint, Anthony Giddens talks of 'pure relationships' to qualify 'a situation where a social relation is entered into for its own sake, for what can be derived by each person from a sustained association with another; and which is continued only in so far as it is thought by both parties to deliver enough satisfactions for each individual to stay within it' (Giddens, 1992: 58). In this context, internet dating sites, like social networking platforms, are useful tools for singles looking to compensate for their lack of affection (Kaufmann, 2010). The first such sites even seemed ideal for coordinating such uninhibited matchmaking in a society where individuals' worth is characterised above all by their ability to take care of themselves and to embark on new projects (Boltanski and Chiapello, 2005). Many single men and women with diverse tastes, physical features and spatio-social properties frequent these sites, which in their design resemble two-sided markets. In industrial economics, 'two-sided markets' consist of two independent and interdependent customer bases (Rochet and Tirole, 2003). In the case in point, there is a market between men and dating websites, and another market between women and those same sites. These two 'sides' of the market can only exist because of the interdependencies between the two 'customer bases'. The role of this technology is to enable them to reveal their respective qualities to others, in order to find the right match. However, a closer analysis reveals a far more complex reality. First, contrary to popular belief, the motivations and levels of commitment of the individuals who frequent these sites vary widely. Some are there to find reassurance after a break-up, others to seduce and others for entertainment or simply to satisfy their curiosity. Second, the information provided is sometimes partial or deliberately false, which implies a prolonged experience and making 'mistakes' before the hope of identifying the fortunate chosen one. Moving from a qualified mode of coordination for market relations to true rapport is the seemingly impossible challenge of internet dating.

The analysis in this chapter is based on a methodology that combines various data collected over a period from 2006 to 2008. These included ethnographic studies, adverts on websites and qualitative confirmatory interviews (three men and two women). Contact was made, via the websites,[1] with fifty-five women aged 30–40, to inquire about their online dating experiences. Each of these interviews served to deepen my knowledge of strategies of self-exposure, predominantly of women, but also via their accounts, of men. Note that the survey concerned only heterosexual exchanges – otherwise the article could be read as a heteronormative account that makes invisible the online market for same-sex encounters. It also excluded many types of dating (one-night stands, partner swapping, religion- or community-based dating, teenage dating, dating between older persons, etc.). Several popular French websites were studied, in particular 'Meetic' and 'adopteunmec'.[2]

The chapter considers the means of creating emotional attachments between heterosexual individuals – to simplify, I talk of romantic ties – using internet dating platforms. In particular, I look at the hurdles that singles have to overcome to switch from a posture formatted for public, market relations, to one more in tune with personal, emotional relationships. There are essentially four such hurdles. The first concerns the risk of being trapped in a 'position of reification' (Honneth, 2008a) by potential lovers that precludes the emergence of emotional ties. The second relates to the opportunities that constructing a profile affords for the presentation of the self in ways that are designed to strengthen ties of friendship and mutual aid. The last two hurdles are closely intertwined: while the third concerns the salience of the initial contact, the fourth is about the need to focus on the singularities of the person selected, and from there to switch from the mode of market coordination – where the quality/price ratio[3] in a situation of incomplete information can always be perfected – to the personal emotional value derived from the meeting.

Reification: from data on the people to people who are like the data

Meeting someone on the internet amounts to going from a mechanism of public coordination where the relevant data are objectified and formatted to make them comparable, to more intimate relations with others where the data – whether they are expressed through words or bodies – are meaningful only for those who share them. The question is not so much the use of the market to initiate the relationship, as the place of this market coordination in the process of meeting in this way, and its compartmentalisation from the other more intimate and personal regime of engagement (Kessous, 2011b; Thévenot, 2006). In reference to Marx, Honneth (2008b) identifies the pathology of the social as the structural blocks preventing the realisation of a 'good life'. In another book (Honneth, 2008a), and as I will explain in greater detail below, he redefines Lukács' concept of reification as a form of 'forgetting' recognition. The other person is treated as a thing rather than being recognised as a partner with whom it is potentially possible to construct his or her life with (or at least go some of the way with, together).

In the social pathologies of dating sites, even if resorting to the market for mediation is not really a problem in itself, the market must remain in its rightful place, that is, the limited place where, in exchange for payment, it affords access to a service. Yet the objectification performed by data is nevertheless imposed on the actors who experiment with the features of dating sites. They use these features to frame a space of choice. When the weighing of these 'cold' data prevails over any other form of adjustment between the individuals, it tilts over into reification.

Naturalised individuals

Creating a matchmaking system based on market coordination requires the construction of categories to classify people. A first, fairly general series of categories sorts individuals by age, height and regional location. Another concerns the ideal partner's education and occupation. Qualification, in the sense of an industrial judgement of objectification, is at work even when a person has to characterise him or herself by the colour of their eyes or their hair, weight, religious beliefs or marital preferences. Singles looking for love thus find themselves with a list of individuals classified by category, presented in an order determined by criteria they have entered into the search engine as an initial filter. In this context, it is understandable that the media, in their – often critical – review of these types of dating, evoke the image of a supermarket. Turning this common perception around with humour, not unlike the way advertising frequently does, the site *adopteunmec* [*adoptaguy*] played with these symbolic representations, by presenting possible choices as if on the shelves of a supermarket, in which women place their chosen men into their shopping carts.

The list and types of categories that can be used to make these matches are one of the elements differentiating the sites. Some only have general pre-specified categories based on a user's cultural tastes (e.g. for country music, jazz, etc.), while others offer far more detailed options (e.g. the name of a musician, an album or the title of a film), based on a more detailed index in the database. It is thus possible for users to select fans of Transylvania Boogie by Frank Zappa, or those who prefer Lisboa Antiga by Amalia Rodrigues. These specifications concern a full range of social activities, from travelling to sexual practices. For instance, the site *adopteunmec* even allows women who wish to do so to specify their favourite sexual positions and whether they perform fellatio and/or practise sodomy.[4] Men are asked to specify their type of accommodation (house or flat) and the way in which it is fitted out: what sanitary fittings (bath or shower) it has, the size of the bed (single or double), its audio-visual equipment (computer, DVD player, projector, etc.). They can also specify their mode of transport (bicycle, scooter, motorbike, car, etc.) and any 'extras' they may have (garden, swimming pool, garage, jacuzzi, etc.).[5] Despite these gendered stereotypes, the website is presented by the designers as being respectful towards women because it is ultimately they who 'call the tune', given they can end a conversation at any point. When these selections are added to the site's other categories,[6] a broad palette of possible combinations opens up while reducing the number of candidates likely to correspond to the chosen criteria. It is thus possible for women, for example, to select a bisexual man with a good sense of humour and a paternal sensibility, who lives with his parents and owns a king-size bed, or, in contrast, a photographer who is good at DIY, does the cleaning, lives in a flatshare, has a goldfish and rides a scooter. Other more conventional categories (occupation, income – when specified, age, weight) are better calibrated for making calculations between equivalent matches.

Irrespective of the degree of detail in the categories proposed by the different websites, they all place on an equal footing information that is measured in conventional, standardised ways (size, weight, etc.) or framed in legal terms (nationality, marriage) and categories that are qualified far more subjectively (e.g. ethnic origin, dress style, character). In so doing, these platforms fulfil the wish of the hedonist: they break down the desired merchandise into a set of elementary properties so that consumers can fully exercise their rationality (Lancaster, 1966). The website categories open choice extensively to personal data – considered to be 'sensitive' under French law – and thus validate marginalist approaches. The latter consider that information on individuals in 'matchmaking' markets (whether the job market or the marriage market) should not be limited to the conventional qualities of the supplier (productivity or qualifications, on the job market) but should also include character and personality traits (Posner, 1981).

Yet if we look closer, we see that it would be difficult to obtain consensus on what a 'sensitive', 'lively' or 'demanding' person actually is. Moreover, all this information is very likely to trigger projections of the future relationship's daily life, of its success or failure. It is as if when two people meet via these sites, they have to make the best choice the first time round, without any knowledge derived from experience or trial and error. The cold and distant information supplied by users on these forms frames the start of relationships as a utopian ideal match. If the calculation is extremely well adjusted, theoretically it should be impossible for one partner in a couple to discover after a year, in the intimacy of the relationship, that the other person does not actually have all the characteristics specified on the forms. Yet it is entirely possible that the ties binding a couple form and strengthen, cementing their mutual attachment, despite – sometimes thanks to – individual imperfections. Also, certain selection criteria involve interpretation, despite their binary appearance. This is particularly true in the case of self-qualifications about marital status. Admitting that there is an existing relationship (a couple, a temporary partner, etc.) is a clear announcement of a preference for a short-lived affair. The opposite is true for other selections: for example indicating never to have been married or stating the wish for a permanent relationship. Ambiguity results either from the fact that this psychological introspection about which category to choose is not always as obvious as it seems for those making the selection, or because a user deliberately and strategically chooses to mask the truth to get their way. In other words, such information, apparently highly qualifying, is undecidable (Livet, 1994). Even if, as certain sociological approaches claim, people seek to match themselves up with someone who has the same or a higher social status (Singly, 1984), in reality they are in a situation of radical uncertainty. They cannot obtain this outcome through an act of economic calculation based on explicit, unquestionable variables. On the contrary, they have to rely on principles of judgement (Karpik, 2007).

Reification as forgetting recognition

As we can see, relying exclusively on data made public to make a match would involve inexorable difficulties. It would lead to people being treated 'as things', that is, to enter a process of reification. Before going any further and analysing how this reifying approach can be avoided, we need to clarify the concept. Georg Lukács argued that the process of rationalisation described by Max Weber, and the natural extension of the market to all social relations, makes reification second nature to the human species in a capitalist society. Axel Honneth sums up Lukács' position as follows: 'every subject involved in the capitalist form of life will necessarily acquire the habit of perceiving himself and the surrounding world as mere things and objects' (Honneth, 2008a: 23). Thus, for Lukács, reification is a market disposition, a *habitus*, corresponding to the contemplative attitude that enables subjects to be detached from the process through which they act on their social environment. Hence, reification implies an emotional shortcoming. Since it does not stem from a subjective choice, it cannot be considered as immoral. Honneth sums up the argument as follows: 'In the constantly expanding sphere of commodity exchange, subjects are compelled to behave as detached observers, rather than as active participants in social life, because their reciprocal calculation of the benefits that others might yield for their own profit demands a purely rational and emotionless stance' (pp. 24–5).

Honneth's reflection leads him to identify a different form of reification to Lukács. He analyses it as a matter of 'forgetting to recognize'. In this specific sense, reification must be understood as a deliberate restriction of attention, a form of amnesia, and not necessarily derived from the extension of a market process. This phenomenon is therefore reversible: 'forgetting' does not signify 'unlearning':

> Instead, a kind of reduced attentiveness must be at issue, which causes the fact of recognition to fall into the background and thus slip out of our sight. Reification in the sense of 'forgetfulness of recognition'; it therefore means that in the course of our acts of recognition, we lose our attentiveness to the fact that this cognition owes its existence to an antecedent act of recognition.
>
> (Honneth, 2008a: 59)

By displaying their personal data and by optimising their baskets of characteristics, actors end up forgetting that they are dealing with other individuals in the same position as themselves, whose bodies and minds are hidden by the mediating work of communications networks and computer screens.

The profile: presenting oneself through friendship connections

How does one go about recreating lost ties and enabling humans to treat one another as humans again? This requires putting aside data on objectified characteristics which, despite their personal appearances, remain rather impersonal, and instead focusing on another aspect of profile pages: the description which candidates use to introduce themselves and to briefly indicate what they are looking for. Many of these descriptions start by introducing a third person: 'I registered on the advice of a friend'. So, whether it is motivated by self-esteem (I'm here to please someone, it's not really me who took the decision), or by beliefs based on someone else's successful experience ('my best friend found her husband on this site, so why not give it a try'), the matchmaking moves from a relationship of two (or to be more exact, of two humans and two computers), to become a relationship of three. The single person is no longer an isolated individual, facing a market seen as a system; he or she has to refer to a third person, who acts as a coach.[7]

Presenting oneself through the personalised description

The description is the section in the profile that is instrumental in capturing the visitor's attention and making them want to get in touch (Cochoy, 2004). Here, more so than in the section listing personal tastes, a person can publicly say who they are and what they like, hate and want. Although the length of the description is rarely limited by the site, for it to be effective it must be short, forceful and positive.[8] In certain descriptions, the quality of the writing is also a social marker advanced as an explicit criterion of selection. Originality is the watchword. To stand out and attract attention, singles must be creative – without appearing too eccentric.

Yet – and more so on some sites than on others – the format of descriptions may differ widely. In some cases it is influenced by the website's registration form, as in the case of *adopteunmec*, where individuals have to answer the question 'Who am I?' The format chosen may be derisive: 'Hah! If I knew who I was, I wouldn't be here... Let's say that I'm a bit crazy but funny'; or lyrical: 'A darling, a chick, a real little devil, just a girl, who's looking for her world champion! Lol'; or using offbeat humour: 'Who am I? There you go, it's starting already... I thought I was the one doing the shopping here! I'll answer if I want to'; or obviously sincere, with a declaration of intent: 'I'm an epicurean who's bored with routine, I like to laugh, I'm curious and passionate. I like to dream outside the box, fantasy is my driver and joie de vivre my slogan.' The description must provide information on the candidate's personality and present their most specific characteristics synthetically, yet without hiding their weaknesses, which are what make them human:

> Spontaneous and rather happy-go-lucky with quite a strong character! Addicted to beautiful tattoos, 'electro' music, nice 'collector' trainers, the sun, shopping, good food, my bed and my job! A bit of a pain I must admit but at the same time that's quite a good sign as it means that I like the person at least a bit.

These elements are all potential affordances that could help to start a conversation. The description is also an opportunity to specify what one is looking for, either by demonstrating hope and an open mind –

> There are those that last a lifetime, those that one should rather not have had, those that shatter you or surprise you, those that change a man, those that make you laugh and uplift you, and those that touch your heart, and then there's the one you never expected... that's it, all your life you meet people

– or by ticking a personal list of sought-after characteristics:

> A sincere and honest young man, interesting (but definitely not full of himself!), who's gotten over his last break-up, who knows how to take the initiative, a bit of a dreamer, a hint of self-deprecation... that's already a lot, isn't it? Yeah, if you can't tick all the boxes, I'm prepared to go some of the way ;-) provided that you like going for walks, having a drink in little Parisian cafés and people watching, chilling out on the couch and watching a movie, going to the movies, the theatre, little gigs... That's it, in the end I'm not all that demanding. ;-)

Other descriptions are however far more unique, whether they present a depressive type or flout all the norms of a positive presentation. For example:

Sirs. Immediately it puts you at ease… Goodbye Ladies! So, what can you say… I'm going to more fully complete the description that's required and then just brushed aside! Well, objectively, I'm not a typical beauty. Sorry, but 1.70m, 50kg, that's just not on!! I like our [French] cuisine and the conviviality of nights out, so good-bye to the 0% figure. While I like to do sports in my spare time, I'll admit I won't go jogging in the rain! What else… oh yes, naturally quite amusing, I really, really don't like arseholes (if this is censored, insert annoying people instead please) and even less so intolerance. Our wealth comes from differences. But anyone who's a bit 'special' please look at the next profile yes yes the cute little blond and forget me! I don't want to upset you but being tolerant doesn't make me a magnet for nutcases… Thanks. So you, Sir, who's got a lil' smile as you read these lines, don't rush off like a thief with the excuse that someone entered your office just as you were about to say hi to me… Yes send me a few lines with your responses and we'll get to know each other. That said, speak soon!

In fact, the profile description is a way of setting the rules of the game, of directly or indirectly showing the other person how the rest of the encounter is envisaged:

Hey Mum, yes it's me. You okay? I'm calling to tell you about my new guy, actually 'Guy' is his username. Why a username? Well… because I don't know him very well yet. We've just exchanged a few (POLITE) words, a conversation that was actually quite enjoyable, on various subjects. That's how we became friends. No, he didn't undress me with his eyes, you know he likes me for who I am, what I do in life. Yes, he's got a good job, he's good looking, he's got many qualities and also some flaws. But still new, as we say, still attractive. At the moment I'm on cloud 9 but he'd better watch out if things turn sour! How did I meet him? Like everyone, on meetic… Okay Mum, I'll be careful. Yes, I'll let you know how things develop. Well, I've gotta go, someone's trying to call me.

Collective support and coaching

This is where our third character enters the scene more directly. Many of the women I met told me that they had shown their profile to someone else to get their opinion. These 'coaches' are supposed to provide reassurance; they enable a person to gain self-confidence and also provide a sort of after-sales service, which often means restoring the person's psychological balance when things don't work out. Some people who are nervous about registering on a dating website do so on a night out with friends. Their entire description, and especially particular catchphrases or disparaging terms, are scrutinised by the group before being published. Many of the people I met said that under the influence of a third party they had totally rewritten the texts introducing themselves. The presentation of oneself thus appears to be teamwork

(Goffman, 1973). Coaches also extend their mission to the choice of photos that complete the profile, and sometimes even take the photos themselves. Their advice continues after online exchanges have been initiated, when the women I interviewed would often consult with their friends about how to move the interaction forward: Where to meet? How to take the first step? Should she refuse to have sex on the first date? The most seasoned users share their personal experiences and urge their friends to avoid the pitfalls that they themselves encountered. But this initiation process is not only a product of a friendship network. Some women told me about how it was also shaped by some of their conquests, even though there was very little emotional commitment on either side. Here is an illustration of the ambivalence of relations formed via these platforms. Very unexpectedly, the men in question had played the role of a big brother, providing advice on how to protect themselves from appearing too fragile or from taking excessive risks. That was the case, for example, with a young woman in her thirties who, not knowing exactly what she wanted after a break-up from a dull relationship, started to multiply her sexual experiences. This is how she related her meeting with one of her first lovers:

> I told him to meet me at my place, he'd given me his name and his phone number so that I'd know who he was. When we parted the next day, he warned me of perverts and nutcases that I could meet on the site, and he made me promise never to do this again. He keeps in touch occasionally by email. Asks me how I'm doing.

Contact and attention: chatting and concentrating to create an intimate relationship

Once a selection of profiles has been made, the candidate for a date must undergo the following test: they have to make contact with the desired person in order to explore the prospects for further attachment. This is the beginning of the end for unrealistic dreams, and where disillusionment first begins. Why? Many polite messages do not get a reply – not even a negative reply. Candidates have to learn to live with this. They are squarely in the information society, where people are so overloaded with information and are so unavailable that they readily shed polite proprieties. As there are far fewer women than men, they tend to receive too many messages and their attention is limited (Kessous et al., 2010; Kessous 2012; Kessous 2015). They cannot provide an after-sales service, especially since some men readily make use of modern emailing techniques – only personalising their message with a short sentence specific to the particular woman before resorting to their standard cut and paste a self-promotion message. These techniques are used so much that some sites have had to ban copy/paste functionalities.

Evaluating non-objectifiable things

Why do men act like this? Why do they not invest more of themselves in the process? These are questions that are often discussed on women's forums about dating sites.[9] One possible answer is that the framework of experience in which individuals meet contrasts sharply with earlier traditions, such as that of nineteenth-century romantic letters. Rivals under threat by other potential seducers do not have the time, even if they have the talent, to pretend to be Alfred de Musset or George Sand. They have to be fast and to multiply the relevant approaches. There is no room for literary prose – especially with the first contact – when so many messages remain unanswered. The most seasoned users deploy certain commercial skills (Kessous and Mallard, 2014): they work fast, look to find an empathetic tone and the best catchphrase to 'grab' the right customer, they are audacious, and withdraw as quickly as they engaged in interaction, turning to another prospect if their efforts are not rapidly productive.

According to most of my interviewees, chatting is preferable to emails for this initial approach, because it's more spontaneous. In this phase, users are no longer acting in public, even if their partner may sometimes be distracted by the arrival of other suitors' instant chat messages. Chatting helps simple tests of compatibility to be carried out: expressing forms of humour – with its possible inferences and misinterpretations – skilfully finding out more about areas in the profile that were unclear or, less skilfully sometimes, by ticking off answers to a list of previously drawn up conditional questions. Usually, in this decisive trial, they act without their coach. Chatting puts them in a natural situation in which it is difficult to camouflage poor writing skills. In populations with a high level of education, those who have cultural references to hand, a talent for repartee and are good spellers are at an advantage. In this phase the two people can learn more about each other since they can, in time, ask more personal questions: 'What do you actually want?' In this kind of personal conversation, each person invites the other to reveal him or herself more genuinely than in their public profile. Most users of these sites know that there is no point chatting online indefinitely: it does sometimes happen that a face-to-face meeting takes place months after the first contact, but usually this preliminary phase is short. Enjoyable contact for one evening may not be renewed the next day, as the desired person has in the meantime chatted to one or more other people whom they find equally interesting. At this stage, short calculations and conquest strategies are usual; memory is volatile and people still have little attachment to each other.

Focusing on someone to exit the market

There seems to be no escaping it. Try as users might, the market relation model is so present that it is difficult to break free from it. They are constantly solicited on the site and curiosity drives them to check the profiles and messages of those who contact them. The system is designed so that every action leaves a trace on members' dashboards as a pop up indicating a visit on their record. This trace, in turn, prompts them to look at the visitor's profile. Yet it is the ability to put the device aside that makes it possible for people to actually meet each other. In order to do so, they have to stop thinking in comparative terms and let go of the range of possibilities, and perceive the other in his or her singularity and uniqueness. It is necessary for them to frame their interactions – that is, not to allow others to interfere with their interpersonal ties and attract their attention – and to resume control over the management of time. Seducing involves providing information bit by bit, without seeming to do so, about oneself, one's personal life, who one is and the things one does. Based on the desired person's emotional reaction and on the ensuing interaction, the two people decide whether to pursue the relationship, to get to know each other better and, sometimes, to take risks. Seducing is in a sense knowing how to manage one's privacy.

The encounter is thus a long journey through which the individuals gradually move forwards towards a state of intimacy that suits them. By taking the time to discover one another and by opting to focus exclusively on one person, users of these sites can switch to an interpersonal regime, one that is not yet of familiarity (Thévenot, 1994). Via these procedural routes the two people 'forget' the market that brought them together in a virtual place, and simultaneously learn to know and recognise each other as individuals worthy of love. In this phase, there is no longer any question of feeding a mass of information into a technical system and of entrusting it with making a suitable choice. The recurrence of their ties ends up with them being strengthened and ensures that the two people become more important to each other than to other prospects. But the timeframe of the market and the choice of a partner based on his or her stated characteristics often leads to premature and irreversible trade-offs, without taking into account the time needed to live this qualitative experience of recognition, in Honneth's sense. The problem is not so much the fact of calculating a decision, but the premature stage at which the calculation is made.

Temporalities and breaking out of the frame

Even if they are aware of these difficulties, apprentice lovers are not necessarily on dry ground. Many of the accounts I analysed show that users of these platforms often lose control of the timeframe of the interaction in those cases when it is suddenly interrupted by the other party, either online or after a first date. This is partly to do with expectations about the pace of the interactions: they seem to be both very fast – sometimes accompanied by the injunction to interrupt any other activity and to answer a message immediately – and very short. Within a few days, sometimes a few weeks, everything is said.

This loss of control over time is often attended by a breaking of the 'frame', in the sense that Goffman (1991: 340) uses it, within which the new relationship proceeds. Confrontations with another human body is one of several causes of disturbance likely to break the frame. But there are other more embarrassing situations. One may arise, for instance, when a suitor decides to initiate contact with a candidate whose profile does not include any pictures. During the subsequent interaction it is necessary to ask, tactfully, without rushing the person, if they would mind sending a picture. But what then happens if, after waiting for a while – the time to send a photo – the requester does not like it? The conversation might – with the associated emotional violence – come to an abrupt end or else carry on briefly until the requester finds an excuse to withdraw.

Another breaking of the frame might occur when protagonists decide to take the plunge and to meet face to face, often in a public place. At this point the information given in the profile and especially the photo are requalified. Interviewees told me about bald men who had submitted photos where they still had hair, and other apparent lies concerning age, height and weight.[10] Even without there being suspected fraud (see Posner, 1981), the face-to-face meeting is a breaking of the frame: in my ethnographic study I was often surprised – sometimes pleasantly so – by the difference between a person's image in real life and their photos. It took me several hours to really take in the shape of a face – a shape that sometimes disappeared after the interview was over. Some of my interviewees also commented on this phenomenon, explaining how it caused them constantly to go back and forth between the photos of their suitors, both before and after a meeting, in an attempt to remind themselves of their physical features and to reach a decision about whether to continue the relationship or not. When they actually meet face to face, people can look different to how they do in mediated interactions: it is easier to adopt a light and empathetic tone when interacting remotely and protected by virtuality. Face to face, shyness and the influence of the other person's emotions come to the fore.

Another factor that disrupts the frame of the encounter is its complete decontextualisation. With very few exceptions, users can mobilise very little of their previous virtual interactions as a preliminary frame. When the meeting takes place in the context of a dinner with friends, engaging with these friends enables an individual to show him or herself as a nice person, even a charismatic one. The stranger who says unusual things under the affectionate gaze of common friends produces an effect of singularity that may seem touching. But imagine that this 'little grain of madness' is expressed in a different context, say a café, where a date has been arranged. What would the reaction be? Would the person not be tempted to see the other's behaviour as somewhat... strange? Might they have psychological problems? During our interview, a young woman called Lucie expressed it to me in the following terms, 'It's as if a magic wand had put us there at a table, we've got nothing connecting us, no past, no friends.'

Conclusion

Shifting from the market to love – what an unusual challenge! Signing up to a dating site affords users a glimpse of the strong possibilities that exist for meeting their need for affection, contact and communication that, for various reasons, many single people in both urban and rural areas genuinely feel. To attract customers, dating sites employ the usual commercial communication stratagems: they promise a dream that will come true and seek to arouse a desire that a transaction on the platform will fulfil. It is above all the mechanisms of market matching that inspire these sites: the price of the sub-scription acts as an economic constraint in the background of interactions. Integrating their membership costs into an investment formula (to which can be added the price of drinks, the meal at a restaurant and/or tickets to a show) appears to cause protagonists to become instrumental in their representations of partners' bodies (Kaufmann, 2010), projecting them into a space containing both antagonistic relations of equivalence and feelings of love (Boltanski, 1990). While the question of price is solved by the membership contract, the design of the sites emulates a competitive market in which users rival one another to deploy the natural skills that they have acquired in other market situations.

The current trend among dating sites in their quest to meet personalised demands is, as in other competitive markets, to fragment into specific niches. It is for instance now possible for dating site users to choose sites for long-term relationships or for 'naughty', 'hot', 'soft' or 'hard' encounters. They can be matched up by cultural, psychological, social or community affinities (e.g. between people of the same religion or political sympathies). It is therefore hardly surprising that those who deliberately engage in the form of interac-tion that most resembles a transaction – the one-night stand – are most likely to get what they want. This type of 'transaction', that is destined to be but a fleeting encounter, requires little more than some reassurance about the per-son's basic features (physical characteristics, appearance of normality, etc.). More complicated situations are those where singles are looking for more lasting relationships. They have to learn to limit their market reflexes, to allow other levels of emotion to be expressed, to live their experiential exploration and to benefit fully from the potential richness of the encounter. The least one can say is that the design of most of these websites – which seem to be inspired more by procedural principles and less by the desire to facilitate an optimised calculation between different qualities – does not really help them. What seems central – and I hope to have shown that this result is less trivial than it seems – is that, be it simply by virtue of the risk entailed by revealing one's private information online, and despite the similarity of emotional motivations between people (curiosity, excitement, seduction, empathy, etc.), one does not so much meet a lover as discover a client (Kessous and Mallard, 2014).

Notes

1 I was single at the time of this survey, and the interviewees were informed of the fact that I was a sociologist and that I intended to write on the subject.
2 For details, see Kessous, 2011a.
3 In this case the price can be ascertained from the cost of membership and the available time spent on the site.

4 With very few exceptions, these categories are not informed by the protagonists. This may mean that the data are too personal to be made public with graphics that enable the person to be identified. A comparison with the American website 'OK Cupid' would be interesting insofar as it requires users to answer a host of questions, ranging from the very general (How often do you use Facebook?) to the most personal (How do you feel about drugs? Are you okay with having sex on the first date?).

5 I have chosen not to spend time on the social representations associated with the men/women relations encompassed by these categories.

6 The site denotes personality traits as 'functions'.

7 On the importance of the coach in a connectionist society where the project prevails, see Boltanski and Chiapello, 2005: 120–3.

8 The statistics of the experimental site *okcupid.com* highlight the fact that certain words used in the first messages trigger more answers than others. See http://blog. okcupid.com/index.php/online-dating-advice-exactly-what-to-say-in-a-first-message/ (accessed 5 October 2015), also see Rosen et al., 2008.

9 Blogs and forums where comments can be left are spaces for interaction, where the protagonists express their dissatisfaction and their difficulties. In contrast, there are also blogs (usually for men) that provide guidelines for getting a woman to agree to a date. This is what sociologist J.-C. Kaufmann based his essay 'sex@amour' on (Kaufmann, 2010).

10 On the 'little lies' concerning the profile to present oneself online, see (Whitty, 2008)   and   http://blog.okcupid.com/index.php/the-biggest-lies-in-online-dating/ (accessed 5 August 2014).

Bibliography

Bloom, A. (1993) *Love and Friendship*, New York, Simon and Schuster.

Boltanski, L. (1990) *L'amour et la justice comme compétences*, Paris: Metailié.

Boltanski, L. and Chiapello, E. (2005) *The New Spirit of Capitalism*, London: Verso.

Cochoy, F. (ed.) (2004) *La captation des publics: C'est pour mieux te séduire, mon client*, Toulouse: Presses Universitaires du Mirail.

Giddens, A. (1992) *The Transformation of Intimacy: Sexuality, Love and Eroticism in Modern Societies*, Cambridge: Polity Press.

Goffman, E. (1973) *La Mise en scène de la vie quotidienne. Tome 1: la présentation de soi*, Paris: Les Éditions de Minuit.

Goffman, E. (1991) *Les cadres de l'expérience*, Paris: Éditions de Minuit.

Honneth, A. (2008a). *Reification: A New Look at an Old Idea*, New York: Oxford University Press.

Honneth, A. (2008b). *La société du mépris: vers une nouvelle théorie critique*, Paris: La découverte.

Karpik, L. (2007) *L'économie des singularités*, Paris: Gallimard.

Kaufmann, J.-C. (2010) *sex@amour*, Paris: Armand Colin.

Kessous, E. (2011a). L'amour en projet: Internet ou les conventions de la rencontre amoureuse. *Réseaux*, 166(2): 193–223.

Kessous, E. (2011b). Usages des TIC et sociologie économique des conventions. In F. Grangon and J. Denouël (eds), *Communiquer à l'ère numérique: regards croisés sur la sociologie des usages*, Paris: Presses des Mines, pp. 223–250.

Kessous, E. (2012) *L'attention au monde. Sociologie des données personnelles à l'ère numérique*. Paris: Armand Colin.

Kessous, E. (2015) The attention economy between market capturing and commitment in the polity. *Œconomia*, 5(1): 77–101. http://oeconomia.revues.org/1123.

Kessous, E. and Mallard, A. (eds) (2014) *La fabrique de la vente. Le travail commercial dans les télécommunications*, Paris: Éditions des Mines.

Kessous, E., Mellet, K. and Zouinar, M. (2010) L'Économie de l'attention: entre protection des ressources cognitives et extraction de la valeur, *Sociologie du travail*, 52(3): 359–373.

Lancaster, K.J. (1966) A new approach to consumer theory. *Journal of Political Economy*, 74, 132–157.

Livet, P. (1994) *La communauté virtuelle, action et communication*, Combas: Edition de L'éclat.

Posner, R. (1981) The economics of privacy. *American Economic Review*, 71(2): 405–409.

Rochet, J.-C. and Tirole, J. (2003) Platform competition in two-sided markets. *Journal of the European Economic Association*, 1(4): 990–1029.

Rosen, L.D., Cheever, N.A., Cummings, C. and Felt, J. (2008) The impact of emotionality and self-disclosure on online dating versus traditional dating. *Computers in Human Behaviour*, 24: 2124–2157.

Singly, F.D. (1984) Les manoeuvres de séduction: une analyse des annonces matrimoniales. *Revue Française de Sociologie*, 25(4): 523–559.

Thévenot, L. (1994) Le régime de familiarité. Des choses en personne. *Genèses*, 17, 72–101.

Thévenot, L. (2006) *L'action au pluriel. Sociologie des régimes d'engagement*, Paris: La découverte.

Whitty, M.T. (2008) Revealing the 'real' me, searching for the 'actual' you: Presentations of self on actual internet dating sites. *Computer in Human Behavior*, 24: 1707–1723.

9 Acquiring associations

On the unexpected social consequences of possessive relations

Hans Kjellberg

This chapter explores social consequences that follow from the acquisition of goods, thus tracing the links that market exchange gives rise to at one remove, so to speak. My starting point is Douglas and Isherwood's (1996 [1977]: 37) claim that consumption is 'the vital source' of contemporary culture. If we accept this as a working hypothesis, and acknowledge that most acts of consumption are nowadays preceded by market exchange, then exploring the consequences of entering into the particular type of relation implied by the acquisition of goods offers one route for inquiring into the social ramifications of market exchange. In short, what kind of sociality springs from possessive relations?

There are several strands of research that have bearing on this issue. First, classic sociology sensitises us to the many social ties that have already been forged to shape possessive relations, and which may place strict requirements on how these relations play out, whether linked to formal sanctions or some collective conscience (Durkheim, 1997 [1893]). Using your Renoir as a fire starter, however well to do you happen to be, would not pass unnoticed and is likely to have social consequences. Second, students of the material world have highlighted the complex sociotechnical organisation that is required to make 'otherwise loose elements adhere' to produce and maintain the stuff we possess (Molotch, 2003: 2). In both these cases, social ties are suggested to precede, render possible and constrain the forging of possessive relations. Students of consumption have suggested that possessive relations also affect social ties through their import on our identities (e.g. Belk, 1988; Holt, 2002), echoing and expanding on Veblen's notion of social differentiation through conspicuous consumption (Veblen, 1994 [1899]). Based on these and other contributions, possessive relations seem steeped in sociality; social ties precede and follow from the forging of possessive relations. In this chapter, I want to highlight that the sociality of possessive relations includes, but goes beyond these well-known arguments.

I propose to do this by exploring the effects that may follow from acts of acquisition. Specifically, I will trace these effects using an autoethnographic account of my acquisition of a classic car. By focusing on the effects of acquisition, I thus turn the table on the situation debated by Miller and Callon (Callon, 2005; Miller, 2002, 2005): my concern is not whether 'Sophie buying a Renault' requires disentangling the agents and object of exchange, but rather what entanglements follow from the consummation of such an exchange.

My method is inspired by the sociology of translation (Akrich et al., 2006), the study of everyday life (de Certeau, 1984) and consumption practices (Holt, 1995). These inspirations have led me to trace 'things you do because you own X' using a number of mundane examples. My focus on *doings* is motivated by adopting a performative stance with respect to the social; I understand society as that which we hold together rather than that which holds us together (Latour, 1986). This leads me to study the interactive forging of associations between entities triggered by possessive relations rather than describe a structure of social ties surrounding consumption (Latour, 1994, 2005). To be sure, some of the associations forged are safely within the realm of classic sociology, such as when possessions lead you to acquaint new friends, give you esteem, status, etc. In these cases, possessions become vehicles for socialisation, although we must recognise that they may also format the kind of sociality achieved. Beyond this, there are many effects of possession that do not seem to imply anything social at all, at least at first glance. These associations, which may come across as *a*social, are the various attachments to other entities that are triggered or altered by possessive relations (Callon et al., 2002). Due to their hybrid character, and sometimes also their transience, these links as well as the interactions between them are typically disregarded in sociological analysis. Yet, I argue that they account for an important part of the associative consequences of market exchange.

The remainder of this chapter is structured as follows. In the first section, I expand on my starting points for studying market ties at one remove, as well as on how I have done so. In the second section I offer an account of the practical consequences of my acquiring a classic car, which offers a rich source of observations concerning possible consequences of possessive relations. In the third section, I discuss a number of themes that emerge from the account and expand on these using other observations of effects that follow from the forging of possessive relations. In the fourth section, I make some concluding remarks on the sociality of markets from the perspective of studying possessive relations.

Studying market ties at one remove

Why examine market sociality through possessive relations? In their pioneering work on the anthropology of consumption, Douglas and Isherwood (1996 [1977]: 37) define consumption as 'a use of material possessions that is beyond commerce and free within the law' and claim that it constitutes 'the very arena in which culture is fought over and licked into shape'. From this perspective, how we use our possessions – what we do with them – becomes an important key to understanding the social. Since a considerable share of our possessions, and hence acts of consumption, are nowadays preceded by market exchange, exploring the consequences of entering into the particular type of relation implied by acquiring goods seems to offer a potentially fruitful route for inquiring into the social ramifications of market exchange.

This starting point begs the question: what kinds of consequences should we be looking for? The answer will depend on how one understands the dependent variable in the equation, i.e. the notion of the social, or of society. Over the course of my academic career I have moved from a predominantly structural approach to this issue inspired by social network analysis (Baker, 1984, 1990; Granovetter, 1973, 1978, 1985; Uzzi, 1996, 1997), to a view of the social as something that is actively and recursively (re)created (Law, 1994). This move was inspired primarily by the performative stance associated with the sociology of translation (Callon, 1986; Latour, 1986, 1987). Rather than examine social structures, identities, status, positions, etc., my attention is directed towards engagements, preoccupations and doings that can be linked to possessions. The question I seek to address can thus be stated as follows: What does the acquisition of things lead us to do?

Without further specification, this question would probably lead the reader to expect a study of human interaction rituals of the sort so skilfully analysed by Erving Goffman (1959, 1963, 1967, 1974). However, as several students of material culture have suggested, the objects we surround ourselves with – 'the missing masses' (Latour, 1992), or 'social relations made durable' (Jackson et al., 1998: 141) – may also be important for our understanding of the social. Hence, my attention will not exclusively be directed towards human interaction, but also take into account interactions with inanimate (naturally occurring or man-made) objects. To make these two distinctions from structural sociology clearer, my approach can be said to involve *studying the interactive forging of associations between entities triggered by possessive relations* rather than describing the structure of social ties surrounding consumption (Latour, 1994, 2005).

This means that I am interested in consumption practices; what people *do* when they consume (Holt, 1995). While the thrust of consumption research, particularly that which is associated with marketing, focuses on consumer *decisions* to buy goods and services, there is a growing literature that moves beyond the acquisition of products to look at what people do with the products that they purchase (Belk, 1982; de Certeau, 1984; Heiskanen and Pantzar, 1997; Kjellberg and Stigzelius, 2014; Shove and Pantzar, 2005; Shove and Araujo, 2010; Warde, 2005). These efforts highlight that consumption is an activity cycle involving not only acquisition, but also use and disposal (Arnould and Thompson, 2005). Furthermore, they suggest that it is not always possible to accurately deduce the uses of objects from what a producer envisions, or from the projected use of the entity envisioned when acquiring it (Shove and Araujo, 2010). Hence, it is my ambition to trace not only envisioned or projected uses of possessions, but also to identify consequences beyond those anticipated. In the next subsection, I expand on *how* I have sought to do this.

Tracing the forging of associations in possessive practices

How, then, to trace the doings triggered by possessive relations? Inspired by the study of (scientific and technical) practice (Latour, 1987; Pickering, 1993) my ambition is to engage in real-time accounting (how), rather than seek retrospective (because) or prospective (in order to) accounts (Andersson et al., 2008). That is, I am not primarily concerned with the ex ante motives for, or the ex post rationalisations of the doings triggered by possessions, but mainly with what these doings are. The method I have chosen for this represents an elaboration of the classic participant observation. Rather than moving in the direction of non-participant, standardised *observiaires*, which have shown to be highly useful for fixed point surveys of doings (Cochoy, 2008), I sought a method that would allow for accounting of doings over time. Among non-participant techniques, *shadowing* would make this possible (Clark et al., 2003; Czarniawska, 2007). However, since I am primarily concerned with everyday consequences, shadowing would be relatively invasive of the private sphere. These considerations led me to consider self-observation.

The use of subjective personal introspection, researcher introspection and autoethnography has been widely debated in consumption studies (e.g. Brown, 1998; Gould, 1995, 2006; Wallendorf and Brucks, 1993; Woodside, 2004). Typically, the method involves 'the researcher reflecting on and analysing his or her own personal experiences... and bringing them together in the form of an autobiographical essay' (Brown and Reid, 1997). Primarily, introspective techniques have been used in studies of consumer experiences (Holbrook, 1986, 1991), in various attempts to 'gain an understanding of consumption phenomena from an insider's view' (Gould, 1995: 720). For instance, Gould (1991) used introspection to inquire into the link between his consumption experiences and his perceptions of vital energy; Shankar (2000) used it to study the role of popular music consumption in his identity formation; Holbrook (2005) used it to investigate the nature and types of customer value experience.

My primary reason for choosing an approach inspired by introspective techniques was that self-observation would allow me to generate a rich account of the potential consequences of possessive relations (cf. Gould, 1991). As it happens, the access to a 'highly motivated informant who can document action as well as internal states in detail' seems to be one of the few merits on which both critics and proponents of these methods agree (Wallendorf and Brucks, 1993: 353). The ability to map processes over time has also been put forward as an important merit of introspective techniques (Woodside, 2004). In the next section, I will thus offer an account of (some of) the consequences, over a period of two years, of my forging a possessive relation to a classic car. (As a clarification: I did not rely on research funding for financing the acquisition in question, in contrast to Holbrook and his jazz records.)

As a method of data collection, researcher introspection has been criticised for being unsystematic (Wallendorf and Brucks, 1993) and for not allowing confirmation (Woodside, 2004, 2006). Since my account differs from standard introspection by mapping doings rather than thoughts, experiences, perceptions, feelings or the like, there are ways to counteract these weaknesses. To reduce the risk of errors and add credibility to my account (Woodside, 2004), I have complemented my personal recollections with those of family members (trying to elicit their recollections of events that were triggered by or followed my buying the car). Inspired by historical methods (Bloch, 1953) and Cochoy's notion of visual archaeology (Cochoy, 2010), I have also used various remnants from the trains of events I describe when constructing the account. Thus, a number of photos, web-forum entries, my email folder containing all emails sent and received related to the car, as well as saved documents, receipts, tools, spare parts, etc. helped me construct the narrative reported in the next section.

A second important critique of introspective methods is that they render difficult the achievement of *di-stance* (i.e. an epistemological break with the actor level) (Wallendorf and Brucks, 1993). The critics suggest that while introspective methods may be good at achieving closeness during data collection, they make it difficult to develop sufficient analytic distance from the phenomena being studied. I have sought to mitigate this critique, by explicitly adopting an analytic stance vis-à-vis the narrative. Based on the narrative and the starting points elaborated on above, I have identified a number of categories of 'things you do when you own X'. In the discussion of these categories, I complement the self-observation with a number of other illustrations, as well as relate it to ongoing theoretical discussions.

Things I did when becoming the owner of a classic car

On 3 August 2008, I found an advertisement on eBay motors for a 1963 Ford Thunderbird Sports Roadster, allegedly in very good condition.[1] For reasons that need not detain us here, I had been looking for precisely this type of car for some time and now it seemed that my search might be over. Since I live in Sweden and the car in question was to be found in California, completing the actual purchase highlighted some aspects of market exchange that are easily overlooked in more mundane purchases.

One such aspect concerned the qualification of the good (Callon et al., 2002). An initial email contact with the seller's agent confirmed that the car was still unsold. My primary concern then was how to establish that the car really was all it was made out to be, i.e. overcome the obvious information asymmetry in used car deals (Akerlof, 1970). Since I had been searching for some time, I had learned that some of the Swedish importers of classic cars also offered to assist buyers who found cars on their own. Via one of these importers, I was able to tap into what could be described as an established business network around international car deals. The importer contacted a specialised agent performing on-site appraisals of classic cars and against a fee they performed an examination of the Thunderbird and sent me a twelve-page appraisal protocol and 127 photographs by 15 August (see Figure 9.1).

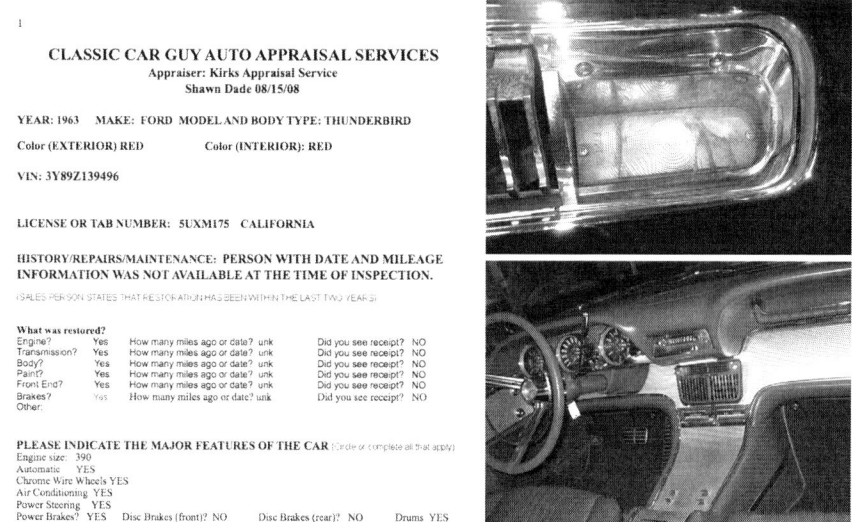

Figure 9.1 Excerpt from the appraisal protocol and sample photos

After carefully studying the photographs and the appraisal protocol – which concluded in a telegraphic style 'Car appears to be in great shape' – and discussing with the importer, I made the seller's agent an offer. A couple of rounds of haggling ensued (via email) before we reached an agreement concerning the price. The contract was then sent back and forth via FedEx, and my bank arranged the money transfer. On 29 August, I became the official owner of a car parked 8,800 km away. This emphasised what Simmel observed more than a century ago: that the forging of possessive relations is intimately linked to the uses to which we put possessions (Simmel, 2004 [1907]: 303–31). Formally the owner of the car, there was still very little I could do with it, including safeguarding it from unfortunate events.

In parallel to completing the transaction, the importer had assisted me in booking an insured transport so that the car could be picked up after it had been paid in full. Once again, the importer's established business contacts proved useful. Via a Swedish shipping agent, he managed to set up a fully insured transport combining a land haul from California to Houston and sea shipment in container from Houston to Gothenburg, in a matter of hours. However, as hurricane Ike swept through the Gulf of Mexico towards Houston in early September 2008, the fact that the car was insured did little to reduce my anxiety. The hauling company explained that the car should be safe since it would be stored on the northern side of Houston. In the end, the car was only picked up in California on 22 September, with Ike now long gone. Given that Ike is considered the third-costliest hurricane ever to make landfall in the United States, I can only conclude that slow service sometimes is good service.

While waiting for the car to arrive I was able to sort out the paperwork for customs and pre-registration. Ten weeks later, the car arrived and after it had passed through customs, a local car-transport company collected it and hauled it to my hometown. I learned of the car's arrival from my wife even before the car-transport company contacted me. She called me up and said: 'Your car is here.' (Not 'the car' or 'our car', signalling at least some distance from the project.) A friend of her boss, who happened to be a fan of classic Fords, but who neither knew me nor that I had bought a T-bird, came into their office saying: 'Do you know what I just saw rolling off a car-transport?!' In the afternoon that day, the whole family went down to the storage facility to have a first glimpse. The day after, the car-transport company hauled the car to our home. There, it ousted my regular car from the garage, which had some practical consequences. Since cold starts are bad (for the engine, the environment, fuel economy, comfort), I now use an electric heater to pre-heat my regular car before going off in the mornings during the cold season. This means that I connect a heater cable to the car and set its timer to start an hour or so before I plan to use it.

Once in my garage, I spent many hours just studying the Thunderbird, feeling it, becoming acquainted with various details, examining the body, the engine compartment, jacking it up to look at the undercarriage, etc. I took notes of things that looked like they needed to be adjusted or replaced, like gaskets, bulbs, oil filter, worn rubber parts, missing details, etc. The list soon became quite long and I started to look for suppliers of spare parts via the internet. Strangely enough, the long list was not coupled with thoughts of having acquired a 'lemon' (Akerlof, 1970), but rather to excitement over the possibility of further improvements. As long as the imperfections were not too serious, the fact that the car was not perfect added to my consumption experience (and to my actual consumption). When placing the first order with a spare parts supplier in the US, I also ordered reprints of the original shop manuals so that I would know how to deal with various technical issues that might arise. I placed the order via the internet, but the owner of the store called me up to discuss the items on my list, making sure they were the ones I needed and that I didn't need others as well. 'Business is slow these days' he said when I commented on his good service; this was December 2008.

When the first shipment of parts arrived I soon discovered that I needed to get new tools as well. The metric system and a classic US car don't go together that well. Plus there were tools that I previously had had no need for, like a dynamometric wrench. My family contributed to this tooling-up as well, giving me a 'creeper' (a low-profile rolling carriage for sliding under a car) for Father's Day. Later, I also discovered that certain actions required tools made especially for the Thunderbird, some of which could be ordered from the spare parts suppliers. By that time, my owning the car had become known not only to friends, but also to various companies through the car registry. This meant that I received spare parts catalogues, subscription offers from magazines called 'Nostalgia' and 'Classic', etc. It was getting relatively easy to find things I needed, but also things I didn't know I needed. On one occasion I got a call from a salesman offering a limited edition Thunderbird leatherjacket. I declined, but bought a T-bird t-shirt instead.

Most things that I had ordered were easy to replace, like the broken lens depicted in Figure 9.2, but one thing that caused me considerable concern was changing the oil pan gasket. I had spotted that the engine was leaking a little oil and had ordered a new oil pan gasket and some gasket cement. After removing the oil pan and fitting the new gasket, I discovered that the oil pan wouldn't slide back into place as it should. That's when I started to study the shop manual. I vividly recall the sinking feeling when discovering the following passage in the manual: 'lift the engine'. Apart from the fact that I had no equipment for it, lifting the engine would mean a lot more work than I had anticipated and thought I could handle. I even registered on a T-bird web forum to inquire whether there was another way, but to no avail. In a move that would make Robert Pirzig proud, I went back and carefully examined why the oil pan wouldn't slide in place. I discovered that a stabiliser bar in front of the engine prevented the pan from sliding in at the right angle and that the crank was obstructing towards the back end. Since the cross bar was suspended in rubber bushings, it could be raised with a jack and the crank could be rotated to increase headroom. After a few attempts, I was able to do the impossible! At least that is what it felt like. With a mixture of relief and satisfaction I was able to bolt the thing back in place, using my dynamometric wrench to torque the bolts correctly. About a month later I passed on my discovery of how to replace the oil pan gasket without lifting the engine to another grateful forum member, which made me feel even better.

On other occasions, I got useful advice from the forum myself. Usually I could find out what I needed to know by simply browsing previous discussions, but at one time I posted a direct question. I had discovered that the ashtray did not open and close as it should. I removed the ashtray housing and discovered that there were some fittings that appeared to have held springs in place, but that the springs were no longer there. I got on the forum and asked whether anyone could explain what the assembly should look like. Within six hours I got a photograph from another forum member who had removed the ashtray housing on his own car and taken a photo of it. Based on his photo,[2] I was able to craft two similarly shaped springs out of the springs from two clothespins.

I also ordered a set of blank spare keys since the car came with only one set of keys. I took the keys and the blanks with me to a key shop, handed them over to the proprietor and asked him to make copies. The service was instant and the proprietor soon returned from the back of his shop with two pairs of keys. Much to my surprise, I discovered that he had managed to copy the round key onto the square blank, and vice versa. As a consequence, neither of the new keys fitted. I may have raised my voice, and I distinctly remember that I refused to pay for the service. Back to square one, I ordered a new set of blanks with my next order of spare parts a few months later. This time, I succeeded in having working copies made after explicitly instructing which key to copy onto which blank. Before leaving the shop, I also bought a 'Ford' keyring for the new pair of keys.

Come spring it was time for the obligatory vehicle registration inspection. US and Swedish rules differ so you need to make a number of adjustments on a US car for it to pass the Swedish inspection. For instance, you need a speedometer that shows km/h not mph. With the help of my Macintosh, a laser printer and a laminating machine I prepared a new scale, which I placed above the original mph scale. (Surprisingly enough, adjustments to current standards concerning safety and environmental effects are not required; the car in question only needs to conform to the regulations that were in effect when the model was first approved.) At the inspection, I learned that registering a classic is special also to the inspectors. Apart from giving me the opportunity to resume the inspection after a short break to change two bulbs that were the wrong colour – which I had forgotten about – the inspecting officer called up one of his friends during the inspection just to tell him what he was driving at that moment.

Passing the inspection meant that the car could be legally driven on public roads, provided that it was properly insured. Getting the appropriate insurance required me to fill in a detailed application form and append photos not only of the car, but also of the garage in which it would be stored. The approval of the application took almost two weeks and threatened our first planned trip with the new car to visit some friends over a weekend.

Figure 9.2 One typical use: the special occasion (driving to our oldest daughter's confirmation on 30 May 2009)

Looking back at how I have used the car since then – which is not that often, maybe once a week during summer – one group of uses could be labelled 'special occasions'. Driving to church for my oldest daughter's confirmation is one example (see Figure 9.2), taking the same daughter and her best friend to their graduation ball another. On weekends, we sometimes take the T-bird rather than the regular car when going to visit friends. Using the car for special occasions is also something that others are interested in. I have received a few queries from friends and acquaintances whether it would be possible to hire me and the T-bird to drive final-year baccalaureate students to their proms or newly wed couples from church.

A second typical use situation is 'the drive'. Most of the time, this involves making some excuse for taking a spin if the weather is nice, for instance to take the kids to buy ice cream. I also learnt that car enthusiasts gathered at a café outside my hometown every Tuesday evening from April to September and have made a few trips there, usually with some family member. At one time, when I was parked outside a supermarket waiting for my wife, a man came up to the car and asked whether I was a member of the club or not. I had no idea what he was talking about, but soon learned that there was a Swedish T-bird club that I 'just had to become a member of'.

Besides letters from companies trying to sell parts and magazine subscriptions, I was also contacted by an international society dedicated to the Ford Thunderbird Sports Roadster, asking if it was correct that I had acquired one of these cars and whether I would be interested in becoming a member. Against a fee I would not only become a member, but also receive a copy of the 'gate release form' for my car (the original Ford factory invoice for the vehicle) and a certificate that my car was an authentic Sports Roadster. Since I was interested in the details and also because I knew provenance is important in antiques, I filled in the application form. Thus, I am now included in the membership roster of the International Sports Roadster Society. About a year later, I got a call from another member who also lived in Sweden, who had been surprised to discover there was another Swedish member. We talked for the better part of an hour and vaguely committed to meet up with our cars in the spring.

Doings triggered by owning X

What social consequences can we trace from the account above? Based on my reading of the narrative, I suggest that a number of general themes can be identified.

One possessive relation begets others

First, and hardly surprising, entering one possessive relation may trigger entry into others. In the account above, owning the car triggered acquisitions of spare parts, special tools, key manufacturing services, a t-shirt, etc. This seems to be a common consequence and we can quickly identify similar examples related to other acquisitions. Acquiring a computer tends to trigger acquisitions of software, routers, external hard drives; acquiring a razor triggers acquisitions of blades and shaving cream; acquiring a wok pan may trigger acquisitions of new cooking utensils, cook books, food stuffs; etc. As a buyer, you may anticipate some of these effects, while others may come as a surprise. It is worth noting that this is sometimes anticipated and exploited by manufacturers (Molotch, 2003). One example is the so-called captive pricing scheme where the initial purchase, which creates a systemic dependence, is relatively low cost and the subsequent purchases of parts constitute a much larger cost (e.g. printers and ink cartridges, coffee machines and coffee pods, razors and razorblades). Finally, the example of the gift of a 'creeper' for Father's Day suggests that the triggering of other acquisitions is not limited to the person who acquired the original possession. Acquisitions may thus have reverberating effects.

Possessive relations triggering new associations

Second, entering a possessive relation may make you do completely new things, suggesting a sometimes surprising reversal of subject and object (Latour, 2000). Am I taking the car for a drive, or is the car taking me for one? At times, I am far from certain. Other examples have been noted, such as the man looking for things to grind with his newly acquired angle grinder (Shove and Araujo, 2010). Many of these effects are likely to be transient in character; I no longer spend time in the garage just studying the Thunderbird, nor do I keep repairing the ashtray. However, even these things become stories that are told, not necessarily by myself, but just as often by my wife or some friend. A friend who recently purchased a new car provided another such example of an unexpected but transient activity:

> The first night after I had picked it up, I couldn't sleep. I just lay there in bed thinking: 'This isn't happening. There is a brand new BMW 5-series parked in my garage.' So I got up and put on some clothes, went out to the garage and just sat in the car for a while. Feeling it. Are you crazy if you do that? Haha!

While sitting in the new car at night surely was a transient effect, it was also food for a merry exchange of thoughts on new cars, as well as crazy behaviours in general, among a group of parents taking their siblings to a football tournament. Similarly, there would seem to be nothing requiring owners of Husqvarna automowers to move from window to window in their houses to observe the automatic lawnmower as it leaves its loading dock and starts mowing the lawn. Yet, this is precisely what many do, for a time at least. The effect is not limited to owners; automowers at work have been reported to draw crowds of curious spectators (http://household-tips.thefuntimesguide.com/2009/08/husqvarna_automower.php). With the crowds come opportunities for interaction. However transient, the new object will trigger interactions between its owners and their neighbours concerning the merits of having your own private gardener, its emancipatory effects (allowing you to leave your house unattended during summer), its environmental merits compared to traditional mowers, etc. These examples illustrate how possessive relations may trigger the forging of other associations, suggesting that entering into possessive relations lead us to socialise.

Possessive relations altering ongoing associations

Third, entering a possessive relation may alter the way you do some of the things you do. Such effects may be unfortunate consequences that you are prepared to accept, e.g. my parking the regular car outside the garage and using an electric heater during the winter, in the account above. In many cases the very alteration of doings is of course the whole point of forging the possessive relation, e.g. you buy a dishwasher so that you no longer have to wash the dishes manually.

In other cases, the alterations may be quite unexpected. On days when my then 15-year-old daughter decided to wear her recently acquired pair of (very) high-heeled boots, she saw fit to change her route to and from school in order to minimise walking distance. This was hardly an anticipated effect. At the same time it would seem to have few associative consequences. However, this behavioural modification became the source of some concern about punctuality from her parents, which led to discussions concerning the (questionable or unquestionable) value of attending certain morning classes. Which in turn made the parents and daughter study timetables for buses together (and occasionally led to modifications of one of the parents' route and time of departure for work).

Possessive relations dissolving ongoing associations

Fourth, entering a possessive relation may make you cease doing certain things. In the account above, there were few straightforward examples of this type, apart from the obvious fact that with the T-bird in my garage I no longer spend hours searching through various websites offering classic cars for sale. Still, I would argue that I did cease to do certain things as a consequence of acquiring the car, although it would be difficult to list what it was that I did not do during the hours spent in the garage, or taking a drive. On the one hand, direct interaction with other family members suffered (spending time in the garage rather than with them), on the other, it was increased (doing things together with the car). For other types of purchases, many of these effects are anticipated, like no longer having to mow your lawn when in possession of an automower. Some, however, can be more surprising, like discovering that your possession of a gaming console has dramatically reduced the amount of time spent outside your home, while at the same time has led you to socialise in new ways.

Living up to standards

Fifth, some of the things you do as a consequence of forging a possessive relation are linked to external standards. Although possessive relations are typically considered to be hierarchical and come with a recognised right for the owner to determine in what situations to place that which is possessed, this is a clearly a circumscribed right. There are also obligations that follow from ownership. These vary depending on the possessed entity and across situations and cultures. For some entities there are formalised possessive spaces, which are elaborately defined and specified. In order to be allowed to drive the new car on public roads, I had to pass the Swedish registration inspection, which required me to make certain adjustments to the car. As an alternative, I could have chosen to let it stay in my garage, which underscores how these rules constituted an external circumscription of my possessive relation. In other cases, the owner is not even given that kind of choice; owning a piece of woodland in Sweden will require the owner to engage in silviculture and adhere to certain rules when doing so.

Other standards for possessive spaces are informal, as are the sanctions linked to them. For instance, there was nothing that formally required me to investigate what the original ashtray assembly looked like and perfect the missing springs. The consequences of not doing so would also seem negligible – after all, what if the ashtray doesn't snap closed? Nonetheless I did this, suggesting the presence of a standard determining my doings. In part, I may have internalised this standard over the years (my father being a collector), but my contact with the forum for Thunderbird owners also played a part, exposing me to a number of individuals who took great pride in bringing their vehicles as close as possible to original specifications. Here as well, then, human beings are the servants of the sociality of things, restoring the proper 'social order' of the objects.[3]

Irrespective of whether they are formally prescribed or not, some owners choose to disregard doings beyond their own intended use of an acquired entity. When there are formal prescriptions this may have considerable consequences, such as when owners of livestock are forced to sell their animals when found guilty of maltreatment. Even without formally sanctioned prescriptions there may be consequences. Our neighbours never change the oil or the spark plugs in their lawnmowers, but instead buy new (cheap) lawnmowers every third year or so. When the possessed entity no longer performs as expected, they forge a new possessive relation to replace the old one instead of acquiring spare parts and restoring the existing possession.

Possessive relations triggering others to do things

Sixth, among the effects of possessive relations that can be gleaned from my account there are several that fit the label 'things *others* do because you own X'. Many of these effects are linked to the fact that this possessive relation was subject to registration. Becoming the registered owner of a classic car resulted in me receiving offers from companies selling spare parts, magazines and T-bird merchandise, but also from an enthusiast society. Similar stories are told by owners of pedigree dogs, or pieces of real estate. These effects are indirectly linked to the possessive relation and follow from an *ascription* of certain characteristics to the owner (Akrich and Latour, 1992), e.g. 'if you own a Labrador, you are probably interested in hunting'. More informal versions of this are effects of possessions on personal identity and hence on how others perceive 'owners of X' (Belk, 1988). These effects can be considerable, as illustrated by the perceived import of owning the right cell phone model in certain youth groups.

Some actions on behalf of others triggered by possessive relations are more direct. Receiving Thunderbird-related gifts from family and friends (like the 'creeper') is one example. Another important class of such effects is linked to temporary infringements on the possessive relation. The queries I received concerning the possible use of my car and me for some special occasion belong here. The effect may be more clearly visible in other cases, however. Possession of a concrete mixer or some other piece of machinery often triggers inquiries from neighbours and friends about the possibility of borrowing the machine for some particular project. In villages and rural areas in Sweden this type of pooling of resources is still fairly systematic. So systematic, in fact, that some chose to adapt their possessions to opt out of resource pooling, e.g. buying a car *without* a towing hook to avoid having to lend it to the neighbour.

Concluding remarks

What kind of sociality springs from markets? In a number of contributions it has been suggested that marketing is inseparable from social ordering at large, that it is 'societing' (Cova, 1999; Firat and Venkatesh, 1993; Woolgar, 2004). Similarly, the import of entanglements with the material world (Thomas, 1991) has been highlighted with respect to the organising of markets (e.g. Araujo et al., 2010; Callon et al., 2007; Cochoy, 2007). In this chapter, I have sought to study these aspects of markets at one remove by attending to the consequences of possessive relations. From this perspective, the consummation of market exchange comes across as important not only for our sense of self, via various identity projects, but also as an engine of socialising.

If society is what we hold together through the things we do, as Latour suggested thirty years ago, then market exchanges are likely to constitute very important sources of the societies we are performing. As I have sought to illustrate, the forging of possessive relations does not exclusively or necessarily lead us to become isolated individuals, but offers important opportunities for social engagements. Nor are the effects limited to those who acquire objects; the forging of possessive relations may have reverberating effects. By triggering the forging of yet other possessive relations, the consummation of market exchanges also has the character of 'a player's piano', triggering us to socialise anew.

And it is here, I believe, that the risks of an ever increasing commercial realm lie. Despite the potential wealth of social consequences triggered by possessive relations, the distribution of such consequences may differ from other situations. A growth of possession-induced socialisation may consequently lead to a crowding out of some forms of socialising. In addition, since there are power asymmetries related to the forging of possessive relations, this growth may not be easily controlled. Anyone interested in a 1963 Thunderbird?

Notes

1 For copyright reasons, Routledge has required the author to remove the image of the original advertisement on eBay motors. It can be viewed here: http://bit.ly/ 2f7qzEr.
2 For copyright reasons, Routledge has required the author to remove the image of the ashtray housing. It can be viewed here: http://bit.ly/2f7qzEr.
3 I thank Franck Cochoy for pointing this out to me and for noting that this is only indirectly a matter of market ties.

Bibliography

Akerlof, G.A. (1970) The market for 'lemons': Quality uncertainty and the market mechanism. *Quarterly Journal of Economics*, 84(3): 488–500.

Akrich, M. and Latour, B. (1992) A summary of a convenient vocabulary for the semiotics of human and nonhuman assemblies. In W.E. Bijker and J. Law (eds), *Shaping Technology/Building Society, Studies in Technological Change*, Cambridge, MA: MIT Press, pp. 259–264.

Akrich, M., Callon, M. and Latour, B. (2006) *Sociologie de la traduction. Textes fondateurs*, Paris: Ecole des Mines de Paris.

Andersson, P., Aspenberg, K. and Kjellberg, H. (2008) The configuration of actors in market practice. *Marketing Theory*, 8(1): 67–90.

Araujo, L., Finch, J.H. and Kjellberg, H. (eds) (2010) *Reconnecting Marketing to Markets*, Oxford: Oxford University Press.

Arnould, E.J. and Thompson, C.J. (2005) Consumer culture theory (CCT): Twenty years of research. *Journal of Consumer Research*, 31(4): 868–882.

Baker, W.E. (1984) The social structure of a national securities market. *American Journal of Sociology*, 89(4): 775–811.

Baker, W.E. (1990) Market networks and corporate behavior. *American Journal of Sociology*, 96(3): 589–625.

Belk, R.W. (1982) Acquiring, possessing, and collecting: Fundamental processes in consumer behavior. In R.F. Bush and S.G. Hunt (eds), *Marketing Theory: Philosophy of Science Perspectives*, Chicago, IL: American Marketing Association, pp. 185–190.

Belk, R.W. (1988) Possessions and the extended self. *Journal of Consumer Research*, 15(2): 139–168.

Bloch, M. (1953) *The Historian's Craft*, trans. P. Putnam, New York: Vintage Books Random House.

Brown, S. (1998) The wind in the wallows: Literary theory, autobiographical criticism and subjective personal introspection. In J.W. Alba and J.W. Hutchinson (eds),

Advances in Consumer Research, 25, Provo, UT: Association for Consumer Research, pp. 25–30.

Brown, S. and Reid, R. (1997) Shoppers on the verge of a nervous breakdown: Chronicle, composition and confabulation in consumer research. In S. Brown and D. Turley (eds), *Consumer Research: Postcards from the Edge (Consumer research and policy)*, London: Routledge, pp. 79–149.

Callon, M. (1986) Some elements of a sociology of translation: Domestication of the scallops and the fishermen of St-Brieuc Bay. In J. Law (ed.), *Power, Action and Belief: A New Sociology of Knowledge*, London: Routledge and Kegan Paul, pp. 196–233.

Callon, M. (2005) Why virtualism paves the way to political impotence: A reply to Daniel Miller's critique of The Laws of the Markets. *Economic Sociology, European Electronic Newsletter*, 6(2): 3–20.

Callon, M., Méadel, C. and Rabeharisoa, V. (2002) The economy of qualities. *Economy and Society*, 31(2): 194–217.

Callon, M., Millo, Y. and Muniesa, F. (eds) (2007) *Market Devices*, Oxford: Blackwell Publishing.

Clark, C., Drew, P. and Pinch, T.J. (2003) Managing prospect affiliation and rapport in real-life sales encounters. *Discourse Studies*, 5(1): 5–31.

Cochoy, F. (2007) A sociology of market-things. On the gardening of choices in big retailing. In M. Callon, Y. Millo and F. Muniesa (eds), *Market Devices*, Oxford: Blackwell, pp. 59–73.

Cochoy, F. (2008) Calculation, qualculation, calqulation: Shopping cart arithmetic, equipped cognition and the clustered consumer. *Marketing Theory*, 8(1): 15–44.

Cochoy, F. (2010) Reconnecting marketing to 'market-things'. How grocery equipment drove modern consumption (Progressive Grocer, 1929–1959). In L. Araujo, J.H. Finch and H. Kjellberg (eds), *Reconnecting Marketing to Markets*, Oxford: Oxford University Press, pp. 29–49.

Cova, B. (1999) From marketing to societing: When the link is more important than the thing. In D.T. Brownlie, M. Saren and R. Wensley (eds), *Rethinking Marketing: Towards Critical Marketing Accountings*, London: Sage, pp. 64–83.

Czarniawska, B. (2007) *Shadowing: And Other Techniques for Doing Fieldwork in Modern Societies*, Malmö: Liber.

de Certeau, M. (1984) *The Practice of Everyday Life*, trans. S. Rendall, Berkeley: University of California Press.

Douglas, M. and Isherwood, B. (1996 [1977]). *The World of Goods. Towards an Anthropology of Consumption*, 2nd edn, Abingdon: Routledge.

Durkheim, E. (1997 [1893]). *The Division of Labour in Society*, trans. L.A. Coser, New York: Free Press.

Firat, A.F. and Venkatesh, A. (1993) Postmodernity: The age of marketing. *International Journal of Research in Marketing*, 10(3): 227–249.

Goffman, E. (1959) *The Presentation of Self in Everyday Life*, Garden City, NY: Doubleday.

Goffman, E. (1963) *Stigma: Notes on the Management of Spoiled Identity*, Englewood Cliffs, NJ: Prentice Hall.

Goffman, E. (1967) *Interaction Ritual: Essays on Face-to-Face Behavior*, Garden City, NY: Doubleday, Anchor Books.

Goffman, E. (1974) *Frame Analysis. An Essay on the Organization of Experience*, New York: Harper and Row.

Gould, S.J. (1991) The self-manipulation of my pervasive, perceived vital energy through product use: An introspective-praxis perspective. *Journal of Consumer Research*, 18(2): 194–207.

Gould, S.J. (1995) Researcher introspection as a method in consumer research: Applications, issues, and implications. *Journal of Consumer Research*, 21(4): 719–722.

Gould, S.J. (2006) Comparing, not confirming personal introspection: A comment on Woodside (2004). *Psychology and Marketing*, 23(3): 253–256.

Granovetter, M. (1973) The strength of weak ties. *American Journal of Sociology*, 78(6): 1360–1380.

Granovetter, M. (1978) Threshold models of collective behavior. *American Journal of Sociology*, 83(6): 1420–1443.

Granovetter, M. (1985) Economic action and social structure: The problem of embeddedness. *American Journal of Sociology*, 91(3): 481–510.

Heiskanen, E. and Pantzar, M. (1997) Toward sustainable consumption: Two new perspectives. *Journal of Consumer Policy*, 20(4): 409–442.

Holbrook, M.B. (1986) I'm hip: An autobiographical account of some musical consumption experiences. In R.J. Lutz (ed.), *Advances in Consumer Research*, 13, Provo, UT: Association for Consumer Research, pp. 614–618.

Holbrook, M.B. (1991) From the log of a consumer researcher. In Russel W. Belk (ed.), *Highways and Buyways: Naturalistic Research from the Consumer Behavior Odyssey*, Provo, UT: Association for Consumer Research.

Holbrook, M.B. (2005) Customer value and autoethnography: Subjective personal introspection and the meanings of a photograph collection. *Journal of Business Research*, 58(1): 45–61.

Holt, D.B. (1995) How consumers consume: A typology of consumption practices. *Journal of Consumer Research*, 22(1): 1–16.

Holt, D.B. (2002) Why do brands cause trouble? A dialectical theory of consumer culture and branding. *Journal of Consumer Research*, 29(1): 70–90.

Jackson, P., Rowlands, M. and Miller, D. (1998) *Shopping, Place, and Identity*, London: Routledge.

Kjellberg, H. and Stigzelius, I. (2014) Doing green: Environmental concerns and the realization of green values in everyday food consumption. In S. Geiger, D. Harrison, H. Kjellberg and A. Mallard (eds), *Concerned Markets: Economic Ordering for Multiple Values*, Cheltenham: Edward Elgar, pp. 203–232.

Latour, B. (1986) The powers of association. In J. Law (ed.), *Power, Action and Belief: A New Sociology of Knowledge*, London: Routledge and Kegan Paul, pp. 264–280.

Latour, B. (1987) *Science in Action: How to Follow Scientists and Engineers through Society*, Cambridge, MA: Harvard University Press.

Latour, B. (1992) Where are the missing masses? The sociology of a few mundane artefacts. In W.E. Bijker and J. Law (eds), *Shaping Technology/Building Society, Studies in Sociotechnical Change*, Cambridge, MA: MIT Press, pp. 225–258.

Latour, B. (1994) On technical mediation: Philosophy, sociology, genealogy. *Common Knowledge*, 3(2): 29–64.

Latour, B. (2000) Factures/fractures: de la notion de réseau à celle d'attachement. In A. Micoud and M. Peroni (eds), *Ce qui nous relie*, La Tour d'Aigues: Editions de l'Aube, pp. 189–208.

Latour, B. (2005) *Reassembling the Social. An Introduction to Actor-Network-Theory*, Oxford: Oxford University Press.

Law, J. (1994) *Organizing Modernity*, Oxford: Blackwell Publishers.

Miller, D. (2002) Turning Callon the right way up. *Economy and Society*, 31(2): 218–233.

Miller, D. (2005) Reply to Michel Callon. *Economic Sociology, European Electronic Newsletter*, 6(3): 3–13.

Molotch, H. (2003) *Where STUFF Comes From: How Toasters, Toilets, Cars, Computers and Many Other Things Came to Be as They Are*, New York: Routledge.

Pickering, A. (1993) The mangle of practice: Agency and emergence in the sociology of science. *American Journal of Sociology*, 99(3): 559–589.

Shankar, A. (2000) Lost in music? Subjective personal introspection and popular music consumption. *Qualitative Market Research: An International Journal*, 3(1): 27–37.

Shove, E. and Araujo, L. (2010) Practices, products and trajectories of co-evolution. In L. Araujo, J.H. Finch and H. Kjellberg (eds), *Reconnecting Marketing to Markets*, Oxford: Oxford University Press, pp. 13–28.

Shove, E. and Pantzar, M. (2005) Consumers, producers and practices: Understanding the invention and reinvention of Nordic walking. *Journal of Consumer Culture*, 5(1): 43–64.

Simmel, G. (2004 [1907]). *The Philosophy of Money*, 2nd edn, trans. T. Bottomore and D. Frisby, London: Routledge and Kegan Paul.

Thomas, N. (1991) *Entangled Objects: Exchange, Material Culture and Colonialism in the Pacific*, Cambridge, MA: Harvard University Press.

Uzzi, B. (1996) The sources and consequences of embeddedness for the economic performance of organizations: The network effect. *American Sociological Review*, 61(4): 674–698.

Uzzi, B. (1997) Social structure and competition in interfirm networks: The paradox of embeddedness. *Administrative Science Quarterly*, 42(1): 35–67.

Veblen, T. (1994 [1899]). *The Theory of the Leisure Class*, New York: Penguin.

Wallendorf, M. and Brucks, M. (1993) Introspection in consumer research: Implementation and implications. *Journal of Consumer Research*, 20(3): 339–359.

Warde, A. (2005) Consumption and theories of practice. *Journal of Consumer Culture*, 5(2): 131–153.

Woodside, A.G. (2004) Advancing from subjective to confirmatory personal introspection in consumer research. *Psychology and Marketing*, 21(12): 987–1010.

Woodside, A.G. (2006) Overcoming the illusion of will and self-fabrication: Going beyond naïve subjective personal introspection to an unconscious/conscious theory of behavior explanation. *Psychology and Marketing*, 23(3): 257–272.

Woolgar, S. (2004) Marketing ideas. *Economy and Society*, 33(4): 448–462.

Afterword
The devices of attachment

Michel Callon

How to explain the fact that consumers attach themselves more to some goods than others, to the point of agreeing to pay for them? In other words, how to account for the improbable adjustment that markets produce and reproduce, between a multitude of offers and requests, an adjustment which sometimes ends with a transfer of ownership set against a corresponding monetary compensation?

The great merit of the texts gathered together in this volume is to provide original and convincing answers to this puzzling question, which is a permanent challenge for all those interested in the functioning of markets. By considering that attachment results from a series of tests, in which both assets and agents are transformed, they make it possible to understand the conditions of success – and failure – of commercial transactions. To solve the puzzle of the market, it is necessary to abandon the idea that it organises meetings between agents and goods that are already present and that just wait… to meet. These encounters should rather be described as so many shared but improbable adventures that take place in a multitude of sites and which shape the co-profiling of both goods and agents. These are the multiple and incessant interactions that develop over the course of this process and that culminate, if done properly, in the production of attachments.

Attachment

The process of attachment always starts with a question, with some trouble that grabs the agent. If everything is straightforward, if things and actions repeat identically, the question of attachment does not arise or no longer arises. The goods are there, they have their uses, their values, their qualities; they are acquired or refused out of habit. But faced by a new event, by a situation which cannot be reduced to any other known situation, agents are affected by what is being proposed to them. They seek an unfamiliar response. A street pitcher encountered on a street corner makes his sales pitch; a piece of advertising shakes up pre-conceived ideas; a start-up offers a new drug or a new financial product; an unusual product on a supermarket shelf attracts the shopper's attention. And with that the process is launched.

Agents are called. To dispel doubt and concern, in order to regain some composure, a certain equilibrium, they will have to investigate, experiment.

In this process of inquiry, verbalisation, a putting into words, is central. Take the example of a meal where the wine offered by the host becomes the subject of conversation. What do you think about this bottle? The collective inquiry (which is a model for similar inquiries conducted at a larger scale) takes the form of a conversation which references the label, the colour, and invites the wine to be tasted and commented on; comments that are themselves in turn commented on, speeches and arguments merging, each responding to the other, interspersed with tests and demonstrations of all kinds. The wine, its bouquet, its length on the palate, emerge bit by bit, with everyone making a contribution. A particular way of seeing, of feeling and of speaking, one that is local but probably shaped by previous conversations or readings, is eventually settled. At the end of this exchange, which is a test both for the guests and for the wine in question, the wine that is drunk is no longer the same, nor are the guests about to drink it. Everything has changed, at least to some extent. A community of amateurs has been formed. It is not for nothing that the words that enter the mouths of the agents become part of the dynamic of these transformations and their forms of expression. But it is important not to forget the wine that is actively involved in this act of putting into words, making the diners speak, all the while affecting their bodies. Our body resonates and our mind reasons, says William James essentially. It is clear that goods emerge from the formation of attachments and from their expression, because they act on bodies that learn to be affected by them. If agents are capable of such reflexivity and this kind of return to themselves ('I really want what I want'),[1] then it is because the process of attachment is equally a process of expression, in which they learn what they are and what they are becoming, and whereby, symmetrically, things and goods express what they are or what they can do and 'make do'.

The preceding illustration, which I take from Antoine Hennion, who has provided a decisive contribution to this analytical stream (Hennion, 2013, 2015), captures nicely what we have learned from recent work on the process of attachment. Yes, as Franck Cochoy suggests, things matter; yes they raise troubles and concerns; yes they affect agents and incite them into initiating inquiries. But agents are only affected if they have learned or have been taught to be affected. In these learning processes, verbal exchanges that articulate percepts and concepts play a central role. Joe Deville, Liz McFall and Alexandre Mallard are therefore right to remind us that attachment is a matter of talk and that, like the latter, it is a matter of expertise. There are no ready-made recipes for producing attachments. But fortunately (for the sellers as much as for the buyers) the attachment process is one that is structured and can be organised, from the trouble that the good (for sale) provokes, to the inquiries and investigations that this trouble causes, and over the course of which affects are produced, identities are transformed and become entangled, long-lasting relationships are created and strong associations between goods and agents are constituted.

The organisation of this process is not obvious. It happens through the design and implementation of devices that allow the time and the space for things that surprise and for actors to be surprised. This is a requirement that becomes more pressing with the increasing importance of the singularisation of products and the intensive process of innovation it implies. Never before, in order to be accepted and integrated into social life, have goods been as strongly required to make use of frameworks as flexible, to be unfolded and deployed. Never before, in their unfolding and their deployment, have goods been as required to produce emotions and affect agents previously rendered receptive and attentive.

A good illustration of these devices and their functioning is provided by Emmanuel Kessous' contribution to this book. On the dating platforms he studies, the first operations demanded of the candidates are profiling operations that make it possible for users to evaluate and classify the various participants. Once this has been completed, the time comes for bilateral relations which, after numerous adventures, in a few cases end up taking the form of a relationship that will last for a few hours or an entire lifetime. Nothing is given from the off; everything has to be acquired. Attachment is progressive, the result of successive trials. It progresses according to the rhythm of the investigation conducted by the protagonists embarking on the exploration, I should say an invention, not only of themselves and others but also of the type of relationship they will secure. This investigation would be impossible if it were not framed, channelled and structured by the platform, its technologies, its algorithms, its formulas, which constitute a quasi-pure form of (sociotechnical) attachment device. It arouses surprise, invites conversation, organises tests, stages the body as initially conveyed in the form of words and photos, potentially resulting in a physical meeting.

Dating platforms provide, for a fee, a market supply. They provide the customer a service: helping find a soulmate. And in order to attach customers, to *have* them, as McFall and Deville put it so nicely, the platform must produce another form of attachment: between the members of the platform themselves. That is why the case is so meaningful and helpful. Processes of attachment and their organisation are the sole focus. Kessous shows conclusively that, contrary to what is said in a long critical tradition, rather than the market excluding personal relationships, it instead multiplies and nourishes them. Attachments are at the heart of market activities that variously frame, orient and discipline them. Cochoy, in a striking summary, perfectly synthesises this movement, by proposing the two complementary concepts of collection and selection, understood at once as actions and as results, reflecting the fact that markets on one hand proliferate relations between agents and goods (collections), while on the other rendering them scarce (through successive selections).

Three attachment devices

In order to describe these attachment devices, I suggest an entirely programmatic distinction between three types of devices: *listening* devices; *co-production* devices; and *addiction* devices. The modalities of participation and the importance of goods in the process of attachment varies from one family of devices to the other. *Listening* devices only leave a discrete space for goods, which are present almost in the manner of the décor on a theatre stage, a décor that discreetly provides to words some of the reference points they need to make sense. These devices are designed to convince potential customers that the good being offered to them corresponds precisely to what they want and expect, and that they should therefore become attached to it. With *co-production* devices, consumers are involved in the design and production of the goods intended for them. These devices directly involve agents with goods and, by organising their interaction and mutual adaptation, promote attachments: 'this good is for you because you have designed it'. With *addiction* devices, the influence of things on the bodies of agents peaks. The goods are designed to create a dependency on them that deters agents from breaking free, consequently and almost mechanically ensuring their attachment.

Actual attachment devices tend to combine all three types. A successful attachment implies that agents recognise that, one way or another, what is being offered corresponds to what they want; but if this agreement can be achieved, it is because, at one time or another, consumers have been directly or indirectly involved in the process of designing the good; in the end, so that customers do not disappear before the transaction occurs, their bodies and minds must have been made, at least to some extent, dependent on the good. In the following lines, I will provide an overview of these three families of devices, selecting a few examples from the various contributions to this book. Then I will briefly discuss mechanisms of detachment (sellers must agree to dispose of the goods in which they have nonetheless invested) without which no market transaction could be imagined.

Dialogue: here's what you need!

For sellers, the simplest way to engage the process of attachment is to convince potential consumers that the good in question is just what they need, that it provides a response to problems that must or should be solved.

The function of devices that belong to this family is to progressively identify what customers expect, want or desire by getting them to express it. To achieve this, the conversation takes the form of a dialogue similar to the *chjam'è rispondi* of those Corsican songs in which impromptu questions and answers follow one another. If this dialogue is properly conducted and all goes well, an agreement may be reached ('this is what you want', to which the answer is: 'yes, that's the good I want') as well as the promise of a successful attachment.

The easiest way to get consumers to recognise that they really want the proposed good is to organise a face-to-face encounter between the seller and the customer. They can then engage in dialogue. Whatever the trade, whether a grocer, a butcher, a hardware store or a tour operator, if they want to succeed, they have to learn to manage this sort of conversation, whether with a regular or a first-time customer. The conversation is supported by the presence of goods. Whether displayed on the stall, in catalogues, brochures or videos, they can be valued, scrutinised or touched. At any time, when a reluctance or an objection surfaces, a return to the goods may help to resolve the difficulty and to advance the attachment.

'Pitchers' (*bonimenteurs*) are masters of this difficult and ancient art (Pinch, 2010). Mallard (2011), in his work on small and medium enterprises, recounts how a merchant, travelling with his van into the Vendée countryside, realised that it was useless to go to the market to wait for customers. Instead, he sought them out at home. Two honks of his horn signalled his arrival. 'It's me, it's you, I'm here for you Madame, look at this fish, it's the one you love. I am at your service, I am here to help you, I'm here to solve your problems.' Conversations continue and are picked up again from one visit to the next. A continual *chjam'è rispondi*. This type of conversation, in which seller, customer and goods in search of buyers meet in the flesh, can be conducted on an industrial scale. McFall and Deville describe the growth of the market for life insurance for the poor in the UK. Seasoned agents were sent to homes to present the product and to attend to sceptical customers. Agents succeeded beyond expectation; they became close friends, confidants of this mass of poor people, renewing short contracts week after week. Not one pitcher but tens of thousands of pitchers, encountering and conversing with a multitude of customers, each processed as a singular person.[2]

The internet provides a fantastic platform for launching and maintaining, on a large scale and at low cost, this kind of personalised conversation, which leads customers to make explicit what they like and what they expect. Kevin Mellet distinguishes three strategies. The first consists of the company using the internet as a vector of contagion. The conversation will fail if there is no 'buzz'. The second begins from the idea that there are opinion shapers and opinion makers, and that they need to be reached and convinced. If the operation succeeds, they will relay and extend the conversation amongst their circles of followers. Twitter is a well-suited tool for this type of conversation. The third and final strategy, using tools like Facebook, is to instigate genuine dialogue by stimulating the network of those who claim to be your friends and establishing an unmediated conversation with them.

These tools are part of a more general movement involving research on consumers, their practices, their aspirations and their problems (Tomas Ariztia). These types of research are not disinterested. They aim to make companies aware of the diverse and sometimes contradictory expressions of consumers. They are conducted by myriad stakeholders who work to talk to consumers in order to better 'have them'. The methods used are numerous and complementary. They might involve statistical analysis, perhaps using data on social and occupational categories, or the compilation of information collected by sellers, or face-to-face interviews, or the in situ observation of particular practices, or focus groups, or local meetings in which products are presented and discussed. Anything goes. Imagination has no limits. These investigations allow for an incessant back and forth. As Ariztia points out, they do not establish a truth, but many truths, each of which are provisional and changeable. They play a central role both in the development of advertising campaigns and in the conversations that feed each other.

Consumer research does not lose sight of the goods themselves, managing to involve them in the conversation to varying degrees. It uses tests, notably the food industry with its tasting sessions, or also in showrooms, where real consumers like you and me can see, touch, feel, react, discuss and directly comment on the strength of attachments. But there is no guarantee of success. Attachments, before they are definitively certified and measured according to flows of money, have something in them that makes them uncertain and fragile.

By the way, the reversible, temporary and partial character of attachments is not necessarily a problem. Of course consumers need to be attached, but they should not be attached too much, otherwise markets would sink into routine and repetition, and would soon fall asleep for good. What is important is that the conversation does not wither away. Conversations keep going. It is necessary to wake up the client, to honk twice, to repeat surveys. This is what loyalty cards in particular do, by maintaining a contact and keeping data up to date.

On the supply side, holding a conversation – in reality several conversations in parallel – requires, as Mallard, McFall and Deville show, considerable energy, resources and an impeccable organisation capable of mobilising multitudes of experts and professionals, both inside and outside the company, and sometimes in real time, who are required to coordinate, deal with feedback and brief the agents sent out into the 'field'. Mallard, in his work on call centres, observes that conversations, even when they are carefully prepared and framed, tend to slide, because the profiling of the interlocutors and their matching were poorly adjusted, or because the organisation of the dialogue is affected by misallocated resources, which leads to an increase in time spent waiting before the conversation begins.

It is also necessary for those who design and offer the good in question to themselves be ready to detach. There is certainly no ambiguity. Each of the protagonists realises that the exchange of words will conclude with a commercial transaction. It is thus an 'interested' conversation that is at stake, one that is not easy to manage, especially when this involves the organisation learning a kind of dialogue that has no other purpose than attaching, having (literally), the customer. To be capable of providing a service, of paying attention, of empathy without forgetting that there is a business to be run, oh this certainly needs to be learned. There are even acting classes for it. Mallard (2012) describes how in a telephone conversation between a customer and a call centre agent, the agent alternates masterfully between personalised talk: 'My name is Dominique, how can I help you?' and exchanges that act as a reminder that there are two roles involved, that of the seller and that of the customer: 'Orange would like to remind you, dear Mr. Callon, that your contract cannot be cancelled without charge until the end of November.' The role-playing can come unstuck at any moment. The seller is moving along the edge of a razor. Too much familiarity or not enough and the conversation will end badly. All the more so when the customer is on guard; he knows he risks being duped by the interaction with either Dominique or the one that reaches out to him anonymously, following the intervention of a cascade of intermediaries, in the form of slogans and advertising messages.

At any moment, the conversation could tip over the edge into lies, bad faith, deception, cynicism, tempting smokescreens or fraud. It can also leave the register of the market. Yet the problem is not whether sellers believe what they are saying and customers what they are saying to the seller, but it is rather making sure that the discourse of the seller achieves the limited and temporary truth not of facts but of emotions and passions. When the conversation is skilfully conducted, no one is fooled, no one believes it, and yet everyone believes it, because no one demands the truth.[3] It is in the words: the good liar (*boni-menteur*) is the one who knows how to lie well. And knowing how to lie well is not something possible for all; it is infinitely more difficult than telling the truth.

Co-production: your turn!

Conversation is an obligatory passage point. Silent relationships cannot generate attachments. But conversations that would disconnect from the goods and things at stake, or that would not stick close enough to them and would be limited to a simple verbal exchange, would quickly lose (commercial) interest and eventually ring hollow. The designers of conversation devices are not mistaken. In order to facilitate and reinforce the production of attachments, they work to give goods ever more opportunities to express themselves and to intervene. Why not make the goods themselves the principal actors of economic exchanges? And how to achieve this goal, if not by inviting consumers to enter into the process of design and production. The more I am associated with the development of the good that is destined for me, the more I am able to intervene early in a discussion of its qualities and how it is shaped, and the more likely I am to ultimately end up permanently and sincerely attaching myself to it (Akrich et al., 2002).

The organisation of the innovation process attests to the efficacy and generalisation of devices that are designed to engage customers in how innovation is developed to ensure its success. Von Hippel (2004) has advanced the expression of the democratisation of innovation to emphasise that the process whereby new products are designed is expanding. Even if the word democracy is excessive (access to the activities through which goods are designed remains very selective), it reflects the increasing extent to which users are engaged. In confronting goods, their future recipients get to know better what they want. In the case of the development of new therapies, for example, both the engagement of patients' associations and their attachment to the treatments and molecules that they helped to test are irreversible phenomena. The studies that have demonstrated the generalisation of this form of organisation and the concepts that have been conceived to designate are now innumerable. Some talk about a new regime of innovation (Joly et al., 2010), others about the prosumer, or *consommaction*, two neologisms obtained by contracting the words consumer (*consommateur*) and producer (*producteur*). Chesbrough (2003) has recently had great success by introducing the concept of openness, which points towards the multiplicity of agents that may be engaged in the process of design and production of new products. It would be more accurate to speak of open goods themselves, which, during the process of their qualification, are designed to seek the intervention of the agents concerned. The opening up of the good becomes a crucial quality. When it comes to incorporating, often explicitly, the possibility of, or the need for, adjustment and requalification once the commercial transaction has been completed, it is a powerful force for producing affects and attachments. Do-it-yourselfers prefer to buy things that leave open the potential of improvising, of tinkering; in the same way, it seems, real computer specialists prefer Windows, Android, Firefox and all open systems and software, over Apple and its closed systems. Hans Kjellberg, over the course of a very successful piece of auto-analysis, shows convincingly how the acquisition of a vintage car (thus consequently open to its requalification), by entering his life and refusing to leave it, gradually transformed – all the while itself transforming – relationships with relatives, friends and children, in the process redefining ways of life. The transfer of ownership, which is a crucial moment in the attachment process, helps to reinforce this. The thing has the consumer just as the consumer has the thing.

Marketing has not missed this movement (Araujo et al., 2010; Brodie et al., 2015). It has multiplied the forms of consumer solicitation that encourage more direct interaction with the goods intended for them and that extend opportunities for requalification.

The simplest and most rudimentary mechanism relates to the invention of self-service (Kjellberg and Helgesson, 2007; Cochoy, 2014) and to the display it organises between consumers and products. As Cochoy has shown, product displays create consumers who have no choice but to choose. These devices find themselves constituting a 'free' subject (a tightly framed freedom, of course), who, like every free subject, starts by hesitating, by asking questions. This does not concern a simple conversation between oneself and oneself, but rather, in this case, between oneself and the professionals who organised the casting of the products on display. The products on the shelves and the gondolas, emblazoned with inscriptions and messages, speak to consumers, attract their attention, suggest that they should investigate further, explore further. The goods are loquacious, expressive, by the simple fact of being crowded together, one next to the other, collected and selected. Customers pass between the shelves, and the framings change, intertwine and fuse; the shopping cart, this crucial invention, acts as a type of memory, allowing them to see what they have chosen and the possibility of eventually reconsidering the choices that are now before their eyes. Things enter into a dialogue with the consumer (Cochoy, 2004).

With the rise of brands, marketing has been able to go even further in set-ting consumers to work, in activating them. Take the case, as presented by Carolin Gerlitz, of American Apparel (AA), and the campaign it launched in the 1990s as it sought to break into the clothing market. In creating its style, the AA style, the brand becomes a participatory creation tool. It is possible to follow the practices associated with AA without being directly involved in them (for example, by performing a web search with the keywords 'American Apparel'). Ideas, identities, unconventional and quirky practices find them-selves connected, as if the brand were acting as a platform, stimulating ima-gination and proposals that one has then simply to collect. It is not only that the conversation about the existing goods offered by the (clothing) company is extended, but also that there is the emergence from everywhere of novel combinations that are likely to end up as new products. The brand becomes a participatory design device by putting crowds of actors to work for free and with a shared purpose. In some cases, this machinery becomes very produc-tive. Gerlitz gives the example of Dove, which relies on a multitude of stake-holders, working with women's groups, organising forums and projects, and animating a vast movement that questions standards of beauty – particularly those spread by the media – thereby becoming able to involve itself in the development of new practices and new meanings. At the end of this collective and highly mediatised work, that resembles a social movement, consumers are most ready to attach themselves to the brand and the good which are them-selves attached to practices, issues and concerns that they share. The product has been opened up, unfolded; it has been enriched, transformed, entangled in a network of new associations. This work is undertaken by the brand, which is for marketing what collaborative platforms are for the design of new pro-ducts. The brand attaches; and one is attached to the brand. It becomes a collective force that performs the opening of goods and encourages their maximal meshing with the ethical, political or cultural concerns that simul-taneously transform them. It is not (only), as has often been stated, a trust device. It manages, to echo Gerlitz, the flow of values in opposite directions. Now multivalent, the good sees its economic value increase.

Addiction: pay to attach yourself to even more!

Instigating and maintaining a dialogue is good; even better is connecting it to the co-production of goods and allowing those for whom the goods are intended a margin of manoeuvre that enables them to experience and express what they want. From one device to another, things play an ever more sig-nificant role in the allocation process. But is it not most effective, to ensure that goods, by directly conditioning behaviours, become indispensable to those who consume them, leading them into a state of dependence they are unable to contemplate being without?

Addiction devices are not new. In their puzzling simplicity, they are sometimes astonishingly effective. A few years ago, Lucky Strike introduced cigarettes to the market that had a menthol capsule or 'pastille' in the filter. When the capsule heated up, and when the smoker pressed a button, the taste of the cigarette would change. Teenagers seemed to love it, making, as the expression went, 'pop the pastille' (*péter la pastille*), as rapidly as possible. This small device had two effects. The first was to introduce a flavour that was sure to produce a pleasant sensation in young smokers, encouraging them to breathe deeply. Now, starting, at a very young age, by inhaling the smoke means embarking on a serious path, which is the second effect, a long-term addiction … supplemented by lung cancer. Drawing teenagers to 'pop the pastille', remains a more secure and radical attachment strategy than all the various advertising slogans and branding campaigns put together.

In order to understand the mechanisms of addiction, such as the mechanisms of attachment to goods, the decisive steps in the instigation of bilateral transactions, and the willingness to pay, let us head to Natasha Schüll (2012) and to Las Vegas. The games there have become an economic and commercial activity in themselves, being industrially organised and exclusively and extensively directed towards producing addictive behaviour and accumulating the immense commercial benefits that result. To explain this economic success, it would be too easy, as some think, to invoke human nature and its weaknesses, *panem et circenses*. That would be to seriously underestimate the colossal investment, both of dollars and grey matter, needed to activate these inclinations, for them to be expressed, and to transform ever greater numbers of casual players, who come to be entertained, into gamblers dependent on, overwhelmed by and drowning in the game, who seek nothing else than cutting off the world around them. In order to organise this dependence and to ensure that it is as profitable as possible (for the casino), what costly research and experiments are required! Someone wanting to reduce the addiction to the face-to-face encounter between a screen and a player would be completely blind. In the gambler's silent conversation, we find machines, the latest technological innovations, the use of armies of architects, psychologists and marketers, casinos competing to develop the best-performing algorithms, mathematicians attempting (and this is not as easy as you think) to shape the laws of chance so that it is unmistakably true chance, battalions of lawyers and elected officials fighting over whether these practices are legal, governments keeping an interested eye on the taxes that flow into the state's coffers.

Schüll describes the design and operation of this addiction device with surgical precision. First, there is the long labyrinthine journey that draws the customer to Las Vegas (extremely cheap airline tickets, discounted hotel rooms), which leads, without much in the way of thought, to the heart of the casino, into what players call their zone, an enclosed space of a few square metres, an island lost in the middle of an ocean made up of the 10,000 square metres of the playroom, where every variable (temperature, light, colour and scents that stimulate the emotions) have been calculated and tested. Players are then confronted by a machine designed both to test their propensity to addictive practices and, potentially, to their intensification. The goal is to increase the speed of bets; not to interrupt the game when players win (so that they continue to play with their winnings); to avoid, for example by transforming credit cards into gambling instruments, players losing time when collecting their winnings or recovering funds; to keep the players immobile for as long as possible (they should only leave their seat for physiological needs: to go to the toilet, to eat).[4] Everything is controlled: that which is heard (by integrating background noise) and that which is seen. Comfort is attended to in chairs that vibrate subtly depending on the event. If the attachment and the addiction succeed, it is both because the service is designed to include the active participation of consumers and because of the practices of dialogue and co-production that the casinos implement. Machines themselves constitute an environment; they seize gamblers and grasp them emotionally (Thrift, 2006).

Schüll shows in detail how the essential elements of the control of gamblers' affects are to be found in the slot machine's software and microprocessors. For example, the reels give the sense of having been started by the player who presses the button (as if a dice had been thrown), when in fact the number generator runs continuously and changes the draw every millisecond, meaning players can only select what has been generated at the moment the button is pressed. If after losing, a player leaves their place and watches the next person win, they risk regretting it, thinking they could have pocketed the winnings if they had not moved on. This encourages players to continue, even if the probability that they would have pressed the button at the same time is almost nil. Another way of creating the same feeling ('if I go on I will win') is to show the winning configuration next to the losing one the player has just got.

The machine is programmed to determine the rate at which funds are paid out. It can prioritise, in accordance with players and their typical strategies (duly recorded in the computers' memories and constantly being recalculated), large but infrequent wins, or alternatively wins that are more limited but more frequent. But consuming players' money in small doses seems to be the safest way (for the casino!) to rake in the profits. The continuous flow of small gains draws the player inexorably into the zone of addiction, creating the illusion of 'false wins', while losses slowly and steadily accumulate.

The casino thus intervenes heavily in how players experience their losses and gains. Their affects are in the hands of the industry and its experts, computer specialists, architects, designers and experimental psychologists, who, as one of them explains, work to make the player functionally autistic: 'You are the machine, the machine is you. You take a vacation from people.' Attachment reaches its climax; the machine is directly connected to mental states. The player is in a mousetrap. The innovations succeed when the player surrenders any attempt to calculate and eventually allows the machine to play by itself twenty simultaneous games of poker, or even a hundred, if that is what their heart instructs them. The auto-play function confirms that they are nothing more than a programmed cyborg. The player no longer looks at the cards, but simply at the counter that displays losses and gains. And soon there will be no more need to go to the machines; the machine will come to the player, or better yet the player will be able to carry the machine away. The machines offer players what they like and that which they cannot live without, by putting ever more distance between them and the world around them. They will have popped the pastille once and for all.[5]

Addiction devices are spreading across many sectors and are becoming increasingly important. A number of observers have noted the ways in which innovations from the gambling industry, such as biometric identification systems, or fraud-detection software, have been adopted in other areas: in airports, trading rooms, insurance, banking and the homeland security industry. But one of the areas of activity where addiction mechanisms have long played a central role is of course that of food. It is not combinations of cards that are being played with, but combinations of sugar, fat and salt, calculated according to mathematical models and validated by taste tests. And how can we forget the corporeal mechanisms of dependence that attach users to their mobile phones, to their screens, to their video games, to their medication, to their Apple Watches – not to mention tobacco or alcohol.

This book goes further. One of its contributions, in an echo of the etymology of the word addiction, which for Romans referred to the status of being a free man enslaved to another in debt bondage, is to show the strength and persistence of addiction devices related to money and especially credit practices. One of the most lucrative populations for those that provide loans are those impecunious people living on the edge of poverty. These are the main customers of payday lenders, which tend to involve small sums being borrowed for a short period at astronomical rates (interest rates in excess of 5,000% APR). If well managed, this population can be loyal, with one loan following another, generating significant income. But how to achieve this? To answer this question, McFall and Deville analyse the success of Wonga in the UK which, despite charging the highest rates of interest in the sector, over the years succeeded in overtaking all of its competitors, managing to create long-lasting attachments to customers who were poor, certainly, but still in need of money. Wonga's business model, suggest McFall and Deville, is not based on the renegotiation of contracts or extending the duration of loans. The rule of the game is that before you can take out a new loan, you have to have paid off the previous one. The challenge for Wonga is to gradually identify the contours of a population who, while always in need of money, repays its loans on time, just as the casino is looking for those players who press the button as often as possible to initiate a new bet. No sugar, no salt and no fat for bait and for creating dependence. No, a questionnaire of thirty criteria filled online in five minutes. Then a series of complex backstage calculations, using a mass of accumulated data, in order to define behavioural profiles and to identify along the way and measure those actions that respectively correspond to the good, poor and punctual borrower, which is the company's aim. Wonga customers learn to live with permanent debt, repaid without protest. They are dependent on the money lent by Wonga and this dependence... depends on them, on their behaviour: if they cease to repay, they are suddenly free but... penniless. We are back to slot machines, although here it is machines that lend money instead of swallowing it, and which learn, via the interposed questionnaires and algorithms, that carefully selected customers will not detach themselves. The sequences are the same, with small amounts ultimately generating large returns and customers behaving as required for the game to continue. The poor who, because they are poor, are good candidates for repeated demands, the poor to whom the possibility of repetition is promised as long as they behave properly, in a word, the good poor who end up playing the game and behaving appropriately: these, explain McFall and Deville, are what is at stake in the relations that Wonga establishes with its customers, and which it responds to through its calculative platforms and algorithms.

José Ossandón, in his work on the expansion of credit cards, sent out to customers by large distributors, confirms the effectiveness of these addiction devices. The cards that serve as a means of payment can also be used to get cash and to obtain mini short-term, very high-interest loans. Their owners can also lend them to family members and friends. The risks to issuers are not negligible but they are statistically manageable. As for Wonga, the goal is to identify a population that behaves well, that is to say that repays on time and with whom loans can be renewed. The case is particularly interesting because it highlights a phenomenon of growing importance: the emergence and development of private monies (in this case involving the owners and users of cards on one side and, on the other, the distributors that deliver them). Ossandón shows very convincingly that these monies bind those who use them, becoming totally dependent on them to purchase the goods that they need. The card is a self-reinforcing device that attaches by rendering dependent: the more you use it the more you keep using it.

Attachments that become more and more... attaching?

In one way or another, attachments succeed in becoming implicated in conversation, the co-production of goods and addiction. In Las Vegas, for example, the designers periodically tour the players and interview them; they organise focus groups; they work closely with the players to refine the ergonomics of the zone.[6] There is no addiction device that can avoid conversation and co-design,[7] nor is there any co-design not rooted in conversation. The opposite is undoubtedly true. Attachments relying neither on co-design nor on mechanisms of dependence would be so fragile that both the attachment itself and the profits it generates would be jeopardised. Be that as it may, the combinations are infinite in number, leaving space for a wide variety of commercial strategies to play with the more or less partial and ephemeral character of attachments.

My sense is that the addiction devices occupy an ever more important place in the production of commercial attachments. Addiction and profit seem increasingly intertwined and dependent on one another. Addiction becomes a central category, even if historically contingent. Paul Rabinow (1996) suggests for example that it constitutes an entry point for thinking about *anthropos* today. This is the stuff which contemporary humankind is made of, as the engineering of addiction and addictive practices is rendering explicit and establishing on an unprecedented scale.

These few considerations on the devices of attachment cannot conclude without mentioning the question of… detachment. The management of the affects that make agents act is at least as important from the supply side as the demand side. I mentioned this in the case of listening and co-production devices. But with devices of addiction, the question attains a completely different magnitude and inevitably raises concerns. As Schüll's interviews with designers and engineers show, cats can also find pleasure in the gambling industry. It is the pleasure of stalking and best of all capturing players, with the claws of competition withdrawn, but without ruining them: the mouse should continue to live (Cochoy, 2008). The more the influence of machines increases, the more the dependence of players increases, and the more those who are on the supply side rejoice. They also rejoice when they win a lawsuit initiated by an administration that accuses them of not really respecting the laws of chance in order to set up the losing configurations. All in all, they are convinced that customers are responsible for what they do and that they have genuine free choice. A Hannah Arendt would be required to account for the banality of evil, to explain how we arrived at the position of rendering responsible those whom the device seeks to make irresponsible, and to describe the economy of affects where jubilation is exchanged for an accepted dependence. It is to avoid becoming the subject of public opprobrium that the gambling industry finances treatment centres for gambling addicts and research to identify those players at greatest risk of sinking into dependency so as to prevent their fall. Just as mobile operators hire psychologists to explain to parents how to manage their children and their phones; just as the food industry employs battalions of dieticians to convince consumers not to abuse the products being offered to them. Market attachment produces concerns that continue to haunt us (Geiger et al., 2015).

Translated by Joe Deville and Franck Cochoy

Notes

1 Completely silent commercial transactions, which prohibit all reflexivity (before, during or after the exchange itself), seem implausible. Moreover, even in the most extreme cases, such as gambling addiction, in which agents are seemingly seized without their knowledge, they are able to explain with striking authenticity and

often against the expectations of the observer, what happens to them, why the things catch them and hold them (Schüll, 2012).

2 Personalised conversation devices are at the heart of contemporary markets. There are a thousand ways to address any individual customer, as if it were possible to know everything about them and what they expect. And the simplest way is to call them by name, as has been well understood by that mineral water producer who offers bottles on which are engraved the name and surname of the recipient. Customer Relationship Management specialist Martha Zorn shrewdly notes: 'For instance, isn't it nice to hear your name when you walk in to your local coffee shop? Isn't it nice that they already know what you're drinking without you saying anything?' (Zorn, 2016).

3 On the concept of 'fair trade' as a legal formulation of this regime of truth, see Canu and Cochoy (2004).

4 Some players prefer to wear two pairs of trousers to be able to pee their fill while they pump their coins into the machine.

5 It should be emphasised that the manipulation of players doubles as the manipulation of manipulators. The latter are the target of those who promise ever better addiction devices. It would be more accurate to speak of chains of addiction which derive from and feed into one another.

6 This explains why, when it comes to games, addiction devices differ significantly from one country to another. In Japan, in the pachinko halls, the zone of isolation described by Schüll does not exist. The player must constantly combat the deafening noise of machines, just as the Western pinball player has to. The creation of dependency is essentially a case of experimentation. I thank Franck Cochoy for drawing my attention to this point.

7 As noted above, conversation might be required by objects.

Bibliography

Akrich, M., Callon, M. and Latour, B. (2002) The key to success in innovation. *International Journal of Innovation Management*, 6(2): 187–225.

Araujo, L., Finch, J. and Kjellberg, H. (eds) (2010) *Reconnecting Marketing to Markets*, Oxford: Oxford University Press.

Brodie, R.J., Hollebeek, L.D. and Conduit, J. (eds) (2015) *Customer Engagement: Contemporary Issues and Challenges*, London: Routledge.

Canu, R. and Cochoy, F. (2004) La loi de 1905 sur la répression des fraudes: un levier décisif pour l'engagement politique des questions de consommation? *Sciences de la société*, 62, 69–91.

Chesbrough, H. (2003). *Open Innovation: The New Imperative for Creating and Profiting from Technology*, Boston, MA: Harvard Business School Press.

Cochoy, F. (2000) De l'AFNOR' à 'NF'. Ou de la progressive marchandisation de la normalisation industrielle. *Réseaux*, 102: 65–89.

Cochoy, F. (2004) Is the modern consumer a buridan's donkey? Product packaging and consumer choice. In K.M. Ekström and H. Brembeck (eds), *Elusive Consumption*, Oxford: Berg, pp. 205–227.

Cochoy, F. (2008) Hansel and Gretel at the grocery store: Progressive grocer and the little American consumers (1929–1959). *Journal of Cultural Economy*, 1(2): 145–163.

Cochoy, F. (2014) *Aux origines du libre service. Progressive Grocer (1929–1954)*, Lormont: Le Bord de l'eau.

Geiger, S., Harrison, D., Kjellberg, H. and Mallard, A. (eds) (2015) *Concerned Markets: Economic Ordering for Multiple Values*, Cheltenham: Edward Elgar Publishing.

Hennion, A. (2013) D'une sociologie de la médiation à une pragmatique des attachements. *SociologieS*, June. http://sociologies.revues.org/4353.

Hennion, A. (2015) Paying attention: What is tasting wine about? In A.B. Antal, M. Hutter and D. Stark (eds), *Moments of Valuation: Exploring Sites of Dissonance*, Oxford: Oxford University Press, pp. 37–56.

Joly, P.-B., Rip, A. and Callon, M. (2010) Reinventing innovation. In M. Arentsen, W.V. Rossum and A. Steenge (eds), *Governance of Innovation: Firms, Clusters and Institutions in a Changing Setting*, Cheltenham: Edward Elgar, pp. 19–32.

Kjellberg, H. and Helgesson, C.F. (2007) The model exchange and the shaping of markets: Introducing self-service in Swedish post-war distribution. *Industrial Marketing Management*, 36(7): 361–378.

Mallard, A. (2011) *Petit dans le marché. Une sociologie de la Très Petite Entreprise*, Paris: Presses des Mines.

Mallard, A. (2012) Cadrer et encadrer la vente. Réflexion sur l'avenir des relations interpersonnelles dans une société d'organisations commerciales. In F. Cochoy (ed.), *Du lien marchand. Comment le marché fait société*, Toulouse: Presses Universitaires du Mirail, pp. 81–106.

Pinch, T. (2010) Performativity and economic demonstrations: Pitching quality and quantity. In M. Akrich, Y. Barthe, F. Muniesa and P. Mustar (eds), *Débordements. Mélanges offerts à Michel Callon*, Paris: Presses des Mines, pp. 369–380.

Rabinow, P. (1996) *Essay in the Anthropology of Reason*, Princeton, NJ: Princeton University Press.

Schüll, N.D. (2012). *Addiction by Design: Machine Gambling in Las Vegas*, Princeton, NJ: Princeton University Press.

Thrift, N. (2006) Re-inventing invention: New tendencies in capitalist commodification. *Economy and Society*, 35(2): 279–306.

von Hippel, E. (2004) *Democratizing Innovation*. Cambridge, MA: MIT Press.

Zorn, M. (2016) State of sales. Salesforce Research. https://secure2.sfdcstatic.com/a ssets/pdf/misc/state-of-sales-report-salesforce.pdf.

Index